THE Heart OF THE Artist

THE Heart
OF THE
Artist

A Character-Building Guide for You & Your Ministry Team

Rory Noland

FOREWORD BY BILL HYBELS

WILLOW CREEK
RESOURCES

ZONDERVAN™

GRAND RAPIDS, MICHIGAN 49530

The Heart of the Artist
Copyright © 1999 by Rory Noland

Requests for information should be addressed to:

Zondervan, *Grand Rapids, Michigan 49530*

Library of Congress Cataloging-in-Publication Data

Noland, Rory.
    The heart of the artist : a character-building guide for you and your ministry team / Rory Noland.
       p.   cm.
    Includes bibliographical references.
    ISBN 0-310-22471-3 (softcover)
    1. Church musicians—Religious life.   2. Artists—Religious life.   3. Christian life.   I. Title.
BV4596.M87N65 1999
248.8'8—dc21
                                                    99-18211

All Scripture quotations, unless otherwise indicated, are taken from the *Holy Bible: New International Version*®. NIV®. Copyright © 1973, 1978, 1984 by International Bible Society. Used by permission of Zondervan. All rights reserved.

Scripture marked NASB is from the *New American Standard Bible,* © 1960, 1962, 1963, 1968, 1971, 1972, 1973, 1975, 1977 by the Lockman Foundation. Used by permission.

The following publishers have generously given permission to use extended quotations from copyrighted works.

The song "Audience of One" by Greg Ferguson, © 1991 Ever Devoted Music (Administered by Maranatha! Music c/o The Copyright Company, Nashville, TN) and Maranatha! Music (Administered by The Copyright Company, Nashville, TN). All rights reserved. International copyright secured. Used by permission.

The song "Behind Every Fantasy" by Rory Noland, © 1991 Ever Devoted Music (Administered by Maranatha! Music c/o The Copyright Company, Nashville, TN) and Maranatha! Music (Administered by The Copyright Company, Nashville, TN). All rights reserved. International copyright secured. Used by permission.

The song "He Is Able" by Rory Noland and Greg Ferguson, © 1989 Maranatha Praise, Inc. (Administered by The Copyright Company, Nashville, TN). All rights reserved. International copyright secured. Used by permission.

The song "I'm Amazed" by Rory Noland, © 1991 Maranatha Praise, Inc. (Administered by The Copyright Company, Nashville, TN). All rights reserved. International copyright secured. Used by permission.

The song "Let the Lord Love You" by Rory Noland, © 1989 Ever Devoted Music (Administered by Maranatha! Music c/o The Copyright Company, Nashville, TN) and Maranatha! Music (Administered by The Copyright Company, Nashville, TN). All rights reserved. International copyright secured. Used by permission.

The song "On My Knees" by Rory Noland, © 1991 Ever Devoted Music (Administered by Maranatha! Music c/o The Copyright Company, Nashville, TN) and Maranatha! Music (Administered by The Copyright Company, Nashville, TN). All rights reserved. International copyright secured. Used by permission.

The song "Ever Devoted" by Rory Noland, © 1988 Ever Devoted Music (Administered by Maranatha! Music c/o The Copyright Company, Nashville, TN). All rights reserved. International copyright secured. Reprinted with permission.

The song "Open to the Truth About Myself" by Rory Noland, © 1992 Ever Devoted Music (Administered by Maranatha! Music c/o The Copyright Company, Nashville, TN). All rights reserved. International copyright secured. Reprinted with permission.

The song "Praise God on High" by Rory Noland, © 1998 Ever Devoted Music (Administered by Maranatha! Music c/o The Copyright Company, Nashville, TN). All rights reserved. International copyright secured. Reprinted with permission.

The song "Holy Spirit Take Control" by Rory Noland, © 1984 Ever Devoted Music (Administered by Maranatha! Music c/o The Copyright Company, Nashville, TN). All rights reserved. International copyright secured. Reprinted with permission.

An excerpt from *Addicted to Mediocrity,* by Franky Schaeffer, Copyright © 1981, pages 59-62. Used by permission of Crossway Books, a division of Good News Publishers, Wheaton, Illinois 60187. Reprinted by permission of the publisher.

The poem "Flickering Mind" by Denise Levertov, from *A Door in the Hive,* Copyright © 1989 by Denise Levertov. Reprinted by permission of New Directions Publishing Corp.

An excerpt from *Surprised by the Voice of God,* by Jack Deere, Copyright © 1996 by Jack S. Deere, reprinted by permission of the publisher, Zondervan.

Every effort has been made to contact all the copyright holders of the quoted material. If anyone holding a legitimate copyright feels they have been neglected, we would kindly ask them to write to the author of this book, care of Zondervan, so that proper credit can be given and fees, where appropriate, paid.

Interior design by Sherri Hoffman
Printed in the United States of America

02 03 04 05 /❖ DC/ 19 18 17 16

Contents

Foreword

I have never been able to tell mother-in-law jokes because my mother-in-law is one of the most remarkable women I know. Along a similar line, I have never been able to join in with church leaders as they cry in each others' root beer about the chaos in the choir or the squabbles among the soloists.

For nearly my entire ministry, Rory Noland has led the music ministry of Willow Creek. Rather than my having to justify the misconduct of our musicians to the rest of the church, I frequently hold them up as examples of astonishing levels of servanthood, faithfulness, and humility. No group in our church works harder than the people in our programming department. No group takes as seriously the challenge of telling the "old, old story" a new and creative way. And no group in our church is subjected to the harsh glare of public scrutiny to the extent of our artists. Fortunately, our musicians have been under Rory's tutelage. They draw strength from his humility, his servant spirit, and they rise up to meet the inspiring challenge he puts before them to give their best for God.

In addition to Rory's leadership and exemplary character, Rory himself is a monster musician in his own right. He has written worship songs that have lifted our congregation's ability to see the true God as He really is. Rory has composed orchestra music that has stirred the souls of our people in ways they never forget. But above all else, Rory is a godly man, a fully devoted follower of Christ whose impact on our lives and our church is incalculable.

As you read this book, please keep reminding yourself, "This can really happen!" Artists really can lead exemplary lives as they seek to enrich the souls of people in the church. Through Rory's influence, I've seen it happen firsthand at Willow Creek.

Bill Hybels
Senior Pastor
Willow Creek Community Church

Preface

Selfishness, pride, perfectionism, defensiveness, jealousy, envy, emotional imbalance, and lack of discipline—many people struggle with these character flaws, but Christians with artistic temperaments will face all these issues at various points of their lives if not throughout, simply by virtue of being artists. We don't stumble on these character issues by chance; they're part of our nature. It's what comes with being artists. I didn't consent to write this book because I had done a lot of research on character growth and thought that warranted a book. I wrote it because I've struggled with every character flaw discussed in this book. Most of what I've learned grew out of my quiet times with the Lord. I started sharing what God was doing in my life with my artistic friends at rehearsals, in my small groups, or on retreats. I sensed a kindred spirit with my fellow artists, most of whom also wanted to grow in the areas we all struggle with. I then began to share what I was learning at conferences and workshops and there too found countless others who were hungry for what God's Word has to say about growing in character as a Christian artist. Many of them would ask me to recommend further resources that spoke directly to those of us with artistic temperaments, but unfortunately there isn't much available. This book is written in response to that need.

I've been working with artists in the church for over twenty-five years now, and I've seen churches handle artists in one of two ways. We either coddle artists and put up with their shortcomings or we use and abuse artists. Irving Stone's *The Agony and the Ecstasy*, a biographical novel about the life of Michelangelo, has one long chapter devoted to Michelangelo's relationships with the various popes he worked for. Most of those relationships were stormy ones, and Michelangelo's experience as a church artist was extremely frustrating. As I read about all the abuse heaped upon one of my favorite artists, the thought occurred to me that this tension between the church and artists has been going on for hundreds of years. I dream of the day when the church will stop alienating artists and start nurturing artists and give them a safe place to grow and become the people God wants us to be. I wish we were more sensitive to the needs of artists. And I wish all artists loved the church and were growing in godly character and integrity.

I've come to believe that the best way to experience this material is within the context of a team or small group. You can go through this book by yourself, but the greatest benefit would be gained by going through it in a small-group setting with other like-minded artists. You could study this material with your worship band, your church choir, your drama team, your dance troupe, and so on. This material was originally intended for just those kinds of groups. That's why I included the same group discussion questions I would typically use in my workshops. Because I will often stress the importance of being accountable to someone for changes you want to make in your life, there would also be a lot of value in going through this book as part of a one-on-one discipleship or mentoring relationship with a friend or another artist.

Each chapter of the book begins with a scenario that illustrates the focus of that chapter. Although the names I used and the scenarios are fictitious, they are based on real life—situations I've experienced during my years in the ministry.

I currently have the privilege of serving as the music director at Willow Creek Community Church in South Barrington, Illinois. I was part of the original youth group that started the church, and was hired to my current position in 1984. I might refer to my home church from time to time, but this is not a book about Willow Creek. This is a book for Christian artists. I hope you will be encouraged by this book to fulfill the calling God has for you as an artist. And I hope you will be challenged to grow into the artist God wants you to be.

I am deeply indebted to Bill Hybels, whose leadership I have sat under for most of my life and whose teaching permeates this book more than even I probably realize. I am indebted to my wife,

Sue, for her encouragement and support. And I am indebted to the team of artists at Willow Creek with whom I co-labor, some of whom I have known for over two decades. It is to them that I humbly dedicate this book.

But then, no artist is normal; if he were, he wouldn't be an artist. Normal men don't create works of art. They eat, sleep, hold down routine jobs, and die. You are hypersensitive to life and nature; that's why you are able to interpret for the rest of us. But if you are not careful, that very hypersensitiveness will lead you to your destruction. The strain of it breaks every artist in time.

Irving Stone, *Lust for Life*

Introduction

Those "Artsy Types"

Some time ago I spoke at a church conference in Ft. Lauderdale that was attended mostly by pastors and church leaders. I talked about the current state of church music and the future of the arts in the church. However, my deeper passion is for Christian artists to be living lives of integrity and godly character, so I sneaked in a few words about character and integrity. I hardly mentioned it, yet there was a flurry of questions afterward, all dealing with the issue of character and integrity in the lives of artists in the church. Character is fast becoming the hottest issue facing artists in the church today. In fact, the majority of the questions I get about church music ministry never have much to do with music. They revolve around character issues: How can I get my people to serve with a servant's heart? How can I cultivate unity on the team? How can I get my vocalists or my drama people to get along with each other? What should I do about the attitude problems of a few of my musicians? The music department and other arts-related ministries have become a hotbed for major character problems in the church. I've even seen more than a few music ministries blown apart because their leaders failed to address such character issues.

I've had pastors call me, frustrated over character issues they see in their music staff. "Our music director doesn't listen to suggestions," they'll say, or "He doesn't take criticism well. He's not a team player—he's more interested in doing his own thing."

I've also heard music directors express similar frustrations about their volunteers. "So-and-so is a great keyboard player, but they're just so difficult to work with," or "Our key vocalist throws a temper tantrum and threatens to quit once a month. We're scared because we can't afford to lose any of our best vocalists right now. What should we do?"

For too long churches have ignored the problem, letting character issues in the lives of artists slide. We've turned our heads, hoping the problem would go away by itself, but it never does. A pastor sat with me on the bus back to the hotel at this conference in Ft. Lauderdale, and he said something very revealing: "I just leave those artsy types alone. They're kinda off in their own little world anyway."

What did he mean by "those artsy types"? How do you know if you're one of those artsy types? If you love music, drama, art, film, photography, dance, sound, or lighting, if you love doing artistic things—singing, playing, performing, writing, creating, or expressing—chances are you have some kind of artistic streak, large or small or somewhere in between. You might be someone trying to pursue a career in the arts or someone who dabbles in the arts as a hobby. Maybe the extent of your artistic involvement is that you sing in the back row of the church choir. You might be an "amateur" or you might be a "professional." You might be a performer, a creative person, or both. Perhaps you work with artists or live with an artist, and want to understand us artsy types a little better.

Unfortunately there are certain negative stereotypes that are attached to people with artistic temperaments. Some people say that we are temperamental and eccentric. Some people think we're difficult and strange. Some might say we are moody and emotionally unstable. Others see us as free-spirited, quirky, and undisciplined. Excuses are often made for the shortcomings of the artistic temperament, more so than with any other temperament. The problem occurs when we artists buy into those excuses and use them to justify unacceptable behavior.

The negative stereotypes are unfair because not all people with artistic gifts fit the mold. My son informed me the other day that in school he was learning about how weird musicians are. He had been taking a music appreciation class, and what impressed him the most was that Beethoven had such a bad temper that he would cause a scene in a restaurant if his food wasn't right, that women would throw their room keys onstage at Franz Liszt, and that Wagner was a quirky man with strong anti-Semitic views. Since so many of the musicians he was learning about were very strange, it made me wonder what he thinks about me!

The Melancholy Temperament

For centuries now scholars have been fascinated with the artistic temperament. It started with the ancient Greeks, who divided human personality into four main categories: choleric, sanguine, phlegmatic, and melancholy. Aristotle said that "all extraordinary men distinguished in philosophy, politics, poetry, and the arts are evidently melancholic."[1] As a result, people with an artistic bent were labeled as melancholy, which is somewhat misleading because not all artists are predominantly melancholy. I know quite a few who have only a few melancholy tendencies, and others who aren't melancholy at all.

During the Middle Ages melancholy was considered a physical disorder, and the church regarded it as a sin similar to slothfulness.[2] However, during the Renaissance melancholy made a comeback and was seen as a divine gift. Astrology played a large role in Renaissance thinking. A person's behavior was determined at birth by his or her planet's conjunction with other celestial bodies. Saturn was the planet for the melancholic. Someone born under Saturn would "be either sane and capable of rare accomplishment or sick and condemned to inertia and stupidity."[3] The capability for "rare accomplishment" obviously made the melancholy temperament quite fashionable during the Renaissance. In fact, it was written that "a veritable wave of 'melancholic behavior' swept across Europe" during the sixteenth century.[4] The more eccentric an artist was, the more he or she was considered a "genius."

In spite of this rather exalted view, which continued well into the Romantic period, the melancholy temperament has always had its share of negative press. Even at a time when the melancholy temperament was in vogue, there were those who were expressing concern. Writing in the year 1586, Timothy Bright described the melancholy person as

> cold and dry; of colour black and swart; of substance inclining to hardness; lean and sparse of flesh . . . of memory reasonably good if fancies deface it not; firm in opinion, and hardly removed where it is resolved; doubtful before, and long in deliberation; suspicious, painful in studies, and circumspect; given to fearful and terrible dreams; in affection sad and full of fear, hardly moved to anger but keeping it long, and not easy to be reconciled; envious and jealous, apt to take occasions in the worst part, and out of measure passionate. From these two dispositions of brain and heart arise solitariness, mourning, weeping . . . sighing, sobbing, lamentation, countenance demisse and hanging down, blushing and bashful; of pace slow, silent, negligent, refusing the light and frequency of men, delighted more in solitariness and obscurity.[5]

Not a very flattering picture, is it? Even today there's a certain stigma attached to the melancholy temperament. Whenever I read about the temperaments, the melancholy temperament is always approached with a great deal of ambivalence. The other three temperaments come off smelling like a rose while the dreaded melancholy temperament sounds so awful. We're often seen as analytical to a fault, moody, unsociable, and overly sensitive. What bothers me most is that if you get labeled a melancholic, it is automatically assumed that you are some maladjusted emotional misfit.

Reclaiming the Artistic Temperament for Christ

I believe that God has redeemed the artistic temperament. If you're in Christ, you are a new creature. "The old has gone, the new has come!" (2 Cor. 5:17). In Christ there is such a thing as a transformed, well-adjusted, Spirit-filled artist. Imagine what God could do with an artistic temperament that's completely yielded to Him. He doesn't look at us as "those strange artsy types." After all, He made us. He loves us and He understands us.

I'll admit we are a little different, but it's a good kind of different. Artists look at things differently than nonartists do. We notice detail; we appreciate nuance and beauty. Some people might look at the evening sky and all they see is a bunch of stars. But an artist looks at it and sees beauty and meaning. Artists want to sit under the stars and soak it all in. They want to gaze at the moon and be dazzled. They want to paint a picture of it or write a song or a poem. Debussy was so moved by the evening sky that he wrote *Clair de Lune*. Van Gogh was inspired and painted *Starry Night*. King David was an artist who looked at the evening sky and wrote this: "When I consider your heavens, the work of your fingers, the moon and the stars, which you have set in place, what is man that you are mindful of him, the son of man that you care for him?" (Ps. 8:3–4).

Artists respond differently to things than nonartists do. For one thing, we tend to be more sensitive. And that's okay. That's how God made us. In Ephesians Paul talks about us having the eyes of our hearts enlightened (1:18). Sensitive people have a lot of heart. We might see things differently because we feel deeply. In *Windows of the Soul* Ken Gire writes, "We learn from the artists, from those who work in paint or words, or musical notes, from those who have eyes that see and ears that hear and hearts that feel deeply and passionately about all that is sacred and dear to God."[6]

For this reason artists very often speak out against injustice, inequality, and hypocrisy. They take up the cause of those who are suffering. They make us more sensitive to the lost and lonely and to the plight of the downtrodden. Everyone with an artistic temperament has been told at some point in his or her life to develop a thicker skin. That's nonsense! The world doesn't need more thick-skinned people. It needs more people who are sensitive and tender. Have you ever been moved to tears by a powerful piece of music or held spellbound by a beautiful work of art? Have you ever been moved by a scene from a film? It's because an artist felt deeply about something and communicated in such a powerful way that your heart and soul were touched.

The Arts in the Bible

Let's examine briefly what the Bible has to say about the arts and artists. Along with being the infallible Word of God and an agent of life change, the Bible itself is a work of art. People throughout history have studied it as an example of exquisite literature. One such scholar was Frank E. Gaebelein, who wrote, "It is a fact that over and above any other piece of world literature from Homer down through Virgil, Dante, Cervantes, Shakespeare, Milton, and Goethe, no book has been more fully acknowledged as great simply as a book than the Bible."[7]

The Bible is rich in its artistic use of metaphor. My favorite example is the last chapter of Ecclesiastes, in which the aging process is treated metaphorically and likened to a house. "When the keepers of the house tremble, and the strong men stoop, when the grinders cease because they are few, and those looking through the windows grow dim; when the doors to the street are closed and the sound of grinding fades; when men rise up at the sound of birds, but all their songs grow faint" (12:3–4).

The trembling "keepers of the house" refers to hands that shake when one grows old. The "grinders" refer to teeth and our propensity to lose them as we get older. Losing our eyesight is described as looking though a window and having the image grow dimmer. Other references to being bent over, a loss of hearing, and having insomnia are all included in this clever analogy. Instead of describing the aging process in clinical terms, the writer appeals to our imagination and in so doing gets us to feel a sadness about growing old.

The Bible also contains poetry that is written with a great deal of skill and sophistication. The Psalms, the book of Job, and Song of Songs are the most prominent examples of biblical poetry.

Drama is first mentioned in the Bible when Ezekiel is instructed to "act out" a drama depicting the siege of Jerusalem. He even drew the city skyline and used it as a familiar backdrop (Ezek. 4). Jesus spoke often in parables and told colorful and intriguing stories that had their fair share of drama to them.

The visual arts played a major role in building the tabernacle (Ex. 31:1–11). Francis Schaeffer points out that the tabernacle involved every form of representational art known to man.[8] The visual arts also played a huge role in the building of the temple. In fact, the temple was decked out with the finest carvings and engravings (1 Kings 6:15–36; 7:23–39; 1 2 Chron. 3:5–7; 4:1–7). First Kings 6:4 (NASB) says that Solomon "made windows with artistic frames." Some of the artwork in the temple, like the freestanding columns, had no utilitarian significance (2 Chron. 3:15–17). It was beauty for the sake of beauty.

Music is also mentioned quite often in the Bible. Singing was a big part of Hebrew culture. The book of Psalms is actually a hymnbook, and it continually exhorts us to sing to the Lord (Ps. 149:1). The nation of Israel not only sang during worship; they sang while they worked (Num. 21:16–18). David sang a song he wrote at the death of Saul and Jonathan (2 Sam. 1:19–27). And as you leaf through the pages of the book of Revelation, it's obvious that we're going to be doing a lot of singing in heaven (19:1–8).

There is also plenty of instrumental music in the Bible. The word *selah* that occurs throughout the Psalms (seventy-one times, to be exact) is most likely referring to an instrumental interlude between verses or sections of vocal music. Trumpets were used to summon the nation of Israel for meetings, as a signal to break camp, in feasts, in commemorations, during worship, and in conjunction with various military campaigns (Lev. 23:24; Num. 10:1–10; 29:1; Josh. 6:20; Judg. 3:27; 6:34; 7:19–22; 1 Sam. 13:3; 2 Sam. 2:28; 15:10; 18:16; 1 Kings 1:34; 2 Kings 9:13; Ps. 150:3). Trumpets will also announce the second coming of Christ and the resurrection of the dead (Matt. 24:31; 1 Cor. 15:52). Other instruments mentioned include the flute, lyre, harp, and various percussion instruments (1 Sam. 10:5; 1 Kings 1:40; 1 Chron. 25:1; Ps. 45:8; 92:1–3; 150:3–5; Matt. 9:23).

Dance is also included in the Bible. Psalm 149:3 says, "Let them praise his name with dancing." Psalm 150:4 also says, "Praise him with tambourine and dancing." Miriam led the women in a praise dance in Exodus 15:20. Dancing was also a part of welcoming soldiers home from battle (Judg. 11:34). There was singing and dancing when David defeated Goliath (1 Sam. 18:6), and David danced before the Lord when they brought the ark of the covenant home (2 Sam. 6:14–15).

Artists in the Bible

Maybe I'm biased, but I think God has a special place in His heart for artists, because so many are mentioned in the Bible. Being an artist was one of the first occupations listed in the early days of the Old Testament, along with agriculture and industry (Gen. 4:21). There are several references to teams of musicians (Neh. 10:28–29; Ps. 150:3–5) and other artists (Ex. 31:2–6; 35:30–35). The worship team serving in the temple during David's reign was made up of 288 vocalists (1 Chron. 25:7). One of the judgments made against Babylon in the book of Revelation was that life would be void of the richness that artists bring (18:22).

Several artists are mentioned by name throughout Scripture. We can't list all of them, so I'll just touch on a few. David was a skillful musician and songwriter (1 Sam. 16:18), someone whom God described as a man after God's own heart. Solomon wrote over one thousand songs (1 Kings 4:32). Kenaniah was a great vocalist and a song leader (1 Chron. 15:22). There's a group of musicians in 1 Chronicles whom I call the singing percussionists. Their names were Asaph, Heman, and Ethan (15:16–19), and they were vocalists who kept time for everyone by playing the cymbals. Bezalel was cited as a very gifted visual artist (Ex. 35:30–33).

The Power of the Arts

The arts can be extremely powerful. They can awaken us to truth and can change lives. In 1 Samuel 10 Saul was exposed to a group of musicians who had a powerful ministry in prophecy. Their ministry affected Saul so deeply that he was "changed into a different person" (v. 6). That's the power of the arts! When *Messiah* premiered in London, Lord Kinnoul congratulated Handel afterward on the excellent "entertainment." Like many of us, Handel bristled at the thought of his music being mere entertainment. "My Lord, I should be sorry if I only entertain them. I wish to make them better," he said.[9]

The arts can have a powerful impact if they're produced with the anointing power of the Holy Spirit. God used an anointed musician to open Elisha's heart to prophecy in a powerful way (2 Kings 3:15). In the same way, an inspired piece of art in the hands of an anointed artist can be extremely powerful. An anointed song sung by a Spirit-filled vocalist results in a holy moment. We Christian artists can't do what we do apart from the One who gifted us. Let's never forget that our message is not in glitzy demonstrations of our own talent but in "demonstration of the Spirit's power" (1 Cor. 2:4). One theme running throughout the book of Ezra is that God's hand was upon Ezra and all that he did. We need the mighty hand of the Lord to be upon artists today.

The Arts in the Church

What kind of attitude should we artists have toward the church? We need to love the church, the bride of Christ. In spite of all its short-comings (especially when it comes to the arts and artists), the church is still God's vehicle to redeem a lost world. Charlie Peacock, a Christian songwriter and producer, says, "True artists purpose to love the church despite indifference or opposition to their work. Though indifference is their enemy they separate it from the brother or sister who is seduced by it. They are eager to find their place in the Body and do not consider themselves exempt from fellowship and church stewardship responsibilities. They love the church and do all they can to build it up, for how can you love Christ and hate his church?"[10]

We live in a time, however, when many artists don't give the church a second thought. Even Christian artists. When we think of using our art to impact the world, we usually don't think of doing it through the local church. Or if we do, we see the church as a stepping-stone to something with a wider audience.

For example, there is a whole generation of young people growing up right now with the idea that real music ministry is found not in the church but in the Christian music industry. In fact, when they hear the term "Christian artist," most people think it refers to someone "in the industry." Yet the alto in the church choir, the Christian actor involved in community theater, and the born-again art professor are each every bit as much a Christian artist as someone in the industry. This opinion never wins me any friends in the Christian music industry, but have you ever wondered if the Christian music industry was God's first choice to reach a lost world, or did we in the church abdicate that privilege because we had no vision for how powerful music could be *in the church?* I don't mean to say that God's blessing is not on the Christian music industry. It has borne a lot of fruit and is still touching lives today. That impact would not be lost if Christian artists were channeled into the church and/or the marketplace.

Those of you who are musicians, I just have to say that if you're doing church music but would really rather be doing something else (like "making it" in the Christian music industry), don't do church music. Do something else. That goes for all of us artists. Don't look at the church as a stepping-stone to something more important.

I want to be careful that people don't conclude that I think the church is the only acceptable avenue for a Christian to use his or her God-given talents. You need to find the right audience for your work, and it may not always be the local church. Not every work of art fits in appropriately with a church service. We should be using our gifts in the church and in the world. We need more Christian artists in the marketplace. We need more talented musicians, actors, dancers, writers, poets, painters, performers, and film directors out in the world impacting our culture for Christ. We are the salt of the earth (Matt. 5:13). Our light needs to shine in such a way that people see our good works and are drawn to the Lord (Matt. 5:16). I praise God that some of our Christian musicians are crossing over into the secular market. They're influencing our mainstream culture. My advice to young artists today is to consider the church and/or the world as outlets for your work. Don't settle for the Christian music industry or any other field that confines you and your art to a Christian subculture.

I've been involved in music ministry for over twenty-five years now, and I confess that at some of the most difficult points along the way I've wanted to quit. But when I entertained the thought of doing something else with my life, nothing else came close to captivating my passion. This is what God has called me to do. Doing church music is what God put me here for! My mission in life is to contribute to the advancement of music in the church. You don't have to work for a church to love the church. God is reconciling a lost world to Himself through the church, and He invites you and me to be a part of this "ministry of reconciliation" (2 Cor. 5:18). The church is the hope of the world. Serving God in the local church is a high and noble calling.

We need artists in the church today who have a passion for the power of the arts. My personal ministry verse is 1 Corinthians 14:24–25: "If an unbeliever or someone who does not understand comes in while everybody is prophesying, he will be convinced by all that he is a sinner and will be judged by all, and the secrets of his heart will be laid bare. So he will fall down and worship God, exclaiming, 'God is really among you!'"

I love that passage because it describes a ministry experience that is so powerful, everyone knows it's from God. Listen to how it affects even unbelievers: they are convicted of sin; they become vulnerable and face the truth about themselves; they're drawn to God; and finally they leave shaking their heads in amazement and exclaiming, "There really is a God! He is certainly among you!" When God anoints the arts, there is an awesome power that He unleashes to penetrate hearts, minds, and souls. We of all people must never lose sight of how powerful the arts can be *in church*.

Let's look at how the arts can be utilized in the local church by examining the role of the arts in worship, evangelism, encouragement, and celebration.

Worship

The New Testament puts a great emphasis on corporate worship. In Ephesians 5:19 and Colossians 3:16 the early church is instructed to sing "psalms, hymns and spiritual songs." Leland Ryken points out that "music in the New Testament ... is no longer priestly and professional. It is solidly social, congregational, and 'amateur.'"[11] The work of ministry was no longer done by a few full-time professionals. It is the responsibility of every Spirit-filled

Christian to do the work of ministry (Eph. 4:11–13; 1 Peter 2:5, 9). This is a by-product of the new covenant philosophy of a priest-hood of believers.

These days a large number of churches are experiencing Spirit-led worship, and it's added a deep richness to the life of the church. The arts can facilitate worship in a very powerful way. A moving piece of worship music, a stirring drama, a dramatic reading, an expressive dance, or a gripping piece of visual art can create those holy moments when we as the body of Christ experience God's presence in a real way.

The resurgence of worship has unfortunately ignited contro-versies that each local fellowship needs to work through. For exam-ple, the issue of spontaneous versus planned worship seems to cause people to take sides over which is more spiritual. Scripture gives us examples of each. When the nation of Israel crossed the Red Sea, right there on the riverbank they erupted with spontaneous wor-ship that included singing, playing, and dancing (Ex. 15). On the other hand, the worship time that accompanied the dedication of the temple was highly organized and choreographed (2 Chron. 5:11–7:7).

The traditional-versus-contemporary controversy also faces the church that wants to grow in worship. I've seen two extremes: churches that throw out all the old hymns in favor of contemporary worship choruses, and churches that hold on to those old hymns so tightly that they don't consider using the new worship choruses. The New Testament church was a healthy blend of both. First Tim-othy 3:16 is an example of one of those "new" worship choruses for the early church, but believers were also instructed to sing the "old" psalms (Eph. 5:19; Col. 3:16).

I've also seen churches get somewhat narrow-minded about what worship can be, by insisting that all forms of worship be addressed to God. In other words, they only sing songs *to* God and not *about* Him. I understand that this is an attempt to personalize worship and focus on the Lord, and that's good. We are instructed to sing to the Lord (Ps. 33:3), but I don't believe we should be dog-matic about this, because we would eliminate a lot of good worship choruses that can truly edify the church. Also, what many believe to be fragments of hymns found in Scripture (Eph. 5:14; Phil. 2:6–11; Col. 1:15–20) are about the Lord and are not all sung to Him.

Evangelism

The arts can be especially effective in evangelism because they often reflect the seeker's hunger and search for God. John Fischer, in his book *What on Earth Are We Doing?* says that "much of the art of thoughtful non-Christians expresses a longing for God." Fischer goes on to say that when

> artists reach into their colors or to the notes of a musical score, into the developing solution in a darkroom tray or to the flow of words on a page, they are interacting with the eternity God has placed in their hearts. They are trying to be significant in their universe—trying to mean something more than a random collision of molecules. Though modern philosophy tells them they are nothing, their hearts tell them something else. Because their minds cannot fathom what their hearts know, they feel the weight of the God-placed burden. Art often seems irrational, because the heart is reaching beyond the mind. A modern art museum displays the heart reaching beyond what the mind knows, trying to find the meaning of its existence.[12]

Indeed, people are longing for God, and we artists can help point seekers to Him. I would not dispute the evangelistic potential of Spirit-led worship. Psalm 40:3 says that when we worship, it causes many others to turn to Christ. However, as one who has spent the majority of my ministry years in a seeker-driven church, I would plead for churches to consider using the arts also for strategic evangelism. The arts can play a major role in reaching the unchurched. I've had countless people tell me that they first started coming to a seeker church service because they liked the music. Having said that, though, I should also say that great care must go into selecting artistic expressions that the unchurched person can relate to. When Paul wanted to relate to non-Christians, he would go out of his way to speak to them where they were at. In Athens he used the writings of the people's own secular poets and philosophers to present the gospel (Acts 17:28). He used their art, the expression of their popular culture, to reach out to them. Without talking down to our lost friends and neighbors, we must learn how to relate to a postmodern culture and speak meaningfully to them. I would avoid music lyrics that have a lot of Christian jargon that the unchurched person wouldn't understand. I would avoid music or drama that treats serious life issues in a trite manner. If you're targeting the unchurched, make sure you're speaking a language they can understand clearly.

Encouragement

The arts can encourage and edify the church. Music, drama, dance, literature, and the visual arts can encourage someone who's down, someone who's struggling in his or her walk with Christ, someone who's facing trials and temptations. David ministered to Saul by playing the harp, and it encouraged and refreshed him (1 Sam. 16:23). Both Job and David talk about God giving "songs in the night," encouragement for the dark times (Job 35:10; Ps. 42:8; 77:6). We must never lose sight of people and their needs. The church can use us to bring encouragement to those who need a touch from God.

I love it when a hymn or a worship chorus stays with me after I've heard it, and the lyrics are some rich gem from God's Word that ministers to me throughout the day. It reminds me of the psalmist who says, "Your decrees are the theme of my song" (119:54). I had that experience the first time I heard the song "Turn Your Eyes Upon Jesus" and with the praise chorus based on Matthew 6:33, "Seek Ye First." I couldn't get them out of my head and I didn't want to. I'm a different person with a different attitude when God's Word permeates my heart. The arts can make that happen.

The arts excel at identifying with people's pain and ministering the truth of God's Word with sensitivity. There are times when a speaker will say something and it falls on deaf ears. Take the same message and put it to a beautiful melody or any other sensitive art form, and it moves people. It's because the arts speak to the heart. The arts make us more sensitive and tender to the voice of God. If you really want to encourage people in the church, consider allowing the arts to assist you.

Celebration

Just as the arts played a significant role in the nation of Israel celebrating special events such as the crossing of the Red Sea or the dedication of the tabernacle or the temple, the arts can play a significant role in helping the church celebrate. I'm not talking about celebrating just Christmas and Easter. We in the local church could celebrate a lot more than we do. We of all people have so much to celebrate. Baptisms, church anniversaries, God's faithfulness, and answers to prayer are all good reasons to celebrate. Don't wait until Christmas and Easter. The church should throw more parties, and when we do, we should pull out all the stops and really celebrate! What better way to celebrate than to let the arts run free with creativity aimed at honoring God.

On New Year's Eve 1989, Leonard Bernstein conducted Beethoven's Ninth in a concert that celebrated the fall of the Berlin Wall. In his book *Letters to My Son*, Kent Nerburn writes about watching it on television and how moved he was by the piece.

> The instruments sang as if with one voice. The music rose and expanded and became pure emotion.
>
> Tears streamed from my eyes. I wept uncontrollably. It was more than I was, and more than I could ever be. It was a healing and a testament to the best of who we are and the worst of who we are. It was confession, it was celebration. It was us at our most human.
>
> By the time the concert was over, I had been transformed. Into my daily life had come a moment of sheer beauty. Though at an electronic distance, I had been in the presence of one of those moments that only art can provide, when we humans bring forth something from nothing, and invest it with a majesty and beauty that seems to rival the visions of the gods.[13]

This is the power of art, and the person who has not experienced it is only half alive.

Exciting Days for the Arts

These are exciting days for artists in the church because God seems to be awakening the church to the ministry potential of the arts. A few magazines devoted to the arts from a Christian perspective have emerged recently. When I read them, I sense that the arts are alive and well in our local churches. Many churches today have an arts department or their own programming department. I see good changes on the horizon. For example, the role of the artist is changing, starting with the role of the church musician. Twenty years ago if you told your friends that you were involved in the music ministry of your church, they would assume that you sang in the choir. Twenty years ago if I told people that I worked as a music director in a church, they would assume I directed the choir. Yet there are many churches these days that don't even have a choir. It used to be that if you wanted to use your musical gifts in church, you were out of luck unless you could sing in the choir or play the organ. But today there are guitarists, drummers, sax players, synth players, string players, and vocalists of every style leading or participating in church music ministry. Seeker ministry and the worship movement have brought new life to music in the church. God is calling studio players and jingle singers out of the professional music business to serve in the church. He's also calling nonprofessionals to serve, people from all walks of life who used to play an instrument or sing but ended up in a nonmusic career. They're discovering the joy and reward that comes from using their talent to serve the Lord.

These are exciting days also for drama in the church. It used to be that churches featured drama only at Christmas and Easter. Not only was it locked into being used just a couple times a year, but it was confined exclusively to retelling biblical stories. People used to think of church drama as actors standing around in bathrobes in front of a manger scene. But praise God, more and more churches are using drama, to the point that it's becoming a regular part of their programming. Drama sketches are being used very effectively in many church services today. As a result, the quality of the writing and the acting keeps improving. People who used to do drama in high school and college are experiencing joy and fulfillment in serving God in their local church. Others are discovering drama gifts they never knew they had before.

In the technical area, churches are waking up to how important good sound and lighting are to a church service. We're seeing churches investing money in this area and in some cases even hiring full-time sound and lighting people.

Dance is experiencing a revival in the church, especially as an expression of worship. I've seen reports of churches sponsoring workshops and conferences devoted entirely to dance in the church.

Some churches are displaying the works of their visual artists for people to view as they come into the sanctuary. Others are sponsoring galleries or art fairs.

I'm excited about the progress we're seeing in these areas, because I long for the church to be "the happenin' place" for the arts, as it was during Bach's lifetime just 250 years ago. It used to be that when you wanted to hear great music or experience great art, you went to church. It used to be that when you wanted to play or sing great music, you went to church. We've come a long way from that, haven't we?

I believe we are on the verge of a golden era for the arts in church. I believe we are entering an era in church history when God is calling thousands of artists to use their gifts for Him as He never has before. I believe God is trying to raise up a global community of Christian artists who are fully devoted to the lordship of Jesus Christ in their lives. My friend, if that's a desire of your heart, forsake all else and follow Him. He's calling us to play a major role in the church. What an honor. What a privilege. Oh, may we be found trustworthy (1 Cor. 4:2)! It's time we take stock of where we are all at spiritually and make sure that we are honoring God not only with our gifts but with our lives as well. Let us make whatever adjustments we need to make to become all that God wants us to be. I think it's time we got just as serious about godly character as we are about our craft or our art. We can't be concerned about the arts in the church without being concerned about the lives of artists in the church. Our character as church artists, our walk with Christ, our spiritual growth are all a vital part of creating the kind of ministry experience in which God unleashes the power of His Holy Spirit. We need artists in the church who are known not only for their talent but also for their walk with Christ.

Batter my heart, three-personed God; for you
As yet but knock, breathe, shine, and seek to mend;
That I may rise and stand, o'erthrow me, and bend
Your force to break, blow, burn, and make me new.
I, like an usurped town, to another due,
Labor to admit you, but O, to no end;
Reason, your viceroy in me, me should defend,
But is captived, and proves weak or untrue.
Yet dearly I love you, and would be loved fain,
But am betrothed unto your enemy.
Divorce me, untie or break that knot again;
Take me to you, imprison me, for I,
Except you enthrall me, never shall be free,
Nor ever chaste, except you ravish me.

John Donne, Sonnet no. 14

One

Proven Character

S ean and Abigail were both excited and nervous at the same time. Sean had just finished Bible school, and this was his first job interview. He had always dreamed of being a music director at a church, so he had applied for several positions across the country, hoping to find the church that was a "perfect fit." Pastor Blair from Out in the Country Community Church had responded right away to Sean's application. He had scrutinized Sean's résumé and called all his references. They'd had several conversations over the phone and felt it was time to meet face to face. So here they were—Sean and Abigail having dinner with Pastor Blair at the best restaurant in town.

The meeting was going extremely well. Sean was making quite the impression. When Pastor Blair told Sean that he thought he was the best man for the job, Sean and Abigail were ready to burst, but of course they had to remain cool, calm, and collected because we all know that adults should never get overly enthusiastic. All that was left was the interview with the elders, a mere formality if Pastor Blair and his wife approved. Sean began to ask Pastor Blair some questions about the church and the people he'd be working with.

"What's the morale of the music department like right now?"

"It's okay," Pastor Blair responded. "It's what you'd expect from a church." Sean wondered if that was good or bad as Pastor Blair continued. "You see, we have some people who want us to have a more contemporary approach to music and worship, and others who are fighting it tooth and nail."

"Where do you stand?" Sean asked in a friendly way.

"I'd like us to keep both camps happy," Pastor Blair answered. "I think that's our job as a church. I don't want to lose anybody over this. I think that between you and me we can make everybody happy."

"What are the people like in the worship choir?" Sean was eager to know.

"Very nice people," Pastor Blair proudly assured him. "There are just a few problems here and there. You know, a few rotten apples in the bunch, just like any church choir."

"Like who?" Sean really wanted to know.

"Well, there's Mrs. Johnson, who's been singing in the choir for over fifty years. She'll fight you on any change you want to make, but after she says her piece and quits for the five hundredth time, she'll come back to her place at the front of the soprano section, all happy and proud to be there.

"Then there's Mrs. Smith, who fancies herself a soloist, but I haven't found anyone else to agree, if you know what I mean. Somehow she's got it in her brain that she can sing *The Lord's Prayer,* so once a year, usually in July, we let her sing at a Sunday evening service. It certainly gets me to praying that the song will be over in a hurry." Pastor Blair laughed. "She's real nice, though, and she's married to our best tenor, Mr. Smith, who can be very feisty at times. He's been known to curse up a blue streak when he's upset. He had it out with the last music director in front of the whole choir once. My suggestion would be to get him on your side right from the start. He carries a lot of weight around the church.

"Then there's Mr. Brown, who is one of our newer vocalists, but I can't tell you much about him other than that he's got a great voice. He used to sing professionally, I think, but he's rather undependable. We don't know from one week to the next whether he's going to show. I don't know if he travels a lot or if he's just not committed to the things of God.

"Then there's Mr. and Mrs. Jones, a young couple who just moved here, but I sense they might be having marriage problems."

"Are they seeing a counselor? Is anybody helping them?" Sean asked.

"Well, to be honest with you, I really don't know," Pastor Blair replied. "I've been meaning to give them a call, but just haven't gotten around to it yet."

Sean didn't see any reason to press the issue at this point. Besides, he remembered some more practical things he wanted to ask about. "Does the church have much in the way of sound equipment?"

"No," Pastor Blair said, laughing. "Remember, son, we're not called Out in the Country Community Church for nothing. We don't have the latest and greatest technical gadgets out here. We just get by with whatever the Lord gives us. We do have a sound system, of course. Nothing fancy, but it gets the job done."

"Does anybody know how to run it?" Sean asked.

"Oh, yeah. His name is Wilbur. We call him Will for short. If I were you, I'd call him early every Sunday morning. He has a tendency to oversleep."

"Is he a good sound man?" Sean asked, sounding a little worried.

"Sure," Pastor Blair assured him. "I mean, there's really nothing to it. You just come in and flip on a few switches and cue up a few tapes. I think Will is about as much of an expert as there is. He's got this gadget that tells you how loud things are, like a dB-o-meter. When I tell him things sound too loud or too soft, he'll insist we're okay and he'll show me the dB level on that little gadget—and sure enough, he's right."

Abigail wanted to ask about drama. "Do you think the congregation would be open to using drama during the service?"

"You mean every week?" Pastor Blair asked cautiously.

"Well, maybe eventually every week," Abigail said enthusiastically. "We could start out with a drama sketch once a month that fits the topic of your sermon."

That sounded innocuous enough to Pastor Blair. "I think people might like that," he said proudly. Then he began to reminisce with amusement. "They get a real kick out of seeing me and a couple of deacons dress up as the three wise men every Christmas."

Sean and Abigail both laughed nervously. Sean knew he was pushing his luck, but he wanted to know about any visual artists at the church. "Do you have any artists who draw or paint at the church?"

"Not too many," Pastor Blair said thoughtfully. "We do have a macramé class that has met every Wednesday morning for years now. And we hold a craft fair right before Christmas."

Abigail wanted to venture one last question. "Have you ever seen dance used as worship?"

"No, I haven't," Pastor Blair responded politely. "But I don't think that would go over here. That's a little too far out there for us, I think."

Somehow that seemed to close the door on any more questions. Sean and Abigail had mixed emotions. "It seems that whoever gets the job at your church is going to have their hands full," Sean said, almost in a daze.

"You're right about that, son," Pastor Blair chuckled. "It's not a job for the weak of heart, but I think you'll do just fine."

Questions for Group Discussion

1. If you were Sean, would you take the job at Out in the Country Community Church? Why or why not?

2. What do you think Sean's first year on the job would be like?

3. Do you think Sean and Pastor Blair would make a good team? Why or why not?

4. The music department at Pastor Blair's church seems to have some "problem people." How would you handle some of them?

5. Do you think the problems in the music department at Pastor Blair's church are extreme or typical of many churches?

6. Does the church have any obligation to those who are going through difficult times, such as the Joneses, who are having marriage problems?

7. What would it take for the arts to thrive in a church like Pastor Blair's?

8. What would it take for artists to thrive in a church like Pastor Blair's?

9. If church leaders wanted to start a drama ministry, a dance ministry, or a visual arts ministry, how should they go about it?

10. Do you have any apprehensions about the arts playing a larger role in churches in the future?

Character

People sometimes ask me what I would do if I had to choose between a highly talented musician who wasn't very spiritual or a deeply spiritual musician who wasn't very talented. I think that question captures the dilemma the church has been in with artists for a long time. My answer is, I want both! I want artists who are highly talented and deeply spiritual. There was an artist in Exodus 35 named Bezalel who was gifted in sculpting things out of gold, silver, bronze, stone, and wood. He was a visual artist who was refreshingly creative. He was also filled with the Holy Spirit in wisdom, understanding, and knowledge (vv. 30–31). This spiritual giant also had teaching gifts. He was an artist who was talented and godly. That's what we need to be shooting for! That's the biblical standard. We can't expect to get by on just talent alone. It's imperative that you and I keep growing spiritually and artistically.

The Greek philosopher Heraclitis taught that your character is your destiny. That's a value shift for us because we tend to think that our destiny is all wrapped up in our talent. But our destiny doesn't hinge entirely on what we do as artists; it hinges on who we are as people. My pastor, Bill Hybels, wrote a book whose very title convicts me to the core: *Who Are You When No One's Looking?* Who are you when you're not onstage? Who are you when you're not in the spotlight? Who are you when no one's looking at your work? Who are you really?

Romans 5 says that our perseverance results in "proven character" (vv. 3–4 NASB). We need to be people of proven character. Building character simply means that we're trying to become the people God wants us to be. For those of us with artistic temperaments, it means becoming the artists God wants us to be. I'm not talking about being perfect. I'm talking about a character that's proven over time to be true to the life God has called us to live.

How do you know what God wants you to be? Paul says that our lives should demonstrate "love, which comes from a pure heart and a good conscience and a sincere faith" (1 Tim. 1:5). In other words, a person with character is loving, has a clear conscience, and has an authentic relationship with the Lord. These are telltale signs of someone with godly character.

Are we becoming more loving people, or are we too wrapped up in our art? Are we loving the Lord with all our heart, soul, and mind, or do we love singing, playing, acting, or creating more? Would those around you say that you're a loving person?

Do we have a clear conscience about how we're living our lives? Are we honest people? Are we dealing with sin in our lives or are we hiding it? Are we living as those who are dead to sin and alive to Christ, or are we giving in to the passing pleasures of sin? Are we accountable to each other concerning our sin?

Are we living authentic lives as followers of Christ? The Bible refers to authenticity as living a life of truth in our "innermost being" (Ps. 51:6 NASB) and living a life of "godly sincerity" (2 Cor. 1:12 NASB). In other words, we are who we say we are. We're living what we sing about. We're living what we write about. People won't listen to what we say until they have watched what we do and found consistency. Some of us try to hide behind our talents, and we neglect who we are on the inside, but who we are deep inside is who we really are. That's why Paul says that he tries to "keep my conscience clear before God and man" (Acts 24:16).

We too don't want to be accused of not practicing what we preach. That's hypocrisy—when we look good on the outside for the sake of looking good onstage, but it's not really who we are on the inside. We know the right words to say to come off "Christianly," but we're covering up the truth about ourselves. It's merely a "form of godliness" (2 Tim. 3:5), but it's not who we really are. It looks spiritual, but it has no depth or power. It happens when we perform

a song that says we're "giving our all for Jesus," but our lives in reality don't even come close to that. God does not approve of
hypocrisy. In Amos 5:23 the Lord is fed up with the hypocrisy of His
people, and especially their music: "Away with the noise of your
songs! I will not listen to the music of your harps." God won't listen
to empty songs of praise no matter how creative or beautiful they are
if our hearts are not right before Him. The Bible describes King
Amaziah as a man who "did what was right in the eyes of the LORD,
but not wholeheartedly" (2 Chron. 25:2). In other words, his actions
were good but his attitude was bad. He looked good on the outside
but his heart was far from God. A lot of what I'm talking about has
a great deal to do with the condition of your heart. Is your heart on
fire for Christ these days, or are you just going through the motions?

Authenticity is a powerful witness to the presence of God in
our lives. It doesn't mean that we're perfect. It means that we're
real. It means that we're honest about our imperfections and our
struggles. We don't gloss over them and put on a happy Christian
face to cover up our pain. We admit that we struggle. The non-
Christian can detect when we're being inauthentic. The biggest
giveaway is when we come off as if the Christian life is a carefree
life with no pain or struggle. That's simply not true. If we treat serious life issues in a trite manner, that tells our non-Christian friends
that we are out of touch with reality. Being authentic includes being
real with our struggles and shortcomings.

God never intended our character growth to be a low priority. We
are all supposed to mature spiritually "to the whole measure of the fullness of Christ" (Eph. 4:13). We are to "in all things grow up" into
Christ (Eph. 4:15). Growing in Christ doesn't mean that we acquire a
bunch of head knowledge. It means that we grow in areas such as moral
excellence, intimacy with Christ, self-control and discipline, perseverance, godliness, kindness, and love. "For if you possess these qualities in
increasing measure, they will keep you from being ineffective and
unproductive in your knowledge of our Lord Jesus Christ" (2 Peter
1:5–9). This is the kind of stuff from which character is built.

Some of the things that make us good artists can also bring great
conflict into our lives and can actually work against us as we try to

grow spiritually and minister in the church. For example, it's okay to be introverted but it's not okay to be self-absorbed. It's okay to be in touch with our feelings, but it's not okay to be controlled by them all the time. It's okay to be sensitive, but it's not okay to be overly sensitive or chronically defensive. It's okay to do things with excellence, but it's not okay to be overly perfectionistic.

Any growth that we experience in character will be an asset in everything we do. Any time or energy given to growing in the area of character will be worth the effort. Character growth will improve our relationship with God. It'll improve our relationships with friends and family. It'll improve our relationships with the people we work with. It'll improve our overall well-being. We will be better artists for having grown in character. John Wooden, the legendary college basketball coach, has a great quote about character: "Be more concerned with your character than with your reputation, because your character is what you really are while your reputation is merely what others think you are."[1]

Integrity

In Psalms, David says, "I will walk within my house in the integrity of my heart" (Ps. 101:2 NASB). We artists need to be able to walk through the church lobby with integrity in our hearts. Integrity simply means doing what's right in God's eyes. Character is becoming who God made us to be, and integrity is doing what God wants us to do. Even if it's difficult, even if it jeopardizes our careers, even if no one else is doing it, we need to do what's right. That's integrity. People of integrity want to conduct themselves honorably in all things (Heb. 13:18). People of integrity try to be good examples in all things (Titus 2:7). People of integrity want to honor and please God above all else (2 Cor. 8:21). We need to conduct all our affairs with integrity, to treat all people with love and respect, to speak truth and be devoted to honesty. We need to manage our ministries, our careers, our finances, and our homes with integrity. Our thoughts, our words, our deeds must reflect a desire to do what's right in the eyes of God.

Paul says that his greatest ambition is to please God (2 Cor. 5:9). Is that your greatest ambition? Are you living to please God or are you living to please yourself? Are you trying to bring a smile to God's face with your talents, or is your main goal to gratify yourself artistically?

When it comes to integrity, there is a high road and there is a low road. We need to make sure we're always taking the high road. We don't need the congregation looking at us as those strange artsy types; they need to see us as people of integrity who minister, serve, and shepherd in the powerful name of Jesus. First Timothy 4:12 says that we are to be model examples "in speech, in life, in love, in faith and in purity."

Some of us have grown up with high standards attached to the pastor and the elders but not to the artists onstage. We expect pastors to be godly people. We expect them to walk intimately with Christ and to have godly character. We expect them to be living in righteousness and not leading a double life. Why don't we expect the same from our musicians, our drama people, and all our other artists? We're not just artists. We are ministers too. We stand on the same platform and address the congregation with the same message. Shouldn't we aspire to high standards of integrity, just like the pastor? The qualifications for elders in 1 Timothy 3 and Titus 1 can be applied to *all* leaders in the church, and that includes artists. We are to be above reproach; loyal to our spouses; not self-willed or quick-tempered; temperate; prudent; respectable; hospitable; able to teach; not addicted to anything; not pugnacious but gentle; uncontentious; free from the love of money; able to manage our households well; and we must have a good reputation with those outside the church (1 Tim. 3:2–7; Titus 1:7–9).

Remember what the standard was for people who waited on tables in the early church? They were to be people "known to be full of the Spirit and wisdom" (Acts 6:3)—in other words, people of integrity and high character. This wasn't the standard for high-profile positions only; it was the standard for all servants in the church. We are to be people of integrity and proven character. Lewis Smedes says that "integrity is a bigger thing than telling the truth. It is about being a certain kind of person. It is about being people who know who we are and what we are, and it is about being true to what we are even when it could cost us more than we should like to pay."[2]

Psalm 4:3 (NASB) says, "Know that the Lord has set apart the godly man for Himself." In a similar way, the Lord has set apart the godly artist for Himself. Godly artists have been set apart with a special gift or a unique talent, set apart to experience intimacy with God, set apart to be used by God in so many meaningful ways. I believe that God wants to raise up artists in the church who are set apart for Him. They're not different in a strange way, like so many artists in the world. They're different because they're artists with godly character. They're people of integrity. They're not only greatly talented; they're humble, loving, and approachable. They walk with God. They're so sold out to Jesus that people stand awed not by their talent but by their God (see Luke 9:43).

Testing Brings Growth

Now let's get practical and talk about *how* to grow in character and integrity. How does one go about growing in character? Simply put, we grow when our character gets tested (1 Peter 1:7). Romans 5:3–4 (NASB) says that "tribulation brings about perseverance; and perseverance, proven character." Tribulation, or testing, produces perseverance; and perseverance molds our character. When we encounter difficulty, it demands a response. We can be pulled along by the darker side of our human nature, or we can respond with integrity. The way we respond to certain challenges and even certain thoughts that pop into our mind goes a long way in shaping our character. We must choose whether we're going to respond with integrity when the opportunity arises.

One day a pastor asked me to join his music staff for lunch. They were leading a new start-up church and wanted to pick my brain about music ministry. These two music guys were bright, energetic, and committed. We had a lively discussion, and I was impressed by the depth of thought their questions revealed. As our lunch appointment drew to a close, the pastor asked me if I had any parting words of wisdom for these two young bucks, as he called them. I told them something I would say to anyone embarking on a ministry in the arts: When you're in ministry, your character will be tested as it's never been tested before. Your character will be challenged and stretched to the limit. Let God have His way with you! When the going gets tough, grow.

On many occasions there's been a problem in my ministry, and the problem has been me. It's been my stubbornness, my immaturity, my self-centeredness, my defensiveness, my being overly sensitive, my anger and resentment, my jealousy and envy—basically, my lack of character. Don't let your lack of character stand in God's way. Don't let it inhibit your ministry. Hebrews 6:1 tells us to "go on to maturity." Let God mold you into the person He wants you to be.

Our character gets tested when we're asked to play a behind-the-scenes role instead of the more prominent role we wanted to play. How will we respond when that happens? Our character gets tested when someone gives us constructive criticism. How are we going to react? Our character gets tested every time our feelings get hurt. Are we going to develop a bitter spirit or a forgiving heart? Our character gets tested when perfectionism rears its ugly head and we're tempted to come down hard on ourselves and others for not living up to our expectations. Are we going to give in to perfectionism or not? Our character gets tested when a situation calls for us to put the needs of others ahead of our own. How will we respond to that? Our character gets tested when we face the temptation to sin, when we try to meet our needs apart from God. Are we going to be faithful or not? How we respond to these little tests determines whether we will become artists of character and integrity.

Taking Inventory

How are you doing these days in terms of your character growth? Where are you strong and what areas need attention? One of the crucial steps in any recovery program is to take a moral inventory of yourself. Paul says the same thing in 2 Corinthians 13:5 when he says, "Examine yourselves to see whether you are in the faith; test yourselves" (see also 1 Cor. 11:28). His most passionate plea on the subject comes from 1 Timothy 4:14–16: "Do not neglect your gift, which was given you through a prophetic message when the body of elders laid their hands on you. *Be diligent in these matters; give yourself wholly to them,* so that everyone may see your progress. *Watch your life and doctrine closely.* Persevere in them" (emphasis mine).

That's very strong language Paul is using to exhort us to grow and become the people God wants us to be. Perhaps he felt compelled to be so direct because of our tendency to avoid taking an honest inventory of ourselves. We'd rather judge others than evaluate ourselves.

To avoid being too hard or too easy on ourselves, we must be sure to include God in the process. We should pray what David prays in Psalm 139:23–24: "Search me, O God, and know my heart; test me and know my anxious thoughts. See if there is any offensive way in me, and lead me in the way everlasting."

Right now spend a few minutes taking inventory on where your character growth is at these days. We'll be addressing each of these areas in the remainder of this book, but for now answer the following questions as honestly as you can.

Servanthood

1. How often do you put the needs of others ahead of your own?

    ____Most often.

    ____Sometimes.

    ____I hardly ever think about it.

2. How did you respond the last time you were asked to serve out of the spotlight and behind the scenes?

    ____I did it with joy.

    ____I didn't like it, but I did it anyway.

    ____It made me angry.

Teamwork

1. Are you using your artistic talents at church and experiencing genuine community with a group of Christian artists?

_____Yes.

_____I'm not currently serving at church.

_____I have no meaningful relationships with other Christian artists.

2. How are you at resolving relational conflict in your life?

_____I always try to go straight to the individual and talk.

_____Most of the time I try to talk it out with the other person.

_____I hate confrontation, so I suppress my feelings when people hurt me.

Perfectionism

1. Do you entertain thoughts in your head that you're not good enough as an artist?

_____Not very often.

_____Sometimes.

_____Just about all the time.

2. Are you hard on yourself when you make a mistake?

_____No.

_____Sometimes.

_____Yes, I can be very hard on myself.

Defensiveness

1. Has anyone ever said that they feel as if they have to walk on eggshells around you?

_____Never.

_____Sometimes.

_____I hear that from people all the time.

2. How do you respond to constructive criticism?

_____I welcome feedback and regularly invite it from others.

_____It's hard, but I usually accept it with grace.

_____I feel hurt.

Jealousy and Envy

1. How do you respond to someone with more talent or success than you?

    _____I praise God that He's gifted the person and that He's also gifted me.

    _____It's hard, but I try not to let it affect me.

    _____I turn inward and feel inadequate and inferior.

2. When you run across someone with more talent or success than you, does it make you want to give up being an artist?

    _____Never.

    _____Sometimes.

    _____Often.

Managing Your Emotions

1. Has anyone ever told you that you're too negative or moody?

    _____Never.

    _____Sometimes.

    _____I hear that all the time.

2. Do you ever sense that you're being controlled by your emotions?

    _____Never.

    _____Sometimes.

    _____Yes, I often feel controlled by my emotions.

Leading Artists

1. If you're a leader who is also an artist, do you ever sense any tension between the two?

    _____No, never.

    _____Sometimes.

    _____Yes, I don't see how I can do both.

2. If you lead a team of artists, how well are they following you?

_____I feel inept at leading artists.

_____We've got so much conflict on the team and I don't know where to begin to solve it.

_____We all seem to be moving together in the right direction.

Sin

1. Are there any ongoing sins or bad habits in your life right now?

_____No.

_____No, but there are a couple of areas in which I struggle from time to time.

_____I'm struggling with a certain sin, and I don't know what to do about it.

2. Do you have anybody in your life that you're accountable to regarding sin?

_____Yes.

_____I have accountability in my life, but it's not strong or consistent.

_____I have no accountable relationships in my life right now.

Spiritual Disciplines

1. Do you have a regular quiet time (devotional time with the Lord)?

_____Yes.

_____I try, but it's hard for me to be consistent.

_____I'm just not very disciplined in that area.

2. Do you feel that you have a good relationship with the Lord these days?

_____My relationship with the Lord is going extremely well.

_____I'm feeling dry spiritually these days.

_____I feel far away from Him right now.

Committed to a Process

God keeps working in our lives to conform us to the image of Christ (Rom. 8:29). The greatest miracle He performs is a changed life. Dante says that we are worms destined to be angelic butterflies. This metamorphosis doesn't happen overnight; it takes time. I wish I could say that character growth is quick and easy. But when it comes to the transformation of your character, you're most often going against the grain of who you are naturally and how you were brought up, so it's no easy task. We don't like anything that hurts or anything that takes time. We roll our eyes whenever we encounter anything difficult, and say, "Well, I guess it'll build character," as if it's medicine that's good for us but tastes bad. We've got to change our attitude and embrace struggle, even look for it, because it'll make us better people.

Paul says it's tribulation that leads to perseverance that leads to proven character (Rom. 5:3–4). Character growth is actually a reward. It's the result of being faithful. It's the reward for persevering through difficulty. There will be highs and there will be lows. Most of the time it'll be two steps forward and one backward. Paul never felt that he had arrived. He said, "Forgetting what is behind and straining toward what is ahead, I press on toward the goal to win the prize for which God has called me heavenward in Christ Jesus" (Phil. 3:13–14). Paul was committed to the process of growing in character. I invite you on a lifelong, life-changing journey. It's going to call for day-to-day commitment to die to self and follow God (Luke 9:23; John 12:24). It might be humbling as God brings to light certain things in our character that need to be changed. It might be painful as God performs surgery to remove that which holds us back from being all He wants us to be. However, there will be wonderful breakthroughs along the way. Our God is a God of breakthroughs (2 Sam. 5:20). He's the one conforming us to the image of Christ (Rom. 8:29). He's the one who's at work in us "to will and to act according to his good purpose"(Phil. 2:12–13). He's the one who began a good work in us and will bring it to completion (Phil. 1:6). He is able to make us what He wants us to be. We need to cooperate with Him throughout the process and celebrate each and every breakthrough we experience. So be patient with your progress and trust God with the outcome. Friends, let's present ourselves to God today as artists who are set apart for Him. Let's make a covenant today to be artists of deep character and high integrity for the cause of Christ.

Follow-Up Questions for Group Discussion

1. Does the phrase "artistic temperament" have a negative connotation for you? Why or why not?
2. What kind of art moves you the most?
3. In your opinion, what should the role of the arts be in church?
4. Are you optimistic about the future of the arts in the church, pessimistic, or somewhere in between, say cautious?
5. In your opinion, are the arts utilized effectively in your church?
6. How can the church become more of a safe place for artists?
7. What's the best way for the church to go about helping artists grow in character?
8. Share an area of your life that has changed since you became a Christian. How did that change happen?
9. Why is it hard for people to change?
10. What kinds of things cause us to grow spiritually?

Personal Action Steps

1. Choose for yourself a personal ministry verse—a Bible verse that reflects your passion and/or giftedness.

2. Based on the time and attention given to your artistic growth and your spiritual growth, determine which has been the bigger priority for you and prayerfully consider whether you need to rearrange your priorities.

3. Ask God to reveal to you any areas of your life that don't reflect godly character right now. (For example, family relationships, finances, thought life, attitudes, work ethic, and so on.)

4. Go through the checklist under the "Taking Inventory" section of this chapter and circle the question or topic that reveals the area of your character in which you want to see the most growth during this next year.

5. Decide to whom you could be accountable to grow in that particular area.

He Is Able

He is able, more than able
To accomplish what concerns me today
He is able, more than able
To handle anything that comes my way
He is able, more than able
To do much more than I could ever dream
He is able, more than able
To make me what He wants me to be[3]

Rory Noland

Even now this can be done, but it will lead the grand unity of men in the future, when a man will not seek servants for himself, or desire to turn his fellow creatures into servants as he does now, but on the contrary, will long with his whole heart to be the servant of all, as the Gospel teaches.

Fyodor Dostoyevsky, *The Brothers Karamazov*

Two

Servanthood Versus Stardom

*R*ita is a new member of the worship team at Main Street Community Church. She's a professional singer. She gets hired to perform at weddings, parties, special conferences, and even to record a large number of television spots and radio jingles. She's very good. She's been a believer for quite a while now and thought it would be a great idea to offer her talents for use at her church. At first she was received very enthusiastically. You could tell the music director was thrilled to have her in the ranks. It was certainly a feather in his cap to have someone of such high caliber singing at his church. The other vocalists welcomed her cordially, but if the truth were known, many of them felt threatened by her. They quickly realized she was far and away more talented vocally than most of them and that she had made it in the music business in ways that most of them could only dream about. While they wondered if this immensely talented newcomer meant fewer opportunities for many of them to sing, they nonetheless tried to receive her warmly. But as time went on, it was obvious that Rita knew how good she was compared with everyone else on the team. She quickly rose to prominence and became what everyone referred to as "the featured soloist" at the church.

But eventually Rita's star began to tarnish. More people regarded her as arrogant, and though no one would say it out loud, some even thought she was a prima donna. She was distant, hardly ever talking to or socializing with the other singers. She was often late for rehearsal, sometimes keeping people waiting for up to an hour. Sometimes she didn't show up for rehearsal at all and didn't bother to call. Her antics onstage during a sound check didn't exactly endear her to everyone else, either. She would impolitely demand more of herself in the monitor and call the sound technician to task every time things weren't just right. She would also scold the other vocalists when they weren't exactly "on," and responded with cutting sarcasm to mistakes by the instrumentalists in the band. She often came to rehearsals unprepared, assuming that everyone would cut her some slack because she was an established professional. She didn't sit through the pastor's messages and rarely attended any function of the church that didn't call for her to sing. People in the congregation knew Rita had a great voice. That was obvious, but they wouldn't say she was their favorite singer. She was too distant, too glitzy. It was difficult for people in the congregation to relate to her, hard for them to connect with her.

The pastor of the church invited Rita several times to accompany him during his weekly hospital visits, but she always declined, saying she didn't want to do small venues anymore. The pastor perceived Rita's prima donna attitude and tried to take her aside and gently teach her about servanthood in ministry, but she became offended. She couldn't understand why the pastor was singling her out. "Doesn't the Bible tell us not to judge?" she asked angrily. She was hurt. She felt misunderstood. *These people don't appreciate me,* she thought, so she left the church and never came back. The church, by the way, recovered nicely and went on to have a dynamic music ministry without Rita.

Questions for Group Discussion

1. Rita would never call herself a prima donna, yet she was perceived as one. What specific behavior on her part communicated a "greater than thou" attitude?

2. Do you think the pastor did the right thing in confronting Rita about her attitude? Why or why not?

3. Do you think Rita responded appropriately to her confrontation with the pastor? If not, how should she have responded?

4. Should people like Rita be confronted, or should we just tolerate them in the church?

5. What makes it difficult to confront people like Rita?

6. How would you feel if you were one of the vocalists Rita reprimanded? Or one of the instrumentalists she cut down? Or the sound technician she mistreated?

7. What is it about the stage and public ministry that makes it difficult for an artist to have a servant's heart?

8. In your opinion, what percentage of artists in the church today understand what being a servant is all about?

9. How are artists in the church going to learn about true servanthood?

10. In your mind, what characterizes a true servant of Christ?

Servants or Stars?

I shared the preceding scenario with someone outside the music ministry, and their response was, "Isn't this extreme? Surely there aren't really people out there like Rita." But if the truth were known, we'd all probably admit that we've known a Rita or two sometime in our lives. And while it may be obvious that Rita needs to grow in the area of servanthood, it may not be as obvious that there is a little bit of Rita in all of us. The desire to be served comes easier to us than the desire to serve. We artists can be very selfish and self-absorbed at times. We like the attention that our talents bring us. We like feeling a little more special than most folks, who can't perform or create the way we can. Our society tends to put anybody who has talent on a pedestal. We turn the most successful artists into superstars. The superstars are indulged and pampered. They become rich and famous. So servanthood and being others-oriented doesn't come naturally for any of us.

Let's face it: servanthood is a countercultural notion; it goes against human nature. We'd all rather be served. If given a choice, we'd all choose notoriety over obscurity. We all want to be in the spotlight instead of behind the scenes. Someone once asked Leonard Bernstein what was the most difficult instrument in the orchestra to play. The maestro thought for a second and replied, "Second fiddle."

Barriers to True Servanthood

God's Word has a different standard for those of us who minister in His name. First Corinthians 4:1 says, "Men ought to regard us as servants of Christ." Do our church people see us as servants or stars? Do they see us as ministers or entertainers? I think there are three things that stand in the way of true servanthood.

1. An Attitude of Superiority

The first of these barriers is an attitude of superiority. Very few of us Christians would say out loud that we think we're better than someone else, but we can communicate an attitude of superiority in so many different ways—some of them subtle and some of them not so subtle. For example, the way we treat others reveals whether we think we're better than they are. In our opening scenario Rita never came out and said she was greater than everyone else. She didn't have to. She was distant, she kept to herself, she didn't try to reach out to others, she was always late, she missed rehearsals without calling, she was impatient with the sound technician and other singers, she was sarcastic toward the band, she came to rehearsal unprepared, she didn't sit through the sermon, she didn't come to church unless she was singing, and she had an unteachable spirit. Actions speak louder than words, don't they?

Behind this attitude of superiority is misguided pride. Pride is a hidden desire to be exalted. It's a horrible sin that we artists need to be vigilant about. Pride unfortunately is also one of those sins that is so easy to see in others but not in ourselves. Right now, off the top of our heads, each of us could probably name five people who we think have a pride problem. But the real question is, Where is the sin of pride in each of our hearts? The Bible says that if you want to boast about someone, boast about God (2 Cor. 10:17). If you want to boast about something, boast about your weakness and God's sufficiency (2 Cor. 12:9). Boasting is the way some people cope with insecurity. Many artists are insecure. We're dying to feel good about ourselves, but pridefully building ourselves up is not the right way to do it.

2. Selfish Ulterior Motives

The second barrier to true servanthood is selfish ulterior motives. We need to look deep and keep a watchful eye on our motives, because the Bible says the human heart is "deceitful" and "beyond cure" (Jer. 17:9). We can be very selfish. In Acts 8:17–24 we find a story about a man named Simon who had ulterior motives. Simon saw Peter and John laying hands on people and witnessing glorious manifestations of the Holy Spirit, and he wanted that power for his own selfish reasons. He offered Peter and John money for this Holy Spirit power, but Peter strongly rebuked him and commanded him to repent of his self-serving intentions. We too need to repent of selfish ulterior motives. If we don't, we could think we're serving God and actually be serving ourselves. Sometimes, deep inside, our real motive is to get attention or be noticed. We want to be applauded. We want to be recognized. When our agenda is "me, me, me," we have selfish motives. It happens whenever we manipulate conversations to come around to us and our talent. It happens when we name-drop to make ourselves look important. It happens when we talk about our accomplishments to prove ourselves. What's driving us at those moments is selfish ulterior motives.

3. Confidence in Our Giftedness Alone

The third barrier to true servanthood occurs when we put all our confidence in our giftedness, our natural talent. In Philippians 3:3 Paul says that he puts "no confidence in the flesh." Yet we stand onstage sometimes and perform with a man-made confidence instead of a God-dependent confidence. One of the things that prevents us from experiencing God's fullest blessing on our lives is our self-sufficiency. If we think we can make it on our own because we're smart enough or talented enough, we're sadly mistaken. Sometimes a vocalist will stand onstage and not be quite one hundred percent, because he or she feels a cold coming on. At times like these our confidence is not in our talent but in the power of God to use us in our weakness. When artists have more confidence in their giftedness than in the Lord, they leave the stage more worried about how they looked or sounded than about whether God used them. They're more concerned with technique than with substance.

Christ's Example of Servanthood

Jesus of course is the ultimate example of servanthood. Mark 10:45 says that "even the Son of Man did not come to be served, but to serve, and to give his life as a ransom for many." In Philippians 2 Paul describes how Jesus "made himself nothing, taking the very nature of a servant" (v. 7), and "humbled himself and became obedient" (v. 8). The Son of God left the glory and privilege of heaven to be born in a stable in some remote, backward little country at a technologically primitive point in time. After two thousand years the picture of Jesus washing the disciples' feet is etched in our minds, yet we still fail to grasp the depth of all that it means. Jesus' model of servanthood was a radical departure from the cold, distant, self-centered Greek and Roman gods that preceded Him. His model of servanthood goes against the grain of human history, in which leaders have always ruled through domination. To lead by serving goes against human nature. Can you imagine what it would be like to have Jesus in your music ministry? What would it be like to have Jesus on the drama team? Or in the dance ministry or on the visual arts team or on the production team at church? What it all boils down to is that Jesus would be a servant artist. He said it Himself: "The greatest among you will be your servant" (Matt. 23:11). If you need a visual aid to inspire you to be a servant, picture Jesus washing the feet of the disciples (John 13:2–15). There's an awkward beauty to that scene, isn't there? In a world where might is right, Jesus, the Son of God, was willing to wash dirty feet. Now, that's servanthood. Can you imagine having the God of the universe wash your feet? Have you ever washed someone else's feet?

It's a very humbling experience. When my two sons were younger, every year I would wash their feet sometime during Holy Week to remind myself to be a loving servant-father and to remind them to serve each other. Every year I did that, I was struck with just how awkward it is to serve someone else by performing a menial task. It's a truly revolutionary concept for leaders and people in the spotlight to serve instead of be served.

The Humble Artist

Servanthood starts with humility. Humility means moving from self-centeredness to God-centeredness. But before we talk about what humility is, let's talk about what it's not. True humility is not cutting yourself down or letting people walk all over you. That's false humility. Romans 12:3 says to not think more highly of yourself than you ought, "but rather think of yourself with sober judgment." Don't think of yourself more highly than you should, and don't think of yourself more lowly than you should. Sometimes a bad self-image is mistaken for humility. True humility is not thinking so poorly of yourself that you lack confidence, boldness, or assertiveness. Being humble doesn't mean letting yourself be humiliated. For example, you may think it's fashionable or even spiritual to cut yourself down or to minimize your gifts or to keep quiet because you don't think your ideas are worth sharing, but that's counterfeit humility. And it's wrong because it denies the fact that you matter to God. It contradicts Scripture and violates God's character. Don't beat yourself down and call it humility.

In C. S. Lewis's classic book *The Screwtape Letters* there is a conversation between two demons, Screwtape and Wormwood, who are discussing a strategy to ensnare human beings into this false type of humility. This is Screwtape talking to his fellow demon:

> You must therefore conceal from the patient the true end of Humility. Let him think of it, not as self-forgetfulness, but as a certain kind of opinion (namely, a low opinion) of his own talents and character. Some talents, I gather, he really has. Fix in his mind the idea that humility consists in trying to believe

those talents to be less valuable than he believes them to be. . . . The great thing is to make him value an opinion for some quality other than truth, thus introducing an element of dishonesty and make-believe into the heart of what otherwise threatens to become a virtue. By this method thousands of humans have been brought to think that humility means pretty women trying to believe they are ugly and clever men trying to believe they are fools. And since what they are trying to believe may, in some cases, be manifest nonsense, they cannot succeed in believing it, and we have the chance of keeping their minds endlessly revolving on themselves in an effort to achieve the impossible.[1]

We need to regard ourselves with sound judgment. True humility means having an accurate view of ourselves, thinking we're no more or less than we are. We must know our strengths. We must know our weaknesses. We must know what we're good at, and accept what we're not good at.

How can you embrace true humility as an artist?

Humble Yourself Before God

First of all, humble yourself before God. Jesus said that "everyone who exalts himself will be humbled, and he who humbles himself will be exalted" (Luke 18:14). James 4:10 exhorts us to humble ourselves before God. In fact, God has a special place in His heart for the humble. Scripture says that He dwells with the "contrite and lowly in spirit" (Isa. 57:15) and that He "looks upon the lowly" (Ps. 138:6; see also Isa. 66:2). Pride, on the other hand, is an abomination to the Lord (Prov. 16:5). The Bible says that God is opposed to the proud (1 Peter 5:5). He resists the person who thinks he or she is better than everyone else (James 4:6). Think about how serious that is. You really don't want God opposed to you and your ministry, do you? Psalm 138:6 says that God tends to distance Himself from the haughty. What a dreadful thought: that God could not only oppose the proud but be far away—aloof from them. You don't really want God to be distant and far away, do you? Pride, putting ourselves first, and a lack of humility aren't pleasing to God.

It's imperative that we humble ourselves before God, because apart from Him we can do nothing (John 15:4–5).

Remember that your talent comes from God. You're developing it, but He's the one who gave it to you in the first place. If you have an artistic gift, it's because God has given it to you. Before they entered the Promised Land, Moses warned the people of Israel not to forget that all their blessings were a gift from God. Paraphrasing Deuteronomy 8:17–18, this is what Moses might say to us artists today: "Be humble about your talent. Otherwise you may say in your heart that you did it all on your own. But you shall remember the Lord your God, for it is He who gave you the ability to do what you do."

If you and I accomplish anything artistically, it's because of a gift or talent that came from God in the first place. "By the grace of God I am what I am," Paul says (1 Cor. 15:10). We of all people have every reason to be humble before God and others. That's why Paul warns us in Philippians 3:3 not to put our confidence in the flesh, because our confidence is in God. Humility comes naturally to the person who places all their confidence in God. That's unlike the fool in Ecclesiastes who says, "My heart took delight in all *my* work, and this was the reward for all *my* labor" (2:10, emphasis mine). The prideful person says, "Look what I did." The humble person says, "Look at what God did through me."

Humble Yourself Before Others

First Peter 5:5 tells us to clothe ourselves with humility toward one another. We are to abandon any thoughts of superiority that would cause us to think that we deserve special treatment above others. Arrogance has no place in the heart of the Christian artist.

David was as much of a celebrity to the people of Israel as you could be. He had success, fame, and fortune, but he didn't let it go to his head. The Bible says that "all Israel and Judah loved David, and he went out and came in before them" (1 Sam. 18:16 NASB). *The Living Bible* says that "he was as one of them." In other words, even though he was rich and famous, he was approachable. He was one of them; he was still just one of the guys. He wasn't arrogant; he was humble.

Sometimes in the process of using our talents, we artists get elevated higher than we should. Praise for the artist can be effusive for many reasons: the glory of the spotlight, the impact of the arts, the rarity of the gifts. People say things like, "I love your voice more than anyone else I've ever heard" or "I don't know how you do it; you're absolutely amazing." How do you respond to that kind of adulation? I've heard people (myself included) string a bunch of Christian clichés together in an effort to sound spiritual. The result sounds something like, "Oh, it wasn't really me out there. I had nothing to do with it. It was all God. Praise the Lord. I just open my mouth and He takes over from there." This ends up sounding flippant. Then there is the person who doesn't know how to respond to praise without cutting themselves down. They figure false humility is better than no humility at all. Their response goes something like this: "I'm just a sinful worm filling in until God finds somebody better to do the job."

Sometimes the best response is a simple and humble "Thank you." The Bible says that the way we respond to praise is a mark of our character (Prov. 27:21). Do we let the praise that's heaped upon us cause us to think we're better than other people? Do we really give God the glory, or do we just say the appropriate Christian clichés so it appears we're giving God the glory? Jesus reminds us in Luke 17:10 that when we use our gifts for Him, "we have only done our duty." In God's economy there is no hierarchy of gifts and talents (1 Cor. 12:22–23). Just because we perform onstage, we're no better than anyone else who's faithfully using his or her gifts elsewhere in the church. We're only doing what we ought to be doing.

This verse is not saying that it's wrong to feel good about ourselves or about something we've done. It is quite all right to take pleasure in pleasing God with your talent. In fact, that should be one of our main ambitions in life (2 Cor. 5:9). However, some of us get very uncomfortable when someone applauds our efforts or pays us a compliment. We haven't learned how to receive a compliment with grace. We don't know how to handle it, because we don't think it's okay for people to thank us or say nice things about what we do. Luke 17:10 shows us that Jesus is assuming that people will commend us if we do well, so it's okay. That's why He's teaching about it. The spirit of this verse is one of humility. I'm not suggesting we use this verse as a stock answer whenever someone pays us a compliment. I am suggesting we remember that when we use our gifts and talents for the Lord we're only doing what we ought to be doing. We then can graciously acknowledge and thank all who encourage us, keeping in mind that we are never the main attraction anyway (no matter how high a pedestal people might put us on).

The great composer Franz Joseph Haydn was reputed to be a very humble man. One time an overly adoring fan was fawning all over him, and he responded by saying, "Do not speak so to me. You see only a man whom God has granted talent and a good heart."[2] Haydn responded with the kind of graceful humility that pointed people to God. So let's cultivate humility in our hearts, and we will be humble artists.

Die to Your Desire to Be the Greatest

We need to die to the desire to be the greatest. How do we know if we have a servant's heart? There's a saying that we can tell how much of a servant's heart we have by how we respond to being treated like a servant. We tend to get all bent out of shape if we're not treated like little gods. C. S. Lewis says, "Pride gets no pleasure out of having something, only out of having more of it than the next man. We say that people are proud of being rich, or clever, or good-looking, but they are not. They are proud of being richer, or cleverer, or better-looking than others. If every one else became equally rich, or clever, or good-looking there would be nothing to be proud about. It is the comparison that makes you proud: the pleasure of being above the rest."[3]

For many of us, it's not enough to be talented. We want to be the most talented. There was a man named Diotrephes who brought disgrace to himself and the church because he was so intent upon being prominent that he loved "to be first" (3 John 9). Deep inside many of us hides the same desire to be first. The disciples struggled with this, too, and often ended up arguing about who among them was the greatest (Luke 9:46–48; 22:24–30). We may laugh at them now, but within many of us artists there is a strong desire to be number one. Instead of being the best we can be, we want to be the best there is or the best there ever was. We live in a world in which being average doesn't cut it. There's no glory in being just good. We've been made to feel that if we're not composed of the stuff that legends are made of, we don't measure up. But this should not be so in the church. Ministry is not a popularity contest, and jockeying for position is wrong among Christ's followers. Jesus is the head of the church, and He is to have first place in everything (Col. 1:18). When you and I die to our need to be noticed, we'll fulfill an even greater need: the need for significance in God's eyes. Exchange self-importance for a life of true significance.

The Servant Artist

In Nehemiah's day the musicians were in charge of maintenance for the house of God (Neh. 11:22–23). These janitors-by-day/artists-by-night had a strict, disciplined, daily routine that included doing the custodial work needed for the upkeep of God's house. They were servant artists, and that's what we need to be. If you want to grow in humility, the best thing you can do is serve others. Serving others builds character. Richard Foster writes, "Nothing *disciplines* the inordinate desires of the flesh like service, and nothing *transforms* the desires of the flesh like serving in hiddenness. The flesh whines against service but screams against hidden service. It strains and pulls for honor and recognition. It will devise subtle, religiously acceptable means to call attention to the service rendered. If we stoutly refuse to give in to this lust of the flesh, we crucify it. Every time we crucify the flesh, we crucify our pride and arrogance" (emphasis in original).[4]

Let's face it: it can be a real challenge for us to serve others. We artists tend to be narcissistic and very self-centered. We're sensitive people, but when that sensitivity is turned inward on ourselves, we can be so insensitive to the needs of others. We're very aware of our own feelings, but what about the feelings of others? It's not easy for people with artistic temperaments to become others-oriented. We need to forget about us and throw ourselves into serving others. How do we do that?

Focus on People

First of all, stay focused on ministering to people, as opposed to gratifying yourself artistically. Ministry is not about us and our wonderful talents. It's about people. It's all about serving others. First Peter 4:10 says, "Each one should use whatever gift he has received to serve others." Use your gifts to serve others. If you're trying to gratify yourself artistically and forget all about ministering to people, it will be a very empty experience. We artists spend so much time on technique and style that we often lose sight of the people we're trying to reach. When Jesus looked out on the crowds of people before Him, His heart was moved with compassion (Matt. 9:36). He was sensitive to their needs because He was focused on people. Next time you're onstage or performing for a group of people, try looking out at the people as Jesus would, with a heart full of compassion for each and every one of them.

Paul defined servanthood by how it affects those around us. He said that "the Lord's servant must not quarrel; instead, he must be kind to everyone, able to teach, not resentful. Those who oppose him he must gently instruct" (2 Tim. 2:24–25).

A good place to start serving is with the people we serve with— our fellow artists. Galatians 5:13 tells us to "serve one another," and Romans 12:10 says to "be devoted to one another." We need to come to a meeting, to a rehearsal, or to a service ready and willing to serve. Instead of always asking, "What's in it for me?" or "What can I get out of this?" we need to ask, "How can I serve? What can I give?"

Remember That the Message Is More Important

Keep in mind that the message is more important than the messenger. Paul talks about this in 1 Corinthians 2:4–5: "My message and my preaching were not with wise and persuasive words, but with a demonstration of the Spirit's power, so that your faith might not rest on men's wisdom, but on God's power." In other words, the purpose of my ministry is not to impress people with my art but to demonstrate God's power and love. We can all tell, for example, when a singer is concentrating more on his or her vocal technique than on what the song is about. If not doing that lick that shows off your voice would cause the meaning of the lyrics to come across with more clarity, don't do the lick. Sometimes a simpler, uncluttered approach serves the message better. If you're an instrumentalist, this means that you play skillfully and with appropriate expression but don't draw undo attention to yourself. The stage at your church does not exist solely as your personal platform. We need to serve the message, not ourselves.

By the way, if you're an instrumentalist, you might want to look at Psalm 68:25. In the worship service described here, the artists come into the sanctuary in a specific order. First there are the singers, followed by the instrumentalists and then the dancers with tambourines. Charles Spurgeon points out that this order is no accident; it's by design. It represents the primacy of vocal music and the need for singers to be heard above the instruments. This is not to say that instrumental music is not important. It simply serves to remind us what every great instrumentalist already knows: they should not distract from or drown out the lyrics.[5] Instrumentalists should not compete with vocalists to be heard. We need to work together in serving the message of the song.

Whatever you do, don't do what Hezekiah did (2 Kings 20). When King Hezekiah became deathly ill, God not only promised that He would heal him but even made the sun regress six hours, from noon back to dawn, as a sign that Hezekiah would be healed. Emissaries from neighboring Babylon came to call on Hezekiah because they saw the sun move backward and had heard that God had done it on behalf of Hezekiah. The Babylonians were sun worshipers, so this was a great opportunity to give witness to the one true God. But instead Hezekiah took his guests up to the treasure room and proudly showed them all the kingdom's gold, silver, spices, oils, and armor. God had done this miraculous thing, and Hezekiah was showing off his personal trophy room. God's doing great things around us all the time. Let's not get stuck on how great we are, because it doesn't compare at all with God's greatness.

Examine Your Motivation

My fellow artists, what's your motivation for creating or performing? Is it to glorify God or yourself? Jeremiah's words are just as pertinent to us artists today as they were to the people of Israel: "Should you then seek great things for yourself? Seek them not" (Jer. 45:5). If we're truly ministering in the name of Jesus, our motivation—what we are seeking—should be Christ Jesus and His glory, not our own. Jesus told us to seek first the kingdom of God, not the kingdom of self or the kingdom of art (Matt. 6:33). Christ is to have first place in everything we do (Col. 1:18). Remember what John the Baptist said? "He must become greater; I must become less" (John 3:30). That's the kind of attitude we need to have onstage at all times. It's not about us and how we sound or look. We can't be in ministry to glorify ourselves. Paul says, "Whatever you do, do it all for the glory of God" (1 Cor. 10:31; see also Col. 3:17; 1 Peter 4:11). True ministry is about Jesus and whether His message is getting across. That needs to be our motivation.

When we started the worship choir here at Willow Creek, somebody asked me if this choir was going to sing background all the time or if the group would get to sing special numbers. The thought that occurred to me in response was that in leading worship, we are *all* background. Jesus Christ is center stage, not us. He must increase and we must decrease. Worship needs to be the most unselfish thing we humans ever do.

I want to put a word of caution in here. I've seen artists get so vigilant about their motivation that they become obsessed with whether they're serving the Lord with a servant's heart. A friend of mine, a musician, admitted to me recently that he doesn't really enjoy playing in church because he's constantly worried that his motives are not right. Even though he's trying his best to live in authentic relationship with Jesus Christ, he becomes easily obsessed with hidden motives that he fears are so well concealed he might never see them. That sounds to me like the work of the Accuser, the Evil One. The Bible says that Satan constantly tries to accuse us (Rev. 12:10). He loves to accuse us of wrong motives, even when we're onstage, to get our focus off Jesus and onto ourselves. When Satan accuses, there is confusion. We wonder, *Is this from God or not?* But when God wants to deal with our motives, He always does it in a loving way (Isa. 42:3). His is not the voice of harsh accusation. His is that still small voice like "a gentle whisper" (1 Kings 19:12) that tenderly convicts us of our sin and our need for Him. When God speaks, there is no confusion. There is heartfelt conviction. He gently leads and bids us to follow.

Along the same lines, every once in a while someone will ask me if it's OK to feel confident onstage. "Does that make me less humble?" they ask. A question like that usually comes from someone who equates humility with being spineless, apologetic, and wishy-washy. God has not given us a "spirit of timidity, but a spirit of power, of love and of self-discipline" (2 Tim. 1:7). That doesn't sound very spineless to me. While it's inappropriate for us to be cocky about our talents, it's OK for a Christian to be confident during a performance. If you acknowledge that your talent comes from God and give Him the glory, it's OK to walk onstage and be confident that you can do what He's calling you to do. It's OK to be confident if your confidence is in Him.

Die to Selfishness

Philippians 2:3–4 is a verse that I think every artist should memorize. It says, "Do nothing out of selfish ambition or vain conceit, but in humility consider others better than yourselves. Each of you should look not only to your own interests, but also to the interests of others."

I don't know how anyone can be a prima donna and have this verse sitting in their Bible. We need to die to selfishness and empty conceit and stop being so self-absorbed. There is no room for prima donnas in the ministry. Similarly, 1 Corinthians 10:24 says, "Nobody should seek his own good, but the good of others." Real love does not seek its own (1 Cor. 13:5). Romans 12:10 says to "honor one another above yourselves." We need to regard others as more important than ourselves. That means other vocalists on the team, other musicians in the band, other drama people, other artists. That means the person who sets up the sound system through which you sing or act, the person back at the soundboard, all the way to the person sitting out in the congregation in the very last row. Regard them all as more important than yourself. This is so difficult for artists because we can be so preoccupied with ourselves.

A few times in this book, I'll be mentioning what I call my daily dangerous prayers. These are thoughts or Scripture verses that are so far from how I naturally think that I need to pray them into my heart and soul every day. They're dangerous prayers because they have the potential to radically change my life. One such verse is John 12:24: "Unless a kernel of wheat falls to the ground and dies, it remains only a single seed. But if it dies, it produces many seeds." Now, dying to self is not how I normally operate, so for a year and a half I prayed every day, "Lord, help me to die to self today. Show me how to apply this verse to my life today." Praying something like that every day made me realize how self-centered I really am. For example, when I came home from work, I just wanted to "veg" because I was tired. But instead I was convicted to die to self and spend time with my wife, Sue, or play with my boys. Also, in several relational conflicts, I recall being nudged by the Holy Spirit to die to being right all the time. And I was challenged time and again to die to the approval of others. I dare anyone to pray John 12:24 every day for a year and see if it doesn't change your life.

This dying to self shouldn't be taken to the other extreme, in which we become doormats. Dying to self doesn't mean you abuse yourself. That's obviously not healthy, either, and many doormats can be just as self-absorbed as the next person. According to 1 Corinthians 12:20–25, no one is more important than anyone else. That's why we need to look out for the interests of others instead of always trying to put our needs at the top of the agenda. This is the key to becoming a humble artist.

When Thomas à Kempis writes about the keys to inner peace, it sounds to me as if he's describing what it means to die to self.

> Endeavor, my son, rather to do the will
>   of another than thine own.
> Choose always to have less rather than more.
> Seek always the lowest place, and to
>   be inferior to every one.

Wish always, and pray, that the will of
    God may be wholly fulfilled in thee.[6]

Remember That Ministry Is a Privilege

Those of us who use our gifts in church need to remember that ministry is a privilege. God is in the business of bringing lost people to salvation. He could have sent angels to do the job, but instead He's entrusted us to spread the Word and "make disciples of all nations" (Matt. 28:19) with the help of His Holy Spirit.

Paul often referred to ministry as a privilege and a high calling. He didn't take it for granted. He saw being "useful to the Master" as being the most important thing you can do with your life (2 Tim. 2:21; 4:11). To Paul, being in ministry was a great honor and privilege.

Serving God is a way to honor Him. It's our sacrifice of praise. What a testimony it is for a talented musician, actor, dancer, or artist to use his or her gifts in serving the Lord. What a wonderful example it is to our kids when they see Mom and/or Dad serving the Lord in some form of ministry. That parent is modeling what it means to serve God with the talents He gives us—God working *through* us. That's the joy and the great reward of the Christian life. That's the great privilege of ministry. Proverbs 3:9 says to "honor the LORD with your wealth." Some of you have been given a wealth of talent. "From everyone who has been given much, much will be demanded" (Luke 12:48). Honor the Lord by serving Him in some form of ministry.

Many of us have a strong desire to do something significant with our lives and our talent. We were created to do good works to the glory of God (Eph. 2:10). In Psalm 90:17 Moses asks God to confirm the work of his hands. The margin of my Bible adds that a more literal translation would be "give permanence" (NASB). In other words, "Lord, give permanence to the work of my hands." Help me to do something meaningful and significant with my life. Help me to do something with my talent that endures. We all long for significance. The only thing that can fulfill this longing is to serve God.

Being used by God in any way can be extremely rewarding. We are merely "jars of clay" (2 Cor. 4:7), yet we carry around with us a treasure: the good news of the gospel, God's plan of salvation, the hope of the world. It's an absolute privilege to be used of God. God not only rescued us from eternal damnation; He's blessed us and continues to bless us abundantly beyond what we deserve. Most of us feel that the very least we can do, after all He's done for us, is serve Him with all our heart. David said, "How can I repay the LORD for all his goodness to me?" (Ps. 116:12). Isaiah had a life-changing encounter with God, and he emerged from that saying, "Lord, I'm available. I'll do whatever you want. Here I am, send me!" (see Isa. 6:8). Really, what other response is there after you've tasted grace? We need to remember that it is not God who is lucky to have you and me in His service; we are the ones who are privileged to have a role, large or small, in advancing His kingdom.

The Difference Between Volunteering and Being Called of God

Early in my ministry I began to notice a distinct difference between those who volunteer out of obligation and those who feel called by God to serve. It's not that volunteering is bad; it's just that there is a deeper level of commitment, joy, and reward with those who know their calling is from God. I want to be careful here because some might associate a calling from God with something so high and lofty that it becomes otherworldly. We've made the call to ministry sound so esoteric, as though it's only for people who hear God calling them to the jungles of Africa. I'm talking about something more down to earth, more obvious, than that: God calling you and me to use our gifts in our local church. In 1 Chronicles 15:16–19 King David appoints the musicians to lead the nation of Israel in worship. This was their calling from God. Colossians 4:17 says, "See to it that you complete the work *you have received in the Lord*" (emphasis mine). In 1 Timothy 1:12 Paul says, "I thank Christ Jesus our Lord, who has given me strength, that he considered me faithful, appointing me to his service." Paul's ministry was not some routine act of volunteerism he did out of guilt or obligation. It was a special calling from God. Frederick Buechner said, "The place God calls you is the place where your deep gladness and the world's deep hunger meet."[7] I know so many people who are experiencing deep joy and reward these days because they're following a calling God has put in their hearts to serve in the local church. They have this sense that they're doing what God wants them to do, and their life has taken on deeper meaning and significance. The following is a list of some of the differences I've seen between people who are merely volunteering and those who are called of God. I'll be expanding on most of these points throughout this book.

1. *Volunteers see their involvement at church as community service, but people called of God see it as ministry.* To people called of God, ministry is not to be taken lightly. It's important work with eternal ramifications. It's an honor and a privilege from God. It's something none of us deserves.

2. *Volunteers whine about what it's going to cost to serve, but people who are called are committed to serving.* People called of God see themselves as stewards of the gifts God has given them. Serving becomes a priority in their lives; it energizes them. You won't hear such people complaining, "Oh no. I have to get up early on Sunday and go to church." They calculate the cost, but they can also see the benefits. Within reason, they try to schedule around their service commitments instead of trying to work service opportunities into their busy schedule.

3. *Volunteers shrink back from resolving relational conflict, but people called of God seek to resolve relational conflict for the sake of unity in the church.* People called of God know it would be disobedient to live in conflict with another brother or sister or to run away from God's calling because of relational conflict. So instead they try to resolve relational conflict in a godly way, as outlined by Jesus in Matthew 18, going first to the individual they're in conflict with and talking it out.

4. *Volunteers look upon rehearsal as another commitment they're obligated to fulfill, but people called of God look forward to rehearsal as another opportunity to be used by God.* Volunteers complain about being out another night, but people called of God say, "Great. I get to go to rehearsal tonight. Maybe I can bring a word of encouragement to one of my fellow artists, or I can see what God's doing in this person's life, or I

can ask if there's anything I can be praying for this person about."
Meetings, rehearsals, setting up or tearing down the stage can be significant serving opportunities to people who are called of God.

5. *Volunteers do no outside practicing or preparation, but people who are called of God come to rehearsals and a performance as prepared as possible.* Some people will do just enough to get by. They'll do the bare minimum because after all they're just volunteers. On the other hand, people called of God want to glorify the Lord with their God-given talents, so they're going to perform to the best of their ability. They believe in giving God their very best.

6. *Volunteers are not open to constructive criticism; they get defensive about it. But people called of God are grateful for feedback because they want to be the best they can be.* Instead of saying, "How dare you say anything negative about my God-given talents," people called of God say, "Lord, I want to be the best I can be for You." As a result, they're open to suggestions and direction concerning their work.

7. *Volunteers feel threatened by the talent of others, but people called of God praise Him for distributing gifts and talents as He chooses.* Instead of being threatened by every new addition to the team, people called of God view newcomers as friends, co-ministers, and coworkers. They deal with jealousy and envy in a godly way.

8. *Volunteers want to quit at the first sign of adversity or discouragement, but people called of God dig in and persevere.* No church is perfect, but for that matter, none of us is the perfect church member, either. When there's a problem, people called of God don't sit back and complain or dump it all on the leader and say, "You'd better fix this, or I'm going to quit." They don't run when the going gets tough. They pray. They choose to become part of the solution instead of part of the problem. They realize that when God calls us to serve, He never abandons us. He's always there to lead us through any difficulties we may face.

9. *Volunteers find their main source of fulfillment in their talents and abilities, but people called of God know that being used of God is the most fulfilling thing you can do with your life.* People called of God get offstage and are more concerned that God was glorified than whether their talents were on display enough. They're concerned that God's will, not theirs, was done.

10. Volunteers can't handle being put in situations in which they're going to be stretched, but people called of God respond to God's call with humble dependence on Him. People called of God know that if God has called them to minister, He will equip them to do the work of the ministry, even though it might call for them to grow as people or as artists. Once I was in a rehearsal with a new drummer we had just added to the team. His name was Tony. In the process of taking the band through some new charts, I found myself stopping quite often to correct Tony or give him some direction. At the end of rehearsal I wanted to check in with him, because I didn't want him to feel picked on. So as we were putting equipment away, I asked Tony how he was doing. He sighed at first and then said, "I've been thinking about taking a few lessons, because there are a lot of new styles that I'm just not up-to-date on right now. But I'm not giving up, because this is what God has called me to do." I just shook my head in amazement. Here was a man who understood what it meant to be called of God. Playing drums at church was something God had called him to do. That calling was the motivation behind his service. That calling allowed him to be fruitful, even in situations that stretched his abilities.

Ministry Minded

If I had to summarize the difference between volunteering and being called of God, I would say that someone who has that sense of calling from God is more ministry minded. God never intended ministry to be the responsibility of the chosen few who do "full-time Christian work." God has equipped all believers to do the work of ministry (Eph. 4:11–12).

A friend of mine named Tim Kuntz has been serving here at Willow Creek for many years, and we've also been in a small group together. Tim's vocation is in the computer field, but his ministry is playing the trumpet in one of our bands and leading a small group. Not too long ago Tim got a nice job offer. It meant more responsibility and more money with a good company, but it also meant a lengthy commute downtown every day. He called me for some advice, and we talked about how this would affect his family and his future, but one thing Tim was really concerned about was how this was going to affect his ministry. He wanted to know if he could commute every day and still do the things God has called him to do at church. My friend Tim knows the difference between volunteering and being called of God. He wasn't getting paid to be involved in ministry, yet his work at church had become such a high priority that he cared about how a job change would affect it. God's given him a calling, a role to play in kingdom work, a sense of purpose, and he takes it seriously.

Healthy Boundaries

Now, let me ask you: Is it possible to serve too much? Can one overdo this serving thing? The answer is yes. You can spend too much time at church and neglect your family, your health, and even your relationship with the Lord. That's a real shame because it doesn't glorify God to burn out on ministry. You have to set healthy boundaries. Maintaining healthy boundaries involves having your priorities in place, resulting in the freedom to say yes but not the fear to say no. If you expect to serve the Lord for any length of time, you've got to develop healthy boundaries. We all have to know how and when to say no, long before we reach personal crisis. The church has often been guilty of using and abusing artists. On the other hand, artists have sometimes played the martyr role and let themselves be used and abused.

As a music director at a church, I really struggle with this because I don't want people to burn out but I still want to provide meaningful and fulfilling ministry opportunities to artists. So there's a tension there, a fine line I try to walk. Over the years I have erred on both sides. I have asked one too many times, and it put some-one over the edge. On the other hand, there are times when I have tried to protect someone's schedule by not asking that person to sing or play, and found out he or she was hurt because I didn't ask. If we could all work on setting healthy boundaries, leaders wouldn't need to second-guess or coerce, and artists would feel the freedom to say yes or no. When I approach someone who has healthy boundaries with a ministry opportunity and they say, "Thanks for asking but I just can't do it this week," I don't feel bad for asking and they don't feel bad for saying no.

There are seasons in church work that are naturally more demanding than others. Busy seasons come and go, and even though we tend to get weary in the middle of those busier seasons, they usually are short-lived. My family knows that Christmas and Easter are busy times for me. It's part of church work. But if I'm committed to having healthy boundaries and not overworking the rest of the year, Christmas and Easter or any other time of intense ministry become blips on the chart, exceptions to the rule instead of the norm. Scripture encourages us to be steadfast and to not grow weary (1 Cor. 15:58; Gal. 6:9–10). We are also encouraged to give with a cheerful attitude, not under compulsion (2 Cor. 9:7). That's not going to happen if we don't have healthy boundaries. Healthy boundaries are a must if we're going to serve the Lord with joy and gladness (Ps. 100:2).

Serving an Audience of One

The ultimate test of servanthood is whether you can be content to serve an audience of One, when it's OK to serve in anonymity, when you can throw yourself into a bit part, when you no longer live for the approval of others, when the size of your audience doesn't matter anymore, and when the size of the role you play is less important than being faithful and obedient. This is difficult for us because we often love the approval of others more than the approval of God (John 12:43). We seek the favor of those around us instead of the favor of God (Gal. 1:10). We want to be noticed. Jesus said to beware of that kind of motivation (Matt. 6:1). When you no longer crave the spotlight, when you don't need to be noticed or recognized, and when you're not above doing grunt work such as stacking chairs, you're on your way to being the kind of selfless servant God really uses. One of the hardest jobs in all of programming is teardown: putting equipment away, cleaning up after a service, striking the set. Could you ever be content in serving in obscurity like that? Could you do that kind of service "as working for the Lord, not for men"? (Col. 3:23; Eph. 6:7). You can if you're serving an audience of One.

Philip Yancey compares serving an audience of One to being a mirror or a stained-glass window.

> Tensions and anxieties flame within me the moment I forget I am living my life for the one-man audience of Christ and slip into living my life to assert myself in a competitive world. Previously, my main motivation in life was to do a painting of myself, filled with bright colors and profound insights, so that all who looked upon it would be impressed. Now, however, I find that my role is to be a mirror, to brightly reflect the image of God through me. Or perhaps the metaphor of stained glass would serve better, for, after all, God will illumine through my personality and body.[8]

Many of us struggle with being a servant when we have to labor in obscurity. I've wrestled with this, too. There have been times when I have felt taken for granted. There have been times when I have felt forgotten or ignored. There have been times when I have felt like the Invisible Man, when the talent of others got recognized and mine didn't. But I've come to the conclusion that I would rather labor in obscurity for God than be famous for doing something insignificant with my life. Besides, God sees in secret (Matt. 6:4, 6, 18). We don't labor in obscurity when we labor for God. He sees. He notices and He will reward.

Some time ago someone in our congregation wrote a very complimentary letter to Lynn Siewert, one of our vocalists, and sent me a copy. Lynn has been on our vocal team for many years and exemplifies the heart of a true servant. The letter reads like this:

> I want to thank you . . . for providing your voice to the worship at Willow Creek. Each time I hear you, I can't get over what a wonderful gift the Lord has given to you, and for our benefit. There is something else that emerges each time you sing. . . . There is humility, purity, reverence—and it really comes through. Others I've sat with have all mentioned the same thing—that you're obviously not onstage for your own purposes, but Christ's. I think if I had your voice, I'm afraid I'd sing to the Lord, yet I'd be plenty pleased with myself, too! So in his wisdom he chose you!

People in the congregation can tell whether we're onstage to serve the Lord or merely serve ourselves.

I'd like to conclude by telling you about a man in my life who epitomizes servanthood. When I was just starting out in ministry, I was discipled by a man who became a treasured friend. His name is John Allen. I learned all about servanthood from John, not because we ever did a Bible study on it but because he lived with a servant's heart toward all people. John is a real handyman (and I am not at all). He would come over and fix broken water heaters, leaky pipes, and dilapidated drywall. He'd come over and help with yard work, because to John it was a chance to serve and to spend time with me talking about the Lord. When I faced major decisions in my life, he offered not only to pray for me but to fast as long as I was fasting, to see if God would confirm His will through both of us. That's a real servant. John earned a modest music teacher's salary, yet he shared his financial resources freely and cheerfully whenever a brother was in need. He was always there when I needed him, always asking, "What can I do to help?" I have since moved several states away from my friend, but I will never forget the impact of watching someone live out the heart of a servant right before my eyes. John showed me what true servanthood is. He showed me what it is like to be overjoyed to serve an audience of One.

Follow-Up Questions for Group Discussion

1. What do you think Jesus would be like at rehearsal?

2. What do you think Jesus would be like onstage?

3. Can you think of someone in your life who's been a positive example of servanthood for you?

4. Where would you put yourself on the humility continuum? With empty conceit on one end and false humility on the other, which end of the spectrum do you lean toward most?

5. Which of the ten differences between volunteering and being called of God do you feel is most important in establishing a prevailing arts ministry?

6. Which of the ten differences between volunteering and being called of God least describes you?

7. What kinds of things keep artists from being able to serve an audience of One?

8. Why, in your opinion, is it so hard for artists to have healthy boundaries when it comes to their work?

9. Can an artist be a confident person and still have a servant's heart?

10. What advice about servanthood would you give a fellow artist just starting out in ministry?

Personal Action Steps

1. Offer your gifts to God. If you've never thanked the Lord for the gifts and talents He's given you, do so and tell Him you're committed to using your gifts not as you please but as He wills. If you really want to make your commitment special, express it artistically in some way.

2. Offer your gifts to the church. Paul saw himself as a servant to the church for Jesus Christ (2 Cor. 4:5). Write a letter to your music director, drama director, choir director, or pastor, and offer your gifts and talents to serve the body of Christ in whatever capacity that person deems appropriate.

3. If you've offended anybody by your lack of true humility, acknowledge your sin to whomever it affected and ask that person for forgiveness.

4. Determine whether you have healthy boundaries when it comes to serving. If not, decide what it would take for you to have healthier boundaries and begin making those changes. Choose someone to whom you could be accountable regarding this.

5. Galatians 5:13 exhorts us to serve each other out of love. Try to serve someone this week in a personal way.

Audience of One

It's such a strong temptation to live for man's applause
But I don't want to buy into the lie
'Cause I know that's not a worthy cause
So to keep things in perspective, I hung a sign
      up on the wall

The sign is nothing special, but it really says it all
And the sign says

I'll be content to serve an audience of One
Only His approval counts when all is said and done
And this is my prayer, when the race is finally run
I want to hear "Well done"
From the audience of One

When the drive for recognition starts to get
      the best of me
All I've got to do is look around at the people
      serving selflessly
And they don't serve for glory, and they're not
      keeping score
There's a sign that's written on their hearts
A sign I've seen before

I'll be content to serve an audience of One
Only His approval counts when all is said and done
And this is my prayer, when the race is finally run
I want to hear "Well done"
From the audience of One

In the not-too-distant future
When the crowds all fade away
I'll stand alone before my Lord
And this is what I long to say

I'm overjoyed to serve an audience of One
It's what I've been created for ever since day one
And this is my song, as I bow before Your throne
I love to hear "Well done"
From the audience of One

So this will be my prayer, 'til the race is finally run
I want to hear "Well done," I long to hear "Well done"
I want to hear "Well done"
From the audience of One[9]

Greg Ferguson

We are the music-makers,
    And we are the dreamers of dreams,
Wandering by lone sea-breakers,
    And sitting by desolate streams;
World-losers and world-forsakers,
    On whom the pale moon gleams:
Yet we are the movers and shakers
    Of the world for ever, it seems.

With wonderful deathless ditties
We build up the world's great cities,
    And out of a fabulous story
    We fashion an empire's glory:
One man with a dream, at pleasure,
    Shall go forth and conquer a crown;
And three with a new song's measure
    Can trample an empire down.

We, in the ages lying
    In the buried past of the earth,
Built Nineveh with our sighing,
    And Babel itself with our mirth;
And o'erthrew them with prophesying
    To the old of the new world's worth;
For each age is a dream that is dying,
    Or one that is coming to birth.

Arthur O'Shaughnessy, "Ode"

Three

The Artist in Community

*T*he scene: *Marlene has just walked in the door of her home after a long and grueling rehearsal at church. It's late. The phone is ringing. She runs to pick it up. She has been the drama director at Countryside Community Church for almost five years now, and she has built a strong ministry at the church. The people at Countryside really appreciate drama in the church and look forward to the sketches that the drama team performs and the special events that include drama. For several weeks now Marlene has been throwing herself into rehearsals for the annual Easter pageant, which is just a week away. She reaches for the phone, assuming that, like everything else in her life these days, it has something to do with the Easter pageant. On the other line is Al from the drama team.*

AL (sounding urgent): Uh, Marlene? I hate to call you at home like this, and I'm sorry for calling so late. Are you busy?

MARLENE (smiling): Well, I can talk. You sound troubled. Are you okay?

AL: Well ... um ... no.... I hate to bother you and I hate to bring this up. I know how busy you are, but I think a lot of people on the drama team are really upset right now. I think we have major communication problems on the team. I don't know if you know how bad it really is. I just got off the phone with Stewart, and he's really upset.

MARLENE: Oh, really? I'm sorry to hear that. What is he upset about?

AL: He just feels like if he were to quit the team, no one would care. And some of us have been talking, and a lot of us are kinda feeling the same way.

MARLENE: You mean, like if you left the team, no one would notice or care?

AL: Yeah. A lot of us have been feeling this way for a long time. No one really feels connected.

MARLENE: How long has Stewart been upset? I just spoke with him tonight, and he didn't mention anything about this.

AL: Well, I'm not surprised. He's pretty confused right now. He doesn't think you like him.

MARLENE: Really. I'm sorry to hear that. I like Stewart very much.

AL: Well, he's thinking about quitting drama and even thinking about going to another church. He's pretty angry.

MARLENE: Is he angry with me?

AL: Well, yeah. He didn't get the part he wanted in the Easter pageant. I think he had his heart set on playing Jesus. I understand why you gave the part to Frank. Frank's new and younger, but really Stewart's got way more experience.

MARLENE: Now that you mention it, I thought it was odd that Stewart suddenly left the room

when the cast gave Frank a standing ovation after the Gethsemane scene tonight.

AL: Well, yeah, I think Stewart was really hurt
by that. After all, the cast never gave him
a standing ovation.

MARLENE: That would explain the tension I sense
between those two.

AL: Oh yeah, they're not speaking to each
other. Stewart's avoiding Frank like the
plague. He's not jealous or anything.
Stewart says that it's just so painful to be
around Frank, because he reminds him of
how bad he is in drama and that he's not
good enough anymore to be on the team.

MARLENE: Wow, I'm surprised. Stewart is a very
competent actor. That's why I gave him
such a demanding part.

AL: Yeah, but playing the part of Judas just
isn't the kind of part you can really sink
your teeth into. Anyway, that's not all. I
should probably remind you that Stewart
hasn't been asked to be in a sketch all
month, and he hasn't had a substantial part
in anything for a couple of months, and
we've all been noticing that you've been
giving most of the good parts to the new
people on the team. I don't think we
should discard those of us who have been
around awhile and helped build this
church up.

MARLENE: Well, I'm certainly not trying to discard
anybody—

AL: (interrupting angrily): You know, this church makes such a big deal about getting involved and using your gifts, but I think it's all just talk. I feel so bad for Stewart. He's really thinking about quitting.

MARLENE: Boy, I'd hate to see that—

AL: (interrupting again): And another thing, you know we talk about fellowship and community all the time, but it's all just talk. We're not a team at all. What's happening to Stewart happens all the time. You expect to see this kind of thing out in the world—certainly not in the church! Aren't we supposed to love and care for each other in the church? No wonder Stewart's hurt. I would be, too!

MARLENE: Al, did you tell Stewart to come and talk to me?

AL: Oh no, he can't do that. A lot of people are very intimidated by you, and besides, we all know how busy you are.

MARLENE: But Al, you're putting yourself in the middle of something that really seems to be between me and Stewart.

AL: Oh, I've really been listening more than anything else, and I've been very careful not to spread this around. That would be gossip. But it does make me angry that one of our faithful members who's been around a long time isn't being used anymore.

MARLENE: Well, I wouldn't exactly agree that he's not being used anymore. You know, I really think Stewart should be talking to me. It sounds as if he's feeling insecure and wants to know where he stands with me. Did he tell you about all the times I've called him to be in a sketch but he was out of town those particular weekends?

AL: No, but I think the problem is deeper than that.

MARLENE: I agree. Stewart needs to come straight to me if he has a problem with me. I don't appreciate it when people are talking behind my back, and it doesn't serve our team well if we're not resolving relational conflict in a godly way. Do you think that if you hadn't called me, Stewart would have eventually approached me with this? You know, Scripture is pretty clear about how we should resolve conflict—

AL (interrupting): Uh, Marlene, I've got another call coming in. Sorry, I need to run. I'll get back to you.

MARLENE: Okay, Al. Please be in touch.

Questions for Group Discussion

1. What do you appreciate the most about the team you're serving on in your church? (For example, the choir, the worship team, the vocal team, the band or orchestra, the drama team, the dance team, the sound and lighting team, the visual arts team, and so on.)

2. In our opening scenario Al uses statements like "*Everybody* feels this way" and "*No one* feels connected." Do you think

statements like that are blown out of proportion, or could they be true?

3. In your opinion, what are some of the advantages to doing ministry in teams?

4. What are some of the challenges to doing ministry in teams?

5. What are some of the causes of relational conflict on a team?

6. Do you think most Christians know how to resolve relational conflict?

7. How was relational conflict resolved in the home in which you grew up?

8. Why do you think it's important for artists to learn how to get along with each other?

9. If Satan wanted to undermine the effectiveness of your team, how might he go about it?

10. Have you ever been on a successful team of any kind? (For example, an athletic team, a team of workers, a music, drama, or dance group, etc.) What made that team successful?

The Church As a Colony of Artists

I've always been fascinated by the artist colonies that emerge around major artistic movements. My favorite example is Paris in the early 1900s, a place where artists congregated and fed off each other, and a time when exciting innovations were taking place in the arts. Composers, visual artists, dancers, choreographers, authors, and poets all mixed and mingled, resulting in a virtual beehive of artistic activity. My favorite composer, Igor Stravinsky, was part of this infamous colony of artists, and his circle of friends included fellow composers Claude Debussy, Maurice Ravel, Erik Satie, and Manuel de Falla. It was a time when the arts overlapped in exciting ways as Stravinsky rubbed shoulders with artists like Pablo Picasso, Henri Matisse, and Jean Cocteau. This group wasn't without its disagreements and jealousies, but the artists were friends. They'd go to concerts and art galleries together. They'd get together at each other's homes and talk long into the night about music, art, and literature. On one occasion Stravinsky sat down with Debussy at the piano, and they played through a transcription of an orchestra piece Stravinsky was developing. It just happened to be *The Rite of Spring,* one of the landmark masterpieces of the twentieth century! I wish I could have been a fly on the wall listening to their conversation. These artists changed the world with their art. All the great new work at that time was coming out of Paris, and artists from all over the world were flocking there to study. Paris in the early 1900s was indeed an exciting place to be. The arts were thriving and artists were flourishing!

Wouldn't you love to be in a place like that? Many of us artists are longing for a place to belong, a place where the arts are flourishing, where God is using the arts in a powerful way. A place where artists can experience meaningful fellowship with other Christian artists, where we can learn from each other and cheer each other on. I believe that's part of what God wants our churches to be: a place that harnesses the arts for His glory and nurtures artists.

The sense of teamwork and camaraderie that the artists in Paris had in the early 1900s has always intrigued me, because artists don't always work well together, nor do they always get along with each other. Many of us are more introverted by nature; we're lone rangers. In a book titled *The Musical Temperament,* author Anthony E. Kemp states that while "musicians are distinctly introverted, there is also a 'boldness' which arises not only from their considerable inner strengths but also from their sense of independence. Musicians tend to share these qualities with several other creative types."[1]

Getting artists who are basically introverted and independent to function as a team is no easy task. Like many artists who are thrown together with others on a team, Igor Stravinsky had to learn how to function as a team player. Howard Gardner, in his book *Creating Minds,* points out that when Stravinsky was asked to join the Ballets Russes, it changed his life overnight. "Stravinsky became a valued member of what was possibly the most innovative performing artistic group in the world. . . . Now instead of working mostly

alone, Stravinsky had almost daily intercourse with the ensemble
... set designers, dancers, choreographers, and even those responsible for the business end of the enterprise."[2]

Relationships Matter

Some of what we do as artists is done alone. We may practice or
create by ourselves, but at some point we often end up working
with other artists. Even if you don't consider yourself to be very
relational, you need to learn how to relate to, and get along with,
other artists. Even if you're extremely introverted, you're deceived
if you think you can live a meaningful existence isolated from others or live the Christian life apart from other believers. We need fellowship. We can't be lone rangers. We need each other. To know
and be known is a basic human need.

Many years ago an incident occurred that forever changed my
view of the importance of relationships in my life. I had an appen-
dectomy that involved some complications and the need for two
surgeries. I was in and out of the hospital for two weeks, and it took
me three months to fully recover. That was a real dark time for me.
I remember feeling so lonely in my hospital room that I cried every
time Sue and the boys (who were very young at the time) left. I
found myself anxiously looking forward to visits from friends, rel-
atives, anybody. I can only imagine how lonely it must be for people
who are constantly homebound or shut in. My long convalescence
made me realize that I had taken too many relationships for granted.
You really don't know what you've got till it's gone. I realized that
relationships were not as much of a priority for me as they should
have been. I was too busy for people. I wasn't doing anything to initiate new friendships or build into the ones I already had. When I
got out of the hospital, I was determined to change all that, and I
adopted a new motto: Relationships matter. Instead of working
through lunch, I tried to find someone to eat with. I opened up
larger blocks of time to allow for more personal appointments.
Instead of waiting for people to call me, I started calling them, and
I became more proactive about spending time with people.

Relationships are a lot of work. They don't happen overnight; they need to be cultivated. Even those friendships that seem to happen accidentally, when people are thrown together by circumstance, involve work. Some of the people who complain the loudest about not having any friends are the same people who don't work at having meaningful relationships. They think relationships just happen. They don't. If you want to have quality relationships, you have to put in effort. My best friend lives a thousand miles away. We go back a long way and have a lot of history together. Ours is the kind of friendship in which even if we haven't talked in a while, it's easy to pick up where we left off. He's someone to whom I can tell my darkest secrets. It would be a shame to let that friendship die, but it's a lot of work, especially because we live so far apart. We try to call each other regularly or write letters or send email, anything we can do to keep the communication (and the friendship) strong. I'm now convinced that the time I've invested in this and all my other friendships is time well spent, because relationships matter. Many years have passed since my long hospital stay, but that ordeal straightened me out about the importance of relationships. I am very pleased about the quality and depth of my relational world these days. My friendships and my family are very fulfilling to me.

Teamwork

What intrigues me most about the O'Shaughnessy poem at the beginning of this chapter is its emphasis on *we*. One thing that we learned very quickly at Willow Creek is that ministry is best done in teams. The beauty of working in teams is that together we can accomplish greater things for God than if we were on our own. We have a saying around Willow Creek that goes like this: We come together to do what no one of us could do alone. With all of us pitching in and pulling in the same direction toward a goal, we reap huge dividends from our individual investments. If we try to do all alone what is better done as a team effort, the result will be limited—solitary confinement, if you will.

What does it mean to be part of a team? It means you belong. You belong on the team for two reasons.

1. *Your gifts and abilities have created a niche for you on the team.* Proverbs 22:29 says that a person who is talented and works hard will go far. Because you're talented and work hard, you've been invited to participate in ministry. Your gifts and abilities have made room for you on the team. You share the same calling as others who have been entrusted with an artistic talent. As a result, you play an important role not only as a member of your ministry team but also as part of a worldwide community of Christian artists!

2. *Your personality has created a place for you on the team.* First Corinthians 12:18 says that God "arranged the parts in the body, *every one of them,* just as he wanted them to be" (emphasis mine). When God calls you to be part of a team, He takes into account who you are as well as what you can do. Isn't that great? You're welcome on the team not only for what you can do but also for who you are. No one is going to contribute to the cause and community of the team in the exact same way that you do. Even someone who has the same talents and gift mix that you have won't contribute exactly as you do, because you're two different people with two different personalities. You're not indispensable but you are irreplaceable.

The Things That Kill Teamwork

In spite of how powerful and how meaningful team ministry can be, the task of getting a group of people to interact and perform as a team is a difficult one. Besides the fact that we artists have a propensity to shy away from teams and community, the Evil One does everything he can to disrupt teams. He'll try to sow disunity; he'll try to undermine morale; he'll try to sabotage the cause; he'll try to frustrate plans. Believe me, he'll do everything he can to defeat any and every team that's trying to advance the kingdom of God. So let's begin our study of teams by looking at four things that can kill a team.

1. Selfishness

Selfishness is the biggest obstacle for any team to overcome. There's no way any team can function if the team members are constantly first looking out for themselves. People who are focused only on themselves will miss the big picture. This was the problem with the Prodigal Son's brother (Luke 15:11–32). Instead of celebrating his wayward brother's homecoming with the rest of his family, this man's self-centeredness caused him to be resentful. It caused him to miss the more important thing: his lost brother was saved. We can sometimes get so focused on ourselves that we miss what's really important. That's "me first" thinking. When we're angry because we didn't get to sing all the solos we think we deserve, that's "me first" thinking. When we maneuver conversation around to spotlight something about us, that's "me first" thinking. When the team is celebrating a recent success and we're preoccupied with remorse because we didn't get to play the role we wanted to play, that's "me first" thinking.

2. Grumbling and Complaining

Grumbling and complaining are usually the result of selfishness. Have you ever noticed how much we complain? We complain about the weather. We complain about our jobs. We complain about the government. We complain about our sports teams. Complaining seems to be human nature. The people of Israel grumbled against Moses all the time (Ex. 15:24; Num. 16:41; 17:5). And many of us with artistic temperaments have a tendency to complain and grumble whenever things don't go our way.

I received an email the other day from a church music director who quit his job because he couldn't put up with "all the whininess and apathy" anymore. Satan had successfully sabotaged this church's music ministry by getting all the musicians to be negative. Philippians 2:14 instructs us all to "do everything without complaining or arguing," because grumbling and disputing are like cancers that grow and spread and eventually kill a team or even an entire church.

3. A Competitive Spirit

Healthy competition has the potential to bring out the best in us. The upside of competition in the arts, as in athletics, is that it can spur us on to grow as artists. The downside is that being overly competitive can ruin team morale. When people aren't rooting for each other and cheering each other on because they're in competition with each other all the time, they will never function as a team. Instead of competing with each other, we need to learn how to cooperate with each other.

4. Unresolved Relational Conflict

A lack of unity can really hurt a team. We must never forget that unity is extremely important to God. John 17 records one of Jesus' last prayers before His painful death on the cross. Of all the things He could possibly have prayed for, utmost in His mind was the unity of the disciples. He prayed for them to be one (vv. 21–22) and to be "brought to complete unity" (v. 23). Why did Paul single out two women at the Philippian church who were at odds with each other and beg them to put aside their differences and "to agree with each other" (Phil. 4:2)? Because unity is vital to God. It is a witness— sometimes the most powerful witness—of His working in our hearts. Psalm 133:1 says, "How good and pleasant it is when brothers live together in unity!"

However, let's face it: it's not easy for people to get along, is it? It's not easy for a team of artists to achieve unity, because of the constant clash of egos and personalities. If a team of artists can dwell together in unity, it's a major accomplishment. I recently received a letter from a music director who told me that the pastor shut down the choir because there was so much arguing going on all the time. In another example, a young music director once shared with me that there isn't a rehearsal that goes by without someone blowing up at someone else. Bickering and backstabbing had become normal for them. It shouldn't be this way in the church. We've got to learn how to resolve relational conflict.

A Team's Code of Ethics

Every team has a code of ethics, written or unwritten, spoken or unspoken. It sets the standard of behavior for the team. It defines what's acceptable and what's not acceptable. It says, "This is how we do things on this team." When I joined the staff at Willow Creek, I learned very quickly what the code of ethics was for every staff member. One day I was working feverishly on some music in my office. I worked right up to rehearsals and then rehearsals went long. By the time it was all over, I had music strewn all over my office and a desk piled with papers, folders, and unopened mail. I thought about cleaning it all up before I left, but it was late and I was exhausted. Besides, I could do it first thing in the morning. The next morning someone from building services greeted me at my office door. He was very polite but firm. "I noticed you left your office in quite a mess last night," he began. "I know you're new, but I just want you to know that we don't do things like that around here. We try to keep our offices neat and clean." Needless to say, I've tried to keep my office tidy ever since, because that's the standard to which the whole team of Willow Creek staff was adhering at that time.

A team's code of ethics reflects the core values of that team. If rehearsal is an important value, it'll be important for everyone to be on time. Punctuality then becomes a value statement that says in effect, "Rehearsal is a high value to me, so it's important that I show up on time." If respect for others is a high value for team members, punctuality would also be considered a courtesy. It's basically saying, "I don't want to be late, because I don't want to waste everybody else's time by having them wait for me."

A team's code of ethics also puts forth the level of commitment needed by all team members. It sets the standard for how the team operates. In this way it becomes a change agent of sorts. If you don't model the team's code of ethics, you will change your behavior if you want to stay a part of that team. Using punctuality as an example again, I know someone who was habitually late to meetings and rehearsals. (He had the same problem at work, too.) Since he was part of a team that valued punctuality, he decided that if he walked in and the meeting or rehearsal had already started, he would apologize to everyone he had kept waiting. Needless to say, he quickly broke himself of this bad habit.

A friend of mine who is a high school band director sent me a list titled, "The Marks of Professionalism." He put this together for his band, and I can vouch for their sense of team; it's a great-sounding band. If you were to play in my friend's high school band, this is what would be expected of you:

The Marks of Professionalism

1. Be on time for rehearsals.
2. Be ready to perform in all aspects (warmed up, instrument mechanically set, all equipment available).
3. Take care of your instrument.
4. Bring a pencil to rehearsal.
5. Listen to the conductor.
6. Mark your music—do not trust memory to skip ending, take a repeat, etc.
7. Constantly listen and adjust pitch and volume while playing.
8. Be ready for entrances.
9. Sincerely attempt to play the part correctly.
10. Play second or third part with as much enthusiasm as first part.
11. Practice music between rehearsals and continually strive to improve.
12. Interpret as the conductor wishes.
13. Do not miss rehearsals.

I think it's important for every team to have a code of ethics that all can agree upon. Does your team have a code of ethics or "marks of professionalism"? Do you know what they are and do you model them?

What Does It Mean to Be a Team Player?

A team's code of ethics is very specific to that team, but there are some general responsibilities that apply to any team of artists in the church. I'm talking about what it means to be a team player. Most of what I know about being a team player I learned through either music or athletics. In sports there are certain things you do for the sake of the team. For example, my son's Little League coach told the boys to throw and run every day because it's good for them and good for the team. So my son practiced those disciplines, knowing that it was part of his responsibility to the team.

In the same way, if you're part of a team of artists, there are certain things you need to do for the sake of the team. The success of your ministry depends on how well you do this thing called team, so let's talk about what it means to be a team player.

1. A Team Player Is Committed to the Cause of the Team

In ministry being committed to the cause of the team means that we put the church's mission above our own agenda. From time to time I hear stories about arts ministries in which the team members aren't all on the same page. The result is musicians, drama people, dancers, etc. all doing their own thing instead of coming together for the common good. For example, a musician who uncompromisingly pushes a favorite style of music, even though it doesn't fit the occasion, is putting his or her own agenda ahead of the team's.

Philippians 2:2 tells us to be "like-minded, having the same love, being one in spirit and purpose." When everyone on a team is intent on the same purpose, that team will do great things for God. You should be on a team because you believe in its cause.

Here in Chicago we were fortunate to have the greatest player in the history of basketball playing for the Bulls. I think what was most impressive about Michael Jordan was the example he set of a team player. On December 17, 1996, the Chicago Bulls were playing the Los Angeles Lakers, and Jordan was having what for him was an off night. (We later found out that he was battling the flu during the game.) Coach Phil Jackson asked Michael to be a decoy. "We saw Michael was struggling in the third quarter, and I told him to be a decoy and hit the other guys," Jackson said to reporters after the game. Imagine that: asking the greatest player who's ever played the game to be a decoy, to put the team ahead of his own ego and agenda. Did Michael do it? Yes. After the game Coach Jackson said, "Michael did a great job of playing the role and hitting the open man." Did it work? Yes. The Bulls won 129–123 in overtime. Michael Jordan was a great team player because he put the cause of the team first.

Sometimes last-minute changes are suggested for a service. Sometimes a song that someone's put a lot of work into gets cut completely. Are you flexible when that happens or does it cause resentment? Are you more committed to your own agenda than to the cause? Now, as a leader you obviously don't want to make a habit of cutting songs at the last minute, because that can frustrate your volunteers, but if it does happen, it's a good test of character.

Amasai was a soldier who was committed to the cause. In 1 Chronicles 12:18 he speaks on behalf of his men and says to King David, "We are yours, O David! We are with you, O son of Jesse! Success, success to you, and success to those who help you, for your God will help you." In other words, he's telling David he's behind him all the way. He believes in the cause. He's committed to the team. That is music to a leader's ears. Does your ministry leader know you're committed to the team? When was the last time you told your leader as much? Do you stand behind the team, its leader, and its cause? Are you putting the team's mission ahead of your own agenda?

2.　A Team Player Is Committed to Resolving Relational Conflict

Resolving relational conflict in a biblical way is the key to team unity. If each team member owns the responsibility for team unity, that team will be "like-minded, having the same love, being one in spirit and purpose" (Phil. 2:2).

Unity is important to God, and it's not something to be taken lightly. We are to "make every effort to keep the unity of the Spirit through the bond of peace" (Eph. 4:3). That doesn't happen without people working out their differences. It doesn't happen without people putting their egos aside and constantly deferring to one another. When Solomon dedicated the temple, the priests and musicians came forth "regardless of their divisions" (2 Chron. 5:11). They all checked their egos at the door and stood before God not according to status or rank but unified as God's people. They had quite a powerful worship time at this ceremony, and the arts played a major role (vv. 12–13). This passage also shows us that unity is a powerful testimony to the presence of God. In fact, the presence of God was so strong at this dedication that people were literally falling down. And it all started with the people being unified. Don't ever think unity is optional. It's required if we're going to do anything together in God's name.

Unity is also a powerful witness to the unchurched. "How good and pleasant it is when brothers live together in unity!" (Ps. 133:1). If there was a colony of Christ-honoring artists who got along with each other and truly loved each other, the world would sit up and take notice, because that kind of thing doesn't happen out there in the world. I tell our church orchestra that we are the most visible witness of team unity that the church has. We are such a diverse collection of ages, ethnic groups, abilities, and backgrounds, and we have to play together and get along with each other. If we can get along, anybody can. Our unity is often a more powerful testimony than our music.

Conflict, however, is inevitable whenever there are people around. Conflict doesn't bother me. In most cases it's an indication that people are coming together in community and deepening their relationships. When that happens, friction often occurs. What does concern me, though, is that we resolve relational conflict in a biblical way. In Matthew 18 Jesus outlines a procedure for resolving relational conflict. The first step always is to go directly to the person with whom you're in conflict and talk it out (v. 15). I know that's not always easy. Most of us don't like to put ourselves in the vulnerable position of telling someone that they've hurt us. Many of us are held back because that sounds too confrontational. Let's face it: many of us grew up not learning how to resolve relational conflict in a mature way. But when it's done right, the relationship is not only restored; it's deepened. It might take just one meeting, but very often it will take several meetings. If that doesn't resolve the issue, meet again, involving some mature brothers and/or sisters who can help mediate (v. 16). If that doesn't do the trick, bring in the elders or other church staff to help the parties involved resolve their conflict (v. 17).

For a team member who is offended to not go directly to the member who caused the offense really brings a team down, and it's wrong. I repeat: it is wrong for us to go to anybody else but the person with whom we're in conflict. Too many of us, for some reason, think we're exempt from the conflict resolution process laid out in Matthew 18. We think it applies to everyone but us. We think it's better not to confront the people with whom we are in conflict, and all this bitterness and resentment builds up inside us. We think it's okay to talk to others about the problem we're having with so-and-so, but we never go straight to the source. We're guilty of slander or gossip. Even if what we say is true, it's still gossip. And if it's false, it's slander. If we haven't gone directly to the person with whom we're in conflict, we have no business going to anyone else and poisoning his or her opinion of that person. Proverbs 17:9 tells us that someone who gossips and slanders or tries to play the middleman can ruin even the best of friendships. This also pertains to conflicts that team members have with team leaders. If you have a problem with your ministry director or you're unhappy with how things are going for you on the team, go directly to that leader instead of talking behind his or her back.

In our opening sketch Al's first question when he was talking to Stewart should have been, "Have you talked to Marlene yet?" If the answer was no, Al needed to say, "Stewart, I'll be happy to talk with you about this after you talk to Marlene. You need to go directly to her and talk this out. In fact, I'm going to keep you accountable on this by checking in with you in a few days to see if you've talked to Marlene yet." Al thought his intentions were good, but allowing himself to be the middleman in this conflict was doing more harm than good. Now, I know all this is easier said than done. It's not easy to confront someone who has hurt us. It's not easy to say, "I was hurt by that. Can we talk about it?" It's not easy to admit that our feelings have been hurt. Most of the time when it happens to me, my first response is to say to myself, *Oh, grow up. Stop being a baby.* Meanwhile I can tell that my relationship with the person who offended me is being affected. Confronting is not easy. We can procrastinate, we can deny that we're really hurt, we can withdraw, we can even try to act like good little Christians and pretend nothing's wrong, but those things don't heal even the smallest cracks of a broken relationship. If we were all committed to resolving relational conflict as Jesus commanded, our teams wouldn't get bogged down in gossip, slander, and strife.

Early in my ministry I had an experience that solidified for me the importance of team unity. We had a couple of team members who were at odds with each other. They didn't get along at all, and because they sat next to each other in rehearsal, the air was thick with tension all the time. I observed this for a few weeks and realized that their deep hostility toward each other was not going to go away by itself. Meanwhile it was becoming very noticeable to everyone else, and it was hurting the morale of our team. I pulled both members aside separately and encouraged them to resolve their issues in the manner laid out in Matthew 18, then sat back and watched for a couple more weeks. But there was no movement on either member's part, so I had to do something. I approached both of them individually and asked them to meet me in my office after the Sunday service. You can imagine their surprise when they realized they were meeting not only me but each other as well. And it got even more uncomfortable from there because I said, "Friends, I've been after you for a couple of weeks now to resolve your obvious conflict according to Matthew 18, and I have seen no effort on your part to do so. I am going to leave right now, and I don't care if it takes several meetings like this, but you are going to talk this thing out." And I left. I don't know how long it took for them to start, but when I came back they were talking. They both expressed their anger, and they eventually apologized to each other. They walked away with a better understanding of each other. In short, they had resolved their conflict. Both of them admitted to me later that they had grown up in homes in which relational conflict was handled by yelling and screaming and slamming doors and giving the cold shoulder and playing other such games. This was the first time they had ever been challenged to resolve conflict in a healthy way.

If we're going to be a healthy colony of artists, we have got to learn how to resolve conflict in a biblical way. In your life right now are there any broken relationships that you need to mend? Is there anybody with whom you're having a problem that you need to talk to? Are there any conflicts that you need to work through?

3. A Team Player Encourages and Supports His or Her Teammates

When it comes to the arts in the church, we need to cultivate an environment that is encouraging, life-giving, and supportive. That's part of what it means to nurture artists, especially the artists with whom we serve. Most of us have no difficulty encouraging someone whose gifts pose no threat to our place in the ministry. Our character is truly proven when we can root for those who have the same gifts we have. Can you sincerely encourage and pull for someone who has the same gifts you do? Another test of character comes when someone else gets the opportunities we wish we could have. Maybe it's the solo we wanted, the part we wanted to play, or the recording opportunity we wanted. First Corinthians 12:26 (NASB) says that "if one member is honored, all the members rejoice with it." Can you rejoice for someone who gets the opportunities you wanted?

At Willow Creek I love it when I see some of our drama people who aren't in the sketch that particular service encourage their teammates who are just about to go onstage. I love it when I see one of our more established or experienced vocalists wait underneath the stage to congratulate a new vocalist on his or her first solo. Or a keyboard player applaud the efforts of another keyboard player. Do you realize how rare that is in the world? In the world it's unheard of for artists to encourage each other. It's very competitive and very cutthroat. Someone who has talents that overlap yours is looked upon as a threat. This should not be so in the church. Instead of competing with each other, we need to cooperate with each other, to "encourage one another and build each other up" (1 Thess. 5:11). We need to cheer each other on—even those who share similar gifts with us.

I used to play racquetball three times a week, and I was extremely competitive. In fact, I was so competitive that I embarrassed myself on many occasions. I hated to lose and I'd get all angry if I was playing poorly. I would sulk if I lost and snap back in anger at my opponent. Needless to say, I wasn't much fun to play with, and I didn't really enjoy the sport after a while. I had to stop playing, because my temper was getting out of control. That's when God showed me that behind my competitiveness was a dark, prideful desire to dominate, and it wasn't confined to the racquetball court. This desire to control spilled over into my ministry and all my other relationships. I pleaded for God to change me because I was so filled with pride. Well, after several years I'm playing racquetball again. These days I'm playing occasionally with a friend of mine named Terry. Terry is not as good a player as the guys I used to play, but I enjoy playing with him a lot more. He's more laid back. He enjoys life more. He's exactly what I need. We even encourage each other as we play: "Nice shot" or "Good serve." That's unusual for someone as competitive as I am. But God has been using Terry to work on this character flaw in my life. These days I concentrate more on winning than on competing. And I don't mean just getting more points than my opponent. I'm out to win my personal battle of pride. I still like to play hard, but without that competitive edge. Incidentally, I should add that since I've been playing with this new attitude, my love for racquetball is coming back. Win or lose, I'm enjoying playing again.

In the church we artists need to encourage each other. Instead of hoping that other artists fall flat on their faces and fail, we need to cheer each other on. Proverbs 3:27 tells us, "Do not withhold good from those who deserve it, when it is in your power to act." All artists need encouragement, and it's wrong for us to withhold support from each other for any reason. In your life right now is there anybody that you need to encourage?

4. A Team Player Holds On to His or Her Gifts Loosely

In our opening scenario Stewart is holding on to his giftedness too tightly. He has in his mind an idea of exactly how his gift should be used. When things don't go his way, he pouts and gets upset. He's demanding instead of submissive. Every once in a while I run across an artist like Stewart. In effect they're saying, "I'm not going to give of my time and talent unless my gift is used exactly how I think it should be used."

NBA coach Pat Riley says, "Doing your most for the team will always bring something good for you. It means believing that everything you deserve will eventually come your way. You won't have to grab for it. You won't have to force it. It will simply catch up to you, drawn along in the jetstream, the forward motion of your hard work."[3]

Especially if God is in the picture, I think we can say with confidence that good things will come our way if we work hard and don't try to force it. If our talents and abilities are from God, who really owns them? He does. They're on loan to us and we are to faithfully steward them. So we can relax our white-knuckle grip on our gifts and lay them at the feet of Jesus, to be used to edify His church as He sees fit.

There's an attitude of submissiveness in Psalm 123:2 that moves me deeply every time I read it: "As the eyes of slaves look to the hand of their master, as the eyes of a maid look to the hand of her mistress, so our eyes look to the LORD our God, till he shows us his mercy."

Picture the servant artist saying, "Lord, I'm looking to You to show me what You would like me to do with my talent." We need to lay our God-given gifts and talents on the altar, in total submission to His will. When we put our gifts completely in God's hands and trust Him with how they're used, we can be at peace and serve with a cheerful heart. Only then can we truly be team players, holding on to our gifts and our aspirations lightly. Have you totally submitted your gifts and talents to the Lord? Are you holding on to them loosely?

5. A Team Player Tries to Bring a Healthy Self to the Team

One of the best things you can do for your team is to bring a healthy self to whatever the team does. So what does it mean to bring a healthy self to the team? First it means trying to be healthy physically. In some Christian circles it's fashionable to overwork and be burned out; it's a kind of badge of honor. But what's really going on here most of the time is that we're trying to impress each other with how hard we're working or how important we think we are. Ecclesiastes 4:6 (NASB) says, "One hand full of rest is better than two fists full of labor and striving after wind." Rest is important. It's okay to get the rest your body needs. Most people fail to get the rest they need not because they get up too early but because they go to bed too late. We need to work hard for the Lord and not burn out. Most of us are at our best when we're well rested. Over the years I've learned not to schedule myself late into the evening the night before a big service at church, because I know that my team needs me to be sharp and alert. It's just one of the ways I can bring a healthy, rested self to the team. Regular exercise and sensible eating also contribute to our physical well-being. We tend to underestimate the amount of energy it takes to live a proactive, zealous Christian life or to be an attentive spouse or an involved parent. Then we wonder why we're tired all the time. Exercise and a healthy diet create the energy we all need to live life to its fullest. Are you eating sensibly, exercising regularly, and getting enough rest?

Bringing a healthy self to the team also means trying to be healthy spiritually. During the first century there was an awful famine that was sweeping across the continents. In writing to the Corinthians, Paul talked glowingly about the churches in Macedonia and their team effort to help their fellow believers in need. They were poor yet they contributed abundantly to the church's worldwide relief effort. Paul says in 2 Corinthians 8:5 that they were able to give so much because "they gave themselves first to the Lord." They were in such a good place spiritually that giving came easy for them despite their poverty. When you're walking with the Lord, ministry oozes out automatically. You can't serve out of an empty cup, so make sure you're healthy spiritually. Don't you be the one holding the Spirit's anointing back by being spiritually lazy. Make sure you're having regular devotions, that you're praying, that you're confessing and renouncing sin, that you're in fellowship and sitting under biblical teaching.

Bringing a healthy self to the team also means trying to be healthy emotionally. We can't control the circumstances that affect our emotions, but we can do wonders for our emotional well-being by having meaningful relationships and dealing with pain and conflict in a healthy way. Do you have meaningful relationships? Are you paying attention to your emotions and dealing with them, or are you suppressing them? Are you dealing with pain and conflict in your life, or are you coping by denying or escaping?

Many artists don't have good self-care habits. Even if we're healthy in one area, we may be woefully deficient in another. We don't get the rest we need, we don't eat right and exercise, our emotional world is a mess, or we tend to be spiritually lazy. Athletes take good care of themselves off the field so they can perform well on the field. So it is with us. Don't think that your life outside of ministry has no bearing on your ministry. When you and I try to get rest, exercise, and have regular devotions, we're doing something that's not only good for ourselves but good for the team and great for our ministry. A person who is healthy physically, spiritually, and emotionally handles pressure better. They're more apt to better handle disappointment and failure. They're less likely to grumble and complain or be overly competitive. A healthy self always makes for a healthy team.

6. A Team Player Doesn't Care Who Gets the Credit or the Glory

If you really believe in the cause of your team, does it really matter who gets the credit or the glory? Is it more important that you get the credit or that the work gets done? It's typical for us to want to receive all the credit and glory for something we have done, but if you look below the surface, there's almost always an unhealthy, self-serving motivation behind this desire. In many cases there's a craving for attention that drives us to seek the spotlight. And nowhere is this more prevalent than in the world of the arts.

We artists don't like it when someone else gets credit for our work or our ideas. We want everyone to know that we deserve to be in the spotlight. One time Michelangelo overheard some tourists in St. Peter's Cathedral observing his famous *Pieta,* the marble sculpture of Mary holding the crucified Jesus across her lap. They were trying to figure out who the artist was. After hearing them attribute his work to other artists, Michelangelo came back in the middle of the night and across the band that wrapped around Mary, in big bold letters he carved, "Michelangelo Buonarroti of Florence made this." It was the only work he ever signed.

King David wanted so much to build the temple for God. He could envision it. In fact, it was his idea. But it wasn't God's will for David to build it. He wanted David's son, Solomon, to build the temple. Not only would David not get the opportunity to build the temple; he wouldn't even live to see it built. Someone else would build it. Someone else would get the credit and all the glory. So how did David respond? Did he get angry and curse God? Did he sulk and brood? Did he get angry at his son and undermine his efforts to build the temple? No. In fact, he helped Solomon gather the materials needed to build the temple (1 Chron. 22). Did he do it halfheartedly? No, he did it to the best of his ability. He gave it everything he had. He even gave financially above and beyond what he had already given (1 Chron. 29:2–3). Did he do it with a sour attitude? No way. He was delighted to do these things because of his devotion (v. 3). He pitched in and did whatever he could because building the temple was more important than who did it. That's a team player.

Sometimes we get all bent out of shape when someone else gets all the credit we deserve or all the glory we covet. A wise man once said, "It is amazing how much can be accomplished if no one cares who gets the credit."[4] It's always a thrill to play any role, large or small, on any team that's doing something great for God. It doesn't really matter who gets the credit and the glory, does it?

Just a quick word for those of us in leadership: We really need to monitor this so it doesn't get extreme. If credit is constantly attributed wrongly, it can be very demoralizing. It's true that God sees in secret, but it's the wise and sensitive leader who makes sure credit is given to the appropriate people. Sometimes people are not looking for a large display of public recognition. They just want to be thanked and appreciated for their contribution, so let's be sensitive to this on our teams.

7. A Team Player Brings All of His or Her Spiritual Gifts to the Team

I've seen too many artists neglect their other spiritual gifts. They perform and that's it. What about an artist who also has the gift of mercy or encouragement or helps or shepherding or evangelism? The team is incomplete without these gifts. First Corinthians 14:26 paints a beautiful picture of these gifts in full action: "When you come together, everyone has a hymn, or a word of instruction, a revelation, a tongue or an interpretation. All of these must be done for the strengthening of the church." There is such a wide variety of spiritual gifts, and we need to look for opportunities to use those gifts whenever the team assembles. For example, rehearsal is more than just practice. It's yet another opportunity to use our spiritual gifts and edify our fellow artists. Even if you think you don't need rehearsal, you always need the fellowship and the fellowship needs you. If you have the gift of encouragement, you can come to rehearsal looking for someone to encourage. If you have the gift of helps, you can be on the lookout for someone to serve in this way, someone who just might be sitting next to you at rehearsal. Instead of asking, "What do I get out of this?" we should be asking, "What can I give?"

Hebrews 10:24 tells us to "consider how we may spur one another on toward love and good deeds." That's part of my job as a contributing member of a biblically functioning community of artists. I'm supposed to stimulate my fellow artists to new spiritual heights. Next time you're driving to rehearsal, ask yourself, *How can I use my spiritual gift today to stimulate my fellow artists spiritually?* or *Is there anything I could do or say that could benefit someone else on the team?*

8. A Team Player Sees His or Her Role As Valuable, No Matter How Small

Every great team has members who know their roles on the team and perform them well. They're content to play their roles, because they know that if they don't, the group will not function as a team. The best team leaders are the ones who help their members identify their roles and set them up to succeed in those roles. Some roles are more behind-the-scene than others. Some are more prominent than others. But the mature team player knows that a team can't function without all members pulling their own weight, without all members performing the roles they play to the best of their ability. Being dependable—knowing that you can be counted on—is a sign of character. The football player who scores the touchdown gets all the press, but he knows, like anybody who understands teamwork knows, that it wouldn't be possible without the guys on the offensive line who block, pull, and decoy for him. That's what teamwork is all about. In the church there is no lowest common denominator. There are no losers. There is no role that is unimportant and no job that is trivial. Each of us plays a vital role, without which the team could not function successfully. First Corinthians 12:22–25 says, "Those parts of the body that seem to be weaker are indispensable, and the parts that we think are less honorable we treat with special honor. . . . But God has combined the members of the body and has given greater honor to the parts that lacked it, so that there should be no division in the body, but that its parts should have equal concern for each other."

This doesn't mean that we get so locked into a role that we're unwilling to help with something that's outside our area. When somebody on the team needs our help, we can't be saying, "That's not my job" or "That's not my gift." We need to do our fair share whether it's in our job description or not.

I've been in on the ground floor of two church start-ups, and I remember very fondly the sense of team that most churches know in their formative stages. In the early days of any new ministry, everybody pitches in and helps and does whatever needs to be done. I even helped hang drywall for Willow Creek's first offices. I'm not handy at all and can't be trusted with a hammer and nails, so all they would let me do was help hold the drywall. I was way out of my comfort zone, but I showed up to help. I played a part outside my musical role, and though it was very small, I was needed. I was part of the team and I did my job. I'm talking about the instrumentalist who helps the production team tear down the stage, or the vocalist running a spotlight, or the drama person moving props, or the dancer pitching in to stack chairs. That's what teamwork is all about.

Now, what should you do if you're unhappy with your perceived role or you're unclear about what your role really is on the team? I would suggest you talk to your team leader about this right away. If you don't, you will end up frustrated, bitter, and resentful. Don't let this happen to you. If you're confused or disappointed about your role on the team, please talk to your team leader.

9.   A Team Player Submits to Authority

Submitting to authority can be difficult for some of us. We artists don't like anyone telling us what to do. But assuming your leader never asks you to do something contrary to God's will, you have a responsibility to submit to his or her leadership. Hebrews 13:17 says, "Obey your leaders and submit to their authority. They keep watch over you as men who must give an account. Obey them so that their work will be a joy, not a burden, for that would be of no advantage to you." Submitting to church authority is a sign of character. You may think your leader is wrong or incapable or even unfit to lead, but don't add to the problem by being immature yourself. I've seen people get so agitated over the littlest things, and I've seen people leave the church over relatively petty issues. Stubbornness is not a virtue and pettiness is not becoming. Don't be a thorn in the side of the leader. If you disagree with your leader or don't like something he or she is doing, go talk to that person. If you still disagree, pray that God will change your leader's mind or yours. But if nothing ever changes, you still need to submit and cooperate with the person's leadership. When a leader asks you to do something, don't roll your eyes in disgust. That's plainly immature. When a leader asks you to change something about your art or to tone something down or to dress more conservatively, don't fight it tooth and nail. We should be bigger than that and graciously submit.

10. A Team Player Doesn't Lose His or Her Autonomy or Artistic Identity

This may sound as if it contradicts everything else I'm saying, but it really doesn't. It's important for the artist not to get swallowed up completely by the team. When we lose autonomy, we stop taking responsibility for ourselves. I've seen too many artists try to get lost in the crowd and not take personal responsibility for the development of their gifts and the nurturing of their souls. I've also seen too many artists hide behind the spiritual reputation of the leader and not take responsibility for their walk with the Lord or for the sin in their lives. I'm talking about the choir member, for example, who doesn't take the development of his or her gift or spiritual life seriously, thinking that those things go unnoticed when you're part of a large group. Doesn't this person know that any team is only as strong as its weakest link? There is a side to being an artist that is solitary. We need to practice on our own, or we need to write in solitude, or we need to find the inspiration to create on our own. We have devotions and fight temptation on our own. Even though I'm trying to raise the value of teamwork in arts ministry, the arts are not exclusively a team effort. It's our responsibility to do the alone part on our own.

When we lose individual autonomy, we also start living for the team's approval instead of the Lord's. A group mentality sets in that can be very dangerous for a team of artists. When that happens, we go along with the group without questioning. We don't take creative risks anymore for fear of losing our status with the group. We don't speak up if we hold an opinion different from that of the group. We become man pleasers instead of God pleasers. What was Aaron thinking when he misused his artistic abilities and made the golden calf? (Ex. 32:21–24). He created an idol for people to worship. He lost his sense of personal responsibility and listened to the group instead of listening to God. He gave in to peer pressure and betrayed his faith. It is dangerous for any artist to live for the approval of others and stop listening to God.

To Pay or Not to Pay

One topic I should address, because it comes up at nearly all my seminars, is the policy that some churches have of paying their volunteer musicians regularly. I'll address the issue as it pertains to musicians, because that fits my experience, and you can make further applications to other areas of the arts.

If your church is trying to build a team of committed artists, I would strongly recommend that you *not* get into the habit of regularly paying musicians for their services. It undermines your efforts to build a team. First of all, if you're teaching that every role on your team is important and that all members need to pull their own weight for the common good, yet you pay some people but not all people, that's a contradiction. Secondly, it clouds motivation. Am I serving on this team because this is where God is calling me and wants to use me or because I am paid well? Thirdly, it hurts team morale. It can be demoralizing for team members to make the sacrifice needed for the team, only to find out that someone else is getting paid to make the same kind of sacrifice. While there is a precedence in Scripture for paying a church music staff (1 Chron. 9:33), there is no precedence for paying volunteers. Besides, in the new priesthood of believers everybody does the work of ministry, not just a chosen few.

I wish I could share with you one example of a church that regularly pays volunteers and is successfully building a team of committed artists, but I can't, because the two work against each other. I have yet to meet a church music director who's paying his or her volunteers and feels good about it. Instead, what I get most often are phone calls from music directors who have inherited ministries in which the practice of paying volunteers regularly has been in place for years, and now they're experiencing all sorts of conflicts as they try to expand their ministries and take their musicians to that next level of commitment. Paying people doesn't increase commitment. Knowing that God is calling one to ministry makes one more committed. The days of the church-hopping, gigging musician are over. It may have been nice money on the side, but it doesn't serve the musician well at all. It prevents the person from participating fully at any one church because he or she is spread among several. You can't serve two masters (Matt. 6:24). You can't reap the full benefits of serving in community if you're not committed to one church home.

At Willow Creek we might hire some extra string players for Christmas and Easter services, and I've been known to send gas money or baby-sitting money to someone who's putting in time way above and beyond what is expected, but I would never get into the habit of paying volunteers to play. Besides, my vision for our ministry is that we'd see hundreds more artists serving the Lord with their gifts. It would get too expensive to pay all the musicians I believe God wants to bring to our team. In other words, Willow Creek can't afford to pay for the kind of music ministry I think God wants us to have. If you're paying musicians, your music ministry will be only as large as you can afford it to be. I don't want the number of musicians involved in our ministry to be limited by money. I want the Lord to be free to bring to our ministry the number of musicians He wants.

The Story of a Successful Team of Artists

I want to conclude by telling a story from the Bible about a group of artists who did something great for God. In Exodus 35 Moses rallied the people of Israel together to build the tabernacle. The people got so excited about the opportunity to do something great for God and donated so much money and material that Moses had to tell them to stop. Then Moses called the gifted artists together, divided them into teams, and gave them their assignments. There was great attention to detail; the Bible devotes four chapters to describing the artistry that went into the building of the tabernacle. When it was all done, a cloud representing God's majesty rested over them, and His glory filled the tabernacle (Ex. 40:34). Can you imagine how those artists felt? They had worked together as a team and had accomplished something great for God, and He had blessed their work. God's glory shone through their art. God had anointed their efforts. What more could you ask for as an artist? They had come together as artists to do what no one of them could do alone, and God had blessed it!

Follow-Up Questions for Group Discussion

1. As a group come up with a mission statement for your team.

2. As a group write down your team's code of ethics or marks of professionalism. You might want to write at the top of a flip

chart, "This is the way we do things on the (insert name) team" and pool ideas from the whole team.

3. Can you think of something your team has done recently that would be an example of coming together to do what no one of you could do alone?

4. Do you feel, as a team, that you encourage each other enough?

5. How do you best receive encouragement? (For example, verbally or written, how often, etc.)

6. Why is it difficult for most people to bring a healthy self to the team?

7. How can we keep each other accountable about being healthy physically, spiritually, and emotionally?

8. Besides their artistic abilities, what other gifts do your fellow members bring to the team?

9. It has been said that fellowship, or community, is the art of knowing and being known. Are you better at one than the other, or are you pretty good at both?

10. How can your team become even more effective in ministry this next year?

Personal Action Steps

1. Define your role on the team. Determine what you bring to the team that only you can bring—that is, what you do to contribute to the team.

2. If there is anyone on the team now with whom you are in conflict, go to that person and take steps to resolve the issue.

3. If there are any conflicts or lingering bad feelings in your relationship with your ministry director, go to him or her and take steps to clear the air.

4. Offer words of support to someone on your team who needs encouragement today.

5. Determine whether you are healthy physically, relationally, emotionally, and spiritually. If you need to be in better shape in one or more of these areas, decide what steps you can take to be more healthy, and choose someone to whom you can be accountable concerning this.

Holy Spirit Take Control

Holy Spirit take control
Take my body, mind, and soul
Put a finger on anything that doesn't please You
Anything I do that grieves You
Holy Spirit take control[5]

Rory Noland

Be a great painter . . . that will be the only justification for all the pain your art will cause.

Chaim Potok, *My Name Is Asher Lev*

Four

Excellence Versus Perfectionism

*E*llen is a gifted violinist. She started playing when she was only four years old and showed a great deal of promise throughout her early years. She excelled at a rapid pace because she loved to practice. When other girls her age were playing dress up, she was playing Mozart. One of her earliest and fondest childhood memories was when her parents took her to hear a local performance of Beethoven's Ninth Symphony. As soon as the orchestra started to play, she cried. She was mesmerized by the different sounds of the orchestra and was held spellbound watching the violin section. That Christmas she asked for a recording of Beethoven's Ninth and practically wore it out listening to it over and over again. Ellen loved the violin and she loved music.

Ellen also loved church. Her parents were Christians and very involved in ministry at church. When she was eight years old, she accepted Jesus Christ as her personal Savior. She even played a few violin solos in church and enjoyed doing that very much. But her big dream was to perform as a soloist with all the major orchestras of the world and record all the major violin concertos. She felt that was what God wanted her to do with her life. She eventually won a scholarship to attend a very reputable music conservatory. The competition at the conservatory was fierce, and though it was disheartening at first, Ellen realized that she wasn't really good enough to pursue a solo career. So right before graduation, Ellen scrapped her plans for a solo career and set her sights on performing as a member of a major orchestra. She graduated and went from audition to audition, trying to land a job in the string section of a major orchestra. It didn't happen. She was becoming more and more discouraged. She thought maybe she wasn't cut out to play professionally, so she decided to teach violin lessons. She started teaching privately, going to students' homes, and it was rough going at first as she struggled to build up a clientele, but after a few short years she had a thriving teaching business.

Ellen met and married Tom, a fine Christian man, and she and Tom bought a house and set Ellen up to teach in their home. At this time they began to attend a nearby church, and Ellen began to play in the church orchestra. When they started having kids, Ellen had to cut back on teaching, but she was still pretty consistent in playing for church. At first it was a great outlet for her. It was a refreshing break from teaching. She liked the church, she liked the people, and they even asked her to perform a few solos, which she really enjoyed doing. But as time went on, she became more and more restless playing at church. She still liked the church, still liked the people, and still liked the music, but she was unhappy with her playing. Her playing wasn't up to her unusually high standards. She knew what she was capable of doing and felt she wasn't anywhere near that. Someone would catch her in the hallway at church and tell her how moved he or she was by her playing, and in the back of her mind Ellen would be thinking, *Well, yeah, but what about those high notes I played out of tune at the end?* She had a hard time letting things like that go.

Ellen began to complain that she didn't have enough time to practice. She joined a community orchestra to try to supplement and improve her playing, but the same thing happened there. She never got any complaints from the director. In fact, he was thrilled with her playing and moved her up to the first section right away. People would tell her what a good player she was, but she would invariably respond by cutting herself down in some humorous way. She was always frustrated with her playing. She came to rehearsal discouraged and left defeated. She was disappointed because she didn't sound like she did in college when she was practicing eight hours a day. Yet she didn't have eight hours a day to practice anymore. She could maybe squeeze in an hour a day, but certainly no more than that.

Ellen's frustration built to such an intensity that she finally quit playing altogether. She stopped playing in the community orchestra, and she stopped playing solos at church. She didn't even want to play for family and friends anymore. She missed playing, but she didn't miss how playing made her feel about herself. She said that if she didn't have time to practice and couldn't sound like she knew she could, she didn't want to play anymore. In fact, playing had become a source of irritation for her. She was always down on herself because in her mind she didn't sound good. She was convinced that everybody was so much better than she was and that she just didn't measure up. She had high standards and great expectations, and she couldn't bear the thought of falling short. Most people around her had no idea what Ellen was struggling with deep inside. In fact, many of them envied her because she played so well. But Ellen was in turmoil. Music had been a source of joy to her; she used to love music and used to love to play. But now she hated it. All the joy of music had gone out of her.

Ellen felt God must be disappointed in her, too. She felt guilty that she wasn't using her talent, but in all honesty she was angry at God. Why didn't He give her a solo career or a job in an orchestra? How come things never worked out for her? If God wanted her to play the violin, why was her musical experience always so frustrating? Whenever she had played, she had imagined God frowning in disapproval.

Ellen continued to teach, but some say that even her teaching suffered, because Ellen just wasn't quite the same. She seemed to have an edge about her. She was irritable. She hardly laughed or smiled, and she didn't cry anymore when she heard Beethoven. She seemed driven, unhappy, and frustrated.

Questions for Group Discussion

1. Why has Ellen ended up to be so miserable?

2. What are some indications that Ellen is a perfectionist?

3. Isn't it good for artists to be perfectionists? Why or why not?

4. If Ellen came to you for advice, what would you tell her?

5. Is there any way Ellen's extreme perfectionism could have been avoided?

6. What would it take to restore Ellen's love for music?

7. What kind of frustration is in store for those who know or live with a perfectionist?

8. What do you think God feels for the perfectionist?

9. Have you ever walked away from a conversation kicking yourself for something you said? Have you done this recently?

10. Have you ever made a mistake in a performance and played it over and over in your mind? Recently?

Signs of Perfectionism

Ellen suffers from being overly perfectionistic. Perfectionism is one of the artist's biggest battles. I've seen many talented artists like Ellen lose the joy of their art and give up altogether. What can be done for those of us who suffer with perfectionism? Is there any hope for all the Ellens out there whose perfectionism takes the joy out of their art and their ministry? Much of what I learned about perfectionism came from a book that unfortunately is out of print, called *Living with a Perfectionist* by David Seamands. Early in the book the author outlines some of the signs of perfectionism that I'm about to share with you, and I could see every one of those perfectionistic tendencies in my own life. Personally speaking, perfectionism has been a lifelong battle for me. With God's help progress has been there, but it's been slow and often painful. If you don't consider yourself to be a perfectionist, perhaps you know someone who is, or maybe you live with someone who is. Either way, since so many artists suffer with it, we can't talk about nurturing the artistic soul without discussing perfectionism. So what are the signs of perfectionism? How can you tell if you're being overly perfectionistic?

Maximizing the Negative, Minimizing the Positive

First of all, the perfectionist tends to maximize the negative and minimize the positive. I do this a lot. I can get ten letters of encouragement and one from somebody who's unhappy with my work, and guess which one gets all my attention? The negative one. I'll fret about that one negative comment, and I'll blow it way out of proportion. I'll keep playing those negative comments over and over in my mind. Forget the fact that ten people felt so good about something I did that they took the time to write to me. I dwell on the fact that one person didn't like what I did. We shouldn't ignore negative feedback, but to blow it out of proportion isn't right either.

Have you ever heard of the dot syndrome? Look at a newspaper photograph and notice that it's made up of many dots of ink. Now focus on only one of those little dots. See how you miss the "big picture"? The dot syndrome is just like that. You make a little mistake and keep replaying it in your mind, crucifying yourself over and over for it. It's a loss of perspective. Instead of looking at the big picture, you're obsessed with one tiny dot. For the perfectionist, one thing gone wrong means everything's going wrong.

Several years ago I did an arrangement of an old hymn for a Thanksgiving service at Willow Creek. I treated it in a variety of styles, and it was supposed to be fun, celebratory, and worshipful. Well, there was one section that I counted off at a tempo that was too slow, and the band locked on to that tempo and I couldn't get them out of it. The arrangement played on at the wrong tempo. I don't know how long it actually was, but it felt like forever to me. As a result of my little mistake, the dot syndrome haunted me for months. The rest of the service went very well, but I went home depressed because of that one short section (ironically, the hymn was "Count Your Blessings"). I was sure the whole service was ruined and that I had ruined worship for thousands of people. And I was convinced that there were people going to hell on account of my failure. I was suffering from the dot syndrome. This problem also manifests itself when someone tries to encourage me. Sometimes someone will pay me a compliment, but I'll be thinking to myself,

Yeah, but this was off or that was out of tune or something else wasn't quite right. We perfectionists are never happy with our work, because we tend to maximize the negative and minimize the positive.

What's happening with the dot syndrome, and what happens to many perfectionists, is that we tend to internalize disappointment and failure in an unhealthy way. Other people can make a mistake and it's no big deal, but not the perfectionist. Some of us make a mistake and we're utterly destroyed. We can't stand the thought that we messed up or that we let someone down. We beat ourselves up over things we regret saying or things we wish we had said. We can't seem to forgive ourselves for making the simplest of mistakes.

Black-and-White Thinking

The perfectionist is guilty of black-and-white thinking. Something is either all good or all bad. My performance was either all good or all bad. I'm either a good artist or I don't even deserve to call myself one. There's no in between.

Perfectionists tend to be very critical, and they can come down very hard on themselves when they fail. As a result, perfectionists engage in a lot of negative self-talk. For example, "I can't sing. I shouldn't even be on the worship team. I'm no good" or "See, I knew I'd fail. I always fail. I'm not the artist I thought I was. Everybody else is better than me. I'm lousy." Do you know any artists who, like Ellen, gave up performing or writing because they couldn't live up to their own standards? No amount of practice or rehearsal could make them content with their abilities, because they are their own fiercest critics. As a result, they feel under pressure all the time. And they wonder why writing or performing is no fun anymore.

In his book *Abba's Child,* Brennan Manning says,

> It used to be that I never felt safe with myself unless I was performing flawlessly. My desire to be perfect had transcended my desire for God. Tyrannized by an all-or-nothing mentality, I interpreted weakness as mediocrity and inconsistency as a loss of nerve. I dismissed compassion and self-acceptance as inappropriate responses. My jaded perception of personal failure and inadequacy led to a loss of self-esteem, triggering episodes

of mild depression and heavy anxiety. Unwittingly I had projected onto God my feelings about myself. I felt safe with Him only when I saw myself as noble, generous, and loving, without scars, fears, or tears. *Perfect!* (emphasis in original) [1]

Self-Esteem Based on Performance Instead of Identity

We live in an age in which a healthy self-esteem is a very high priority. In fact, in some circles it is the be-all and end-all. At no other time in history have we had such a plethora of self-help books promising to make us feel good about ourselves. Yet so many people still feel inferior and don't like themselves. Manning says, "One of the most shocking contradictions in the American church is the intense dislike many disciples of Jesus have for themselves. They are more displeased with their own shortcomings than they would ever dream of being with someone else's. They are sick of their own mediocrity and disgusted by their own inconsistency."[2]

Many artists are extremely insecure because they're overly perfectionistic. Because they criticize themselves over the smallest of mistakes, perfectionists struggle with self-esteem. When it reaches the point where your talent makes you feel no good or worthless as a person, your self-esteem is too wrapped up in what you do instead of who you are. Perfectionism can also be a way for artists to get people to like them. *If people think I'm perfect or better than I really am, they'll like me and I will be important*—so goes perfectionist thinking.

High and Unrealistic Expectations

The perfectionist often sets high, unrealistic expectations. I frequently notice this in myself. It usually happens with a song or a piece that I've written. The more work I have invested in something, the higher go my expectations for it to come off not well but *perfectly.* So I walk into rehearsal expecting perfection, and I'm disappointed. I come to the service expecting perfection, and I'm disappointed. This is different from setting goals. Setting goals can be motivational and can bring significant growth. Even if we don't achieve all our goals, we're almost always better off for having tried.

Now contrast that with constantly browbeating ourselves and others because we're not living up to perfection.

We artists who suffer from perfectionism also have unrealistic expectations for other areas of our lives. We walk around with great expectations for our careers, our ministries, our marriages, our friends, and our kids. And we get disappointed and disillusioned when those expectations aren't met. We come to the conclusion that we chose the wrong career or the wrong church. Or we married the wrong person. Or we shouldn't have had kids. Or we don't have any friends. I know a few artists whose expectations for a marriage partner are so high, they will probably never marry.

If you and I set unrealistic expectations, we're setting ourselves up for frustration and disappointment every time. That's why the perfectionist lives with a lot of "if onlys." If only I had said this or done that. If only I had gone to that college. If only I had studied with that teacher. If only I had made that audition. If only I had married that person instead of the person I married. We somehow feel that all our expectations would have been met "if only."

People with unrealistic expectations often end up sabotaging themselves. Many artists like Ellen end up quitting altogether because they can't live up to their own standards of perfection. We also see it in the person who tries to have regular devotions, misses a few days, and then feels so guilty about it that he or she gives up completely.

We need to work hard and aim high, but a perfect performance or a perfect life is an unrealistic goal that is more man-centered than God-centered. I think *perfection* should be spelled with an *i* in the middle instead of an *e,* because perfection really is "perfiction." It's pure fantasy to envision ourselves as being perfect. God is the only one who's perfect. Perfectionism is a very subtle form of the sin Adam and Eve were guilty of in the Garden: wanting to be like God. For those of us who expect life to be easy all the time, perfectionism is also a way of being in control; if I can control my environment, I can protect myself from pain and disappointment.

Suggestions for the Perfectionist

Even though perfectionists have a lot working against them, it is possible to change. I have a few suggestions based on what I've learned in my own battle against perfectionism.

Savor the Positive

First of all, savor the positive. Because we tend to maximize the negative, we perfectionists need to celebrate anything and everything positive that comes our way. That means that we don't ignore the ten letters of encouragement that came with the negative one. We read them over and over as much as we would read the negative letter. It's okay to savor notes of encouragement and save them instead of throwing them away. If God uses us in a special way, or if something exciting happens concerning our artistic gifts, it's okay to celebrate what God's doing through us. Some of us are uncomfortable with that because it sounds as if we're patting ourselves on the back. Savoring is not patting yourself on the back for a job well done. It's letting God pat you on the back for doing what He's called and equipped you to do. So it becomes a worship experience. It's thanking and worshiping God for using us, because apart from Him we can do nothing (John 15:5).

In 2 Samuel 6 David had defeated the Philistines and returned the ark of the covenant to Jerusalem. The whole nation celebrated, and David was so overjoyed that he danced "with all his might" (v. 14). And why not? He was savoring a great work of God that he'd had the privilege to be a part of. David danced before the Lord with humility and joy. He wasn't taking the glory for himself. He was worshiping God. David's wife, Michal, on the other hand, wasn't into savoring, and she sharply criticized her husband for his outlandish celebration. But God was not pleased with her negative attitude, and He cursed her with barrenness (v. 23). So you see, God doesn't like it when we pass up an opportunity to savor Him. He delights in worship-filled celebration.

Maximizing the negative is self-centered because it focuses on us and our shortcomings. Savoring is God-centered because it celebrates

God gifting us and using us. For those of us who have a hard time celebrating anything we do, this is going to be a difficult step. But it's such an important one if we're ever going to be healthy, God-glorifying artists. We've got to stop downplaying the good things that happen when God uses us. We've got to learn to savor, for the glory of God, the good things God does in us and through us.

My wife once told me something very interesting about Amish crafts. The Amish, whenever they produce any of their crafts, purposely put a flaw somewhere in their work. It could be one piece of thread that's out of line or a part of a quilt that's slightly off center, but it's there to remind them that only God is perfect. When I gave this teaching about perfectionism to our vocal team years ago, I wanted to give them a visual reminder to savor the good things God does in us and through us—to stop minimizing the positive. My hardworking longtime assistant, Lisa Mertens, graciously volunteered to cross-stitch the phrase "Savor it" for everyone on the team and put each one in a nice frame. But in keeping with the Amish tradition that reminds us of our human frailty, she put a slight mistake in each cross-stitch. She purposely didn't dot the *i* in *it,* to remind us that only God is perfect.

Let God be God. He alone is perfect. It's one of the reasons why we worship Him and not ourselves. Artists who strive for perfection are chasing the wind. It's folly. We're not perfect—never have been and never will be. Paul says, "Not that I have already obtained all this, or have already been made perfect, but I press on to take hold of that for which Christ Jesus took hold of me" (Phil. 3:12). In other words, he's saying, "Folks, I am not perfect. I have not arrived." And he's right. Only God is perfect. We are frail human beings. We are but dust (Ps. 103:14). We make mistakes and that's okay. God wants us to cease striving for perfection and to know that He alone is God (Ps. 46:10).

After the Lord convicted me of my need to savor positive feedback, I began to save meaningful notes of encouragement instead of throwing them away. I put them in a folder that sits in my desk, within easy reach. Sometimes I'll pull that folder out and read a few notes, and I've found that it helps me to put the negative in perspective with the positive. I'm also trying these days not to discount or downplay compliments from people. Instead of writing off what they're saying, I'm choosing to listen and believe them. In short, I'm trying to learn to savor the positive. As a family, we've used going out for dinner as an excuse to celebrate birthdays, special achievements, the end of the school year, or a surprise blessing. It's our way of savoring the good things God has done.

Be Kind to the Artist in You

Whether we perform or create, there's an artist inside who wants so much to blossom and flourish, to be able to grow, and to be given a chance to express. The way we treat each other goes a long way in whether that becomes possible, but the way we treat ourselves is equally important. Some of us are in situations in which it's difficult for the artist to flourish—a discouraging situation at church or too little encouragement or support at home. Some of us have fallen into patterns we learned in childhood, in which we put ourselves down when we don't feel we measure up. Ephesians 4:32 tells us to "be kind and compassionate to one another, forgiving each other, just as in Christ God forgave you." That's a great verse. Have you ever thought of applying it to yourself and the artist in you? The perfectionist is not kind to the artist inside. As we've seen, the perfectionist constantly criticizes the artist inside, sets unrealistically high expectations, and sees only the negative. But God made us to be artists. When we mistreat the artist in us, we diminish someone God made and loves. Some of us wouldn't dream of treating others as badly as we treat that artist inside us.

A fellow artist who also struggles with perfectionism once shared with me a new insight she was learning. "I don't mess up on purpose," she said, "so I just need to relax and not get so down on myself all the time." Easier said than done, of course, but I appreciate the fact that she sees how wrong it is for us to crucify ourselves over something we never meant to say or do. Kindness goes a long way in healing anybody's wounded soul. Be kind to each other and be kind to the artist in you. Life as an artist is tough already. We don't need to make it worse by being our own worst enemy. The next time you're tempted to cut yourself down for not measuring up, remember that no one whom Christ died for deserves to be treated badly, not even you.

Does God Really Like Me?

The world is not always a pleasant place to live. You can start the day off feeling pretty good about yourself, until you encounter a cutting remark that sets you back. You may find yourself in a situation that exposes your weaknesses instead of your strengths. You may run into people who make you feel inferior by the attitude you perceive in them. You may experience one put-down after another. Some intentional, some not. Some said in jest, some not. It's hard to have a healthy self-image in this careless place we call planet Earth.

Even the accolades and applause that an artist receives are nice, but you can't base your self-esteem on them. If you base your self-esteem on what you do instead of who you are, your self-image will go up and down depending on your latest reviews. Building your self-concept solely on your gifts and talents is like building a house on shifting sand. Instead build your self-esteem on who you are as a child of God. I know artists who have become involved with ministry to satisfy their need for approval. The problem is, they only feel good about themselves if they do well. The key to a healthy self-image is not about doing. It's about being: being a beloved child of God.

I have struggled with feeling loved by God. I know He loves the world, but does He love *me?* Okay, I've heard that He loves me, but does He *like* me? The Bible is all about a God who knows us intimately and loves us personally. He demonstrates His love for us daily in the context of our personal relationship with Him. He became a man and walked among us; He looked at people individually—one at a time—with love in His eyes. Then He laid down His life for us—out of love. What people saw in Jesus was a God who was truly interested in their lives and really cared about them. God loves you and me personally. I know that if I understood a fraction of all that means, it would dramatically change my life.

Many of us artists are feelers. We relate to the world around us based on our feelings, but that's dangerous because our feelings change. However, the worst thing you could do to those of us with artistic temperaments is to tell us to ignore our feelings. We can't ignore our feelings. In many of us those feelings are too strong, too real, to ignore. What influences our feelings most, though, is what we believe in our minds. If we fill our minds with the truth about God's love, we will feel more of His love, but making the connection between the brain and the heart is not always easy. I know someone who embarked on an exhaustive Bible study about God's love, listing all the verses that tell us He loves us, and there are a lot of them. It's simply overwhelming to come face to face with the fact that the God of the universe loves you. And He loves me. Whether I feel His love or not, I can't argue with the truth of God's Word.

One verse that helps me feel God's love is Psalm 18:19, because it says that God delights in me. This is also affirmed elsewhere in Scripture (Ps. 37:23; 41:11). Did you know that God delights in you? He created you and He enjoys being with you. He enjoys seeing you grow. He enjoys watching you be what He created you to be. He enjoys watching you use your talent—every time you perform or create. He delights in you.

Another verse that puts me in touch with God's love is Romans 8:38–39: "I am convinced that neither death nor life, neither angels nor demons, neither the present nor the future, nor any powers, neither height nor depth, nor anything else in all creation, will be able to separate us from the love of God that is in Christ Jesus our Lord." This verse has become especially meaningful to me because it reminds me that nothing—absolutely nothing—can separate me from the love of God. Even if I'm having trouble feeling His love, it's still there. Nothing can take it away. Memorizing this verse has helped me feel God's love more deeply. Every time I say it, my heart is filled. It's like food for my soul. It helps me live in the reality that God loves me personally.

The only hope non-Christians have for a healthy self-image lies in their ability to think positively and to focus only on positive feelings about themselves. The only hope believers have for a healthy self-image lies in our concept of God. That's the key. Our God-concept is more important than our self-concept. It's a paradox. You find your life by losing it (Matt. 10:39). You find your worth and your value by losing yourself in God.

Let the Lord Love You

Now, let me warn you that it's not enough to memorize verses about God's love. At some point you've got to let Him love you. Some of us are really good at taking the Bible literally on all points except this one. Have you ever been sitting in church during worship and just been overwhelmed by the thought that God loves you? What was your response? Have you ever sensed God trying to tell you that He is pleased with you? Did you ignore Him when that happened? I've had many experiences like that, and my knee-jerk reaction every time is to think, *No, that's not from God. I must be making it up.* God sent an angel to tell Daniel that He loved him (Dan. 10:11, 19). Why wouldn't He try to get through to us to tell us He loves us?

Once when I was working out at our neighborhood gym, out of the blue I sensed God trying to say to me, "I am pleased with you." (I hope that doesn't sound weird. I didn't hear a voice or anything. I just had that thought quietly but strongly enter my mind.) My initial response was to think, *No, that's not from God. He's not trying to tell me He's pleased with me. I must be making it up.* But then I realized I couldn't be making it up, because at the time I had been struggling severely with feelings of self-doubt and inadequacy. So the thought occurred to me: *Maybe God is trying to tell me He loves me.* So I listened (as I continued my workout), and I sensed God saying to me, "And I like your music." Well, that just about moved me to tears because I had been struggling with disappointment over my songwriting. *Lord, are you sure you like my music?* I asked Him in my mind. *You know I've written some real duds in my day.* "I don't care," I sensed Him saying. "I like them because you wrote them, and you're my beloved child." I had to leave the gym right then and there because I couldn't control my emotions. I sat in my car and cried. I'd had an encounter with the love of God that was deep and real and personal. I shudder to think that I almost missed it. I almost dismissed it and completely ignored it. We need to listen to God's truth about who we are in Him; however, somewhere along the line we have to let it touch us deeply. We have to let Him love us.

My wife has struggled with low self-esteem. The lyrics at the end of this chapter are from a song I wrote for her. When we got married, I thought I could cure her of self-esteem issues by simply loving her unconditionally. That certainly helped, but I could not do for her what only God can truly do. Even though she feels she's not there yet, she would admit that she sees progress. She would also say that it takes time. You can't undo years of hearing negative things about yourself (and believing them) overnight.

Don't Make Self-Esteem Your God

There's one caveat I'd like to throw in here. Don't make self-esteem your god. I know some people who are obsessed with having a good self-esteem. They think they'll never be happy until they can fully love themselves. Their joy level is determined by how good they feel about themselves. As a young Christian, I remember hearing that if you don't love yourself, you can't love others and you'll never be able to truly love God. I couldn't for the life of me get anyone to explain the logic behind that. It seemed as though the world's obsession with self-esteem had infiltrated the church. The Bible doesn't teach that at all. We are to love God above all things and above all people, even ourselves. Jesus said that we are to love the Lord with all our heart, with all our soul, and with all our mind. This is the greatest commandment (Matt. 22:37–38). Loving others *and then* ourselves is the second greatest commandment (Matt. 22:39). We must never get that out of order. Loving Jesus is more important than loving yourself. Loving others is more important than loving yourself. While God wants us to know how precious we are in His sight, loving ourselves was never meant to take the place of loving Him. In fact, when we love God first, we can truly love others and ourselves. So be careful not to make self-esteem your god. Seek first God's kingdom, and things like having a healthy self-image will be granted to you (Matt. 6:33).

Set Realistic Expectations

With God's help set realistic expectations. God deserves our best efforts, but does God expect us to perform perfectly? Of course not.

Can God use something or someone that is imperfect? Can He use a song that is sung or played imperfectly? Of course He can. The major source of frustration in my life stems from me walking into situations with expectations that are unreasonable and too high. Psalm 62:5 tells us, "My soul, wait thou only upon God, for my expectation is from him" (KJV). Our expectations need to come from God. We need to give our expectations over to Him and exchange them for what He expects, not what we expect. While we might be expecting artistic perfection, that might be the furthest thing from God's mind. Try to keep the big picture in mind. God cares about all the details of our artistic endeavors, but He's also in the business of saving souls. What's more important? That our efforts come off perfectly or that God's name be praised and that lost people come to know Him through our ministry? Try to keep things in His perspective.

If God doesn't demand perfection, what does He expect? He expects us to do justice, to love kindness, and to walk humbly with Him (Mic. 6:8). God expects us to grow spiritually. The end result is His responsibility. Our job is to cooperate with the process. We put so much pressure on ourselves to be perfect (the end product), when God is more concerned with the process (that we walk humbly with Him).

So what's realistic to expect when we minister for God? Every time we use our gifts for Him, we need to go into it wanting to do the best we can but trusting God's will to be done, not our self-centered, lofty expectations to be met. People look at the outside and expect the appearance of perfection, but God looks at our hearts (1 Sam. 16:7). He looks at the inside, at our motives and intentions. We can't control how well we perform or how people are going to respond. But we can control our motives and how prepared we are to minister with our talents. We simply have to do our best and trust God for the results He wants.

As I'm writing this, I've been struggling with expectations I had for a weekend service I was just involved in here at Willow Creek. I arranged the music for what I thought was going to be a big orchestra, but illnesses and unexpected emergencies decimated certain key sections, so I ended up with a smaller orchestra. I had some

great players, just not as many as I had arranged for. Nobody had
bailed out on me because of a lack of commitment. Everybody
who couldn't make it had a very valid excuse. I tried hard to get
replacements, calling everybody and anybody who ever owed me a
favor, but to no avail. So I rearranged some parts and we went with
a smaller orchestra. When it was all said and done, we ended up
with no gaping holes in the arrangements, no melody lines missing,
but it didn't sound as good as what I was hearing in my head. Now,
in the past this would have set off a couple of days of mild depression for me, but this time I decided to practice what I preach and
give my expectations to God. Growth in this area has been slow
and painful, and I still have such a long way to go, but—praise
God—I handled it differently this one time. (Maybe there's hope
for me yet.) I told the Lord that this was His battle and that I was
going to trust Him for the results. He reminded me that His grace
is sufficient, that His power is perfected in my weakness, and that the
big picture was not how great my arrangements sounded but
whether people were coming to know Him (2 Cor. 12:9). God
also used some close friends to help me deal with the frustration
created by my unmet expectations. Instead of trying to hide my
insecurity, I confided to those close to me that I was struggling with
perfectionism. (It's hard for perfectionists to admit they're weak.)
People whose opinion I trust said they hadn't noticed any decline
in the music and that I was the only one who would ever know
we'd had any musicians missing. When I heard that from people
who I knew were being honest with me, I realized that I had been
fretting over unrealistic expectations. The size of the orchestra had
changed, and I had never adjusted my expectations. They were way
out of line with the situation.

Pursuing Excellence

By now some of you might be saying, "Now, wait a minute. Didn't
the masters and the great artists of history have a perfectionistic streak
that catapulted their art into greatness? Wasn't perfectionism part of
their genius?" It's my observation that pursuing perfectionism is

destructive to the artist and his or her art. Perfectionism is unhealthy. It inhibits performance and stifles creativity. I think the best artists pursue excellence, not perfection. In fact, I'd like to propose that perfectionism is more or less the evil twin of excellence. While perfectionism is destructive and man-centered, pursuing excellence is constructive and God-honoring. Instead of pursuing perfection, we need to pursue excellence.

Nancy Beach, our programming director here at Willow Creek, defines excellence as "doing the best you can with what you have." No matter how much or how little talent we've been given, we can all try to do our best. For all of you perfectionists out there, note the word *try*. God understands that we're not perfect. All He's asking us to do is try. No matter where you are in your development as an artist, we can all try to do things with excellence. You don't have to be a professional to do the best you can with what you have. You don't even have to be an accomplished artist. You just have to be willing to try to do your best.

Pursuing excellence means we do our best with what we have, to the glory of God. He is worthy of our very best. We serve an ultimately creative God. When He created the world, He imbued it with breathtaking beauty and awe-inspiring majesty. God didn't just throw things together when He created the universe. He modeled creative excellence for us. Seven times during the Genesis account of creation, God stands back, looks at what He's created, and says, "It is good." It's obvious that we serve a God who delights in creativity and values doing things with excellence.

Excellence is also a powerful witness for Christ. Most non-Christians who ever end up in church expect the music to be lousy and outdated. They don't expect to be moved by drama or dance or the visual arts. Wouldn't it be great if they were to come expecting the worst but instead found the arts produced with creativity and excellence? Wouldn't it be great if the local church were leading the way in artistic excellence for our culture? Proverbs 22:29 says, "Do you see a man skilled in his work? He will serve before kings; he will not serve before obscure men." When we do things with excellence, the world will sit up and take notice, and we can point them to the God who created us, gifted us, and loves us.

Artistic Integrity — Developing Skill

When we talk about excellence in the arts, we often talk about artistic integrity. Having artistic integrity simply means that an artist performs or creates with skill. Psalm 33:3 tells us to "play skillfully, and shout for joy." Don't strive to be perfect; instead try to perform or create skillfully. In other words, do the best you can with the talent you've been given. It doesn't glorify God to be mediocre. He's the God who exhibited ultimate skill and creativity in forming the universe. He delights in creativity and assigns value to things produced with skillful artistry. There was a vocalist in the Old Testament named Kenaniah who had a reputation for being skillful (1 Chron. 15:22). He was singled out for leadership and responsibility because of his talent. He had artistic integrity. We need to shoot high artistically. We need to aim for quality over quantity, and substance over show.

We need to take the development of our artistic skill very seriously. First Chronicles 25:7 tells us that the artists in the Old Testament were all trained. We artists need training and ongoing development. We need to take classes and lessons and get good coaching. We need to read books and magazines that will help us improve our craft. After all, how can you develop your singing, your playing, your writing, your acting, your dancing, your painting, your drawing without some type of ongoing training? Many music directors who have been in ministry for a long time don't feel challenged musically anymore. What can you do to challenge yourself artistically?

We also need to expose ourselves to great art and learn from it. How can you be a great artist without studying great art? Don't stay away from great art just because it's not "Christian." Franky Schaeffer points out that there are only "two kinds of art, good art and bad art. There is good secular art and bad secular art. There is good art made by Christians and bad art made by Christians (and all the shadings in between)."[3]

We can learn a great deal and improve our skills by exposing ourselves to quality art inside and outside the church. Philippians 4:8 instructs us to let our minds dwell on things that exhibit excellence. We should be attending art exhibits, concerts, plays, movies, and musicals to broaden our artistic horizons. That's part of our ongoing development as artists. The idea here is to expose yourself to excellence, which unfortunately would exclude much of what's on TV. Don't subject yourself to the brain-numbing junk that's on TV when you could be reading a good book, listening to a CD, or going to a play or an art gallery. That's the kind of entertainment that enriches our lives. Why settle for anything less?

Artistic integrity involves hard work. There is a price to be paid for excellence. Don't kid yourself and think otherwise. If you want to pursue excellence in the artistic disciplines, it takes hard work. This is no time for us artists in the church to be lazy. God is on the verge of using the arts in a mighty way. The days of us in the church producing art in a mediocre fashion are over. Being lazy with our talent is more a sign of being comfortable than being committed. Schaeffer is talking to you and me when he says, "Of all people, Christians should be *addicted to quality and integrity* in every area, not be looking for excuses for second-best. We must resist this onslaught. We must demand higher standards. We must look for people with real creative integrity and talent, or we must not dabble in these creative fields at all. All of this does not mean that there is no room for the first halting steps, for experimentation, for mistakes and for development. But it does mean that there is no room for lazy, entrenched, year after year established mediocrity, unchanging and unvaried" (emphasis in original).[4]

For too long artistry in the church has been thrown together without much regard for quality. For too long we've muttered under our breath, "Aw, it's good enough for church," and the result is that church art (especially music) has come to be associated with insipid mediocrity. Some of us only do enough to get by. God deserves so much more than that. He deserves our very best. A friend of mine once noticed that I wasn't working on my writing gifts, that I was kind of coasting along. He confronted me about this and said, "You've learned how to do just enough to get by. Shame on you." He told me he would kill to be able to do what I can do. Those words, spoken in love, changed me. He was right. I was being lazy. I realized I was taking my gifts for granted. Remember, God has entrusted each of us with a talent, and we are accountable for how we steward that gift (Matt. 25:14–30). It must really grieve Him when we take our talent for granted. It must make Him sad to see people with talent not putting forth any effort. Pursuing excellence involves hard work. Remember, we're not talking about perfectionism; we're talking about doing the best you can do with what you have, and that involves effort. It means that if you're acting and there's one little spot in the script where you're having difficulty, you try to work it out. If you're dancing, you don't keep practicing mistakes over and over again. You put in the hard work to get it right. If you're a writer, you keep rewriting until you get it right. If you're a vocalist, you vocalize regularly and keep your voice in shape. If you're an instrumentalist, you try to keep your chops in shape. You practice. You take the time and put in the effort to fix wrong notes or learn those tricky rhythms. Having a strong work ethic is a sign of character, and people with talent should never settle for less than their best. I saw somebody wearing a T-shirt the other day that said, "Success comes before work only in the dictionary." How appropriate.

I like what the famous conductor Sir George Solti said, near the end of his life, about the need for artists to work hard. He said, "I feel more strongly than ever that I have an endless amount of studying and thinking to do in order to become the musician I would like to be."[5] That was spoken by a man who was already an international success and in his mid-eighties.

Giving God Our Best

King David, a skillful musician according to 1 Samuel 16:18, said something that has always stuck with me in regard to this matter. The Lord told David to build an altar, and a man named Araunah offered to give David everything he needed to build the altar. However,

David refused, saying that he didn't want to offer the Lord that which "cost me nothing" (2 Sam. 24:24). David didn't want to offer the Lord that which didn't take any effort. He didn't want to offer the Lord anything halfheartedly. What a great example for us to follow. We can't be offering the Lord that which cost us nothing. We need to offer God our very best because He deserves it.

The artists who worked on the temple used the best gold they could find for their work, because they wanted to give God their best. Second Chronicles 3:6 says, "Beautiful jewels were inlaid into the walls to add to the beauty; the gold, by the way, was of the best, from Parvaim" (LB). The clay for their bronze work came from the Jordan valley, and it too was the best they could find (2 Chron. 4:17). In Malachi 1 the Lord reproved the nation of Israel because they weren't bringing their best sacrifice to the altar. Instead of offering Him their best cattle, sheep, or goat, the people would offer a blemished animal—one that was sick, old, or lame. It doesn't honor God when we bring Him less than our best. He deserves so much more. Colossians 3:23 says, "Whatever you do, work at it with all your heart, as working for the Lord, not for men." My fellow artists, God is worthy of our best efforts, so let's honor Him by giving Him our very best.

Because I'm addressing artists who struggle in this area, I need to stress once again that I'm not talking about perfection. I'm talking about doing the best we can with what we have. Excellence is a moving target, and hopefully each year our standards reach a little bit higher than the year before. If we resist the human tendency to only do enough to get by, we will grow in the area of excellence. When I look back on what I did five years ago, I realize that it's not as good as what I'm doing now, but it was the best I could do at the time.

Being Creative and Original

Pursuing excellence also means being creative and original. Francis Schaeffer points out something very interesting about the artistry involved in the making of the tabernacle. When they made the priests' garments, the artists were instructed to create blue, purple,

and scarlet pomegranates (Ex. 28:33). Schaeffer draws our attention to the fact that pomegranates can be purple and scarlet during
various stages of their growth, but never blue. Imagine that—a blue
pomegranate. In other words, the artists didn't have to make exact
duplicates of nature. They could bring something new and refreshingly different to their work. Schaeffer's implication is that there is
freedom in God's economy for artists to be creative and original.[6]

That's why God's Word encourages us to sing to the Lord a
"new song" (Ps. 33:3). I feel very strongly that every church needs
to encourage the writing of original music. Original music is an
expression of church life. It's a good way to document what God
is doing in your church. If God is doing something unique in your
church, let's have a song about it as a testimony to the community.
If there's a teaching that God has been impressing upon the congregation, let's have a song about it, like a landmark that enables us
to remember the teaching every time we sing it. If there's something your church is celebrating, let's have a song that commemorates it. This "new song" principle applies not only to music but to
all the arts. Let's encourage the creation of new art to reflect what
God is doing today in every one of our churches.

Effective Communication

We need to pursue excellence in our ability to communicate effectively. Great art communicates a message, an idea, a thought, a feeling, or an emotion. Art at its best stimulates the mind and moves the
soul. If we in the local church don't get serious about how to communicate effectively, our art will move no one. No matter how
accomplished or sophisticated we are, if thought is not given to
communicating clearly, how are we going to reach people with our
art? Paul has an interesting point in 1 Corinthians 14:7–9: "Even in
the case of lifeless things that make sounds, such as the flute or harp,
how will anyone know what tune is being played unless there is a
distinction in the notes? Again, if the trumpet does not sound a clear
call, who will get ready for battle? So it is with you. Unless you

speak intelligible words with your tongue, how will anyone know what you are saying? You will just be speaking into the air."

Isn't it true that if our message lacks clarity, we might as well be speaking into the air? We need to make sure that art produced for the church says something and says it clearly. All artists need to know that communication is just as important as technique. I've been greatly moved at times by singers whose technique was not as developed but whose communication skills were strong. On the other hand, an artist who has great technique but gives no thought to communicating clearly and effectively will move no one. Christian art will never become a force to be reckoned with if we ignore what it takes to communicate meaningfully.

People in theater usually have a better handle on this. They know how important it is to give thought to every line. "How am I going to say this?" they ask. "What should I be feeling, and what's the best way to express it?" Dancers have no spoken lines. The best dancers know that they have to use their physical movements and their faces to tell us what they're trying to say. Visual artists don't have the spoken word or their own facial expressions. Most of the time they're not even present when people observe their art, so they have to fill the canvas or the page with emotion and meaning that effectively communicates.

The artists who I think are more oblivious to good communication are unfortunately the musicians, especially vocalists. There's been a sentiment in the church for far too long that singers who perform without any facial expression or emotion are somehow less distracting and more spiritual. In the churches in which I grew up, vocalists would sing with their arms perfectly still at their sides, and looking straight down at their music. No eye contact, no meaningful gestures, no facial expression at all. The irony here rests in just how unnatural that really is. When we're talking about something important to us, we don't stand at attention like robots. We move our arms to emphasize our point. Our faces register an emotion that matches our words. We look at people when we talk to them. Vocalists, when you rehearse, do you give as much attention to how you're going to communicate a song as you do to your technique? Do you just sing the notes, or do you throw yourself into communicating a message? Unlike the dancer, you have the luxury of words. Are you enunciating clearly? Are there any vocal licks getting in the way of your message? Do you know what the payoff lyrics are, the ones you don't want anybody to miss? Unlike the visual artist, you have the luxury of being able to use your body and especially your face. Does your face reflect what you're singing about? Are you using gestures that are meaningful and natural for you?

Some of us are stiff and reserved onstage because we're more concerned with how we look than with whether we're communicating. We're too self-conscious. I like Peggy Noonan's advice on this: "When you forget yourself and your fear, when you get beyond self-consciousness because your mind is thinking about what you are trying to communicate, you become a better communicator."[7]

Professional dancer and choreographer Mark Morris had this to say about throwing ourselves into communicating effectively: "As a performer there's nothing better than moments where you feel that you have the option—within the given text—to do exactly as you want, where you're not worried about what you look like or whether you've warmed up enough. You just seem to be involved in a pure expression which is completely appropriate."[8]

I don't mean to pick on vocalists. We all must submit to what the art form needs to communicate clearly. For example, if you're an instrumentalist, you don't overwhelm the lyrics with intrusive notes or volume. If you're a songwriter, your songs need to have a clear focus and a logical progression of ideas. We in the church need to take communication seriously, because we've been given the charge to communicate the Good News. We have the most important message there is, so let's communicate it boldly and clearly. Effective communication is a vital part of pursuing excellence.

Spiritual Preparation

I'm including spiritual preparation here in our discussion on excellence because I've discovered over the years how crucial it is for Christian artists to prepare their hearts and minds spiritually before they create or perform. The apostle Paul knew the importance of spiritual preparation before ministry. After his dramatic conversion, he didn't hit the lecture circuit right away. He spent three years in relative obscurity, preparing himself spiritually. He already had speaking and teaching gifts, but he needed to prepare himself spiritually for the ministry ahead of him (Gal. 1:15–2:1). In fact, he put in fourteen years of spiritual preparation before his ministry really took off. And this was one of the greatest religious scholars of all time. We need to take spiritual preparation as seriously as rehearsal. It's as much a part of pursuing excellence as is practicing.

At Willow Creek we are blessed to have Corinne Ferguson leading, shepherding, and coaching our vocalists. She understands how important spiritual preparation is to a fruitful vocal ministry. Rehearsal with Corinne is more than just practicing notes. There is a great deal of soul work that happens as well. Sometimes she'll lead the vocalists in a discussion of the lyrics, by asking probing questions. Or the group might pray over the lyrics or pray for the congregation to receive those lyrics with open hearts. Many of us refer to Corinne as our secret weapon, because she literally works behind the scenes and greatly impacts our ministry by inspiring the vocalists to let each song they sing reflect their souls. She gets them to personalize every lyric of the song, to own what the song is saying, and to communicate that message in the most effective way. If a song doesn't first minister to the one singing it, it won't minister to anyone else.

I've also learned a lot about spiritual preparation by watching some of our veteran vocalists here at Willow Creek. I've seen them take lyrics to a song they're working on and journal on them. They'll pursue a Bible study on the main theme of the song during their quiet time or meditate on Scriptures that relate to the lyrics. I've heard them share insights they've gained from applying the truth of a particular song to their own lives. During the days leading up to a service, many of them pray fervently that God would use them to their fullest. This is all part of what it means to prepare yourself spiritually to minister in the arts.

The most important ingredient for effective communication is sincerity. If you can communicate what you believe with sincerity, people will sit up and take notice. Sincerity was a trademark of

Paul's ministry and gave his ministry power and integrity (2 Cor. 1:12; 1 Tim. 1:5). More than anything else, the world is wondering whether we Christians really believe what we sing about. They're wondering how sincere we are, how real Jesus is to us. And you can't act sincere. It's not something you can fake or manufacture. Either you are or you aren't. But you can cultivate a sincere heart. That's where spiritual preparation comes in. Scripture can renew our passion for the things of God and strengthen our convictions. It constantly challenges me to know what I believe and then to live what I believe. Saturate your mind with God's Word so that when you perform a song or drama or dance about God's grace, for example, you feel a conviction down to the depths of your soul about how wonderful that grace is and how no one should live without it. Don't neglect the potential for God's Word to deepen the sincerity of your soul. If your heart is passionate about the things of God, you will communicate with sincerity.

The other thing we need to do for the sake of our spiritual integrity as artists is to live a Spirit-filled life. Acts 1:8 says that when we are filled with the Holy Spirit, we become powerful witnesses for Jesus Christ. If you and I want to have spiritual integrity, we need to walk in the Spirit (Gal. 5:16; Eph. 5:15). That involves a day-to-day, moment-by-moment decision to walk intimately with God, to seek Him first and follow Him wholeheartedly (Matt. 6:33; Luke 9:23). If we walk in the Spirit, the Lord will anoint our work as artists, and we will minister powerfully in His name.

Come to Me

What would Jesus say to the perfectionist? I think He'd look us straight in the eyes, hold out His hand, and say, "Come to me, all you who are weary and burdened, and I will give you rest. Take my yoke upon you and learn from me, for I am gentle and humble in heart, and you will find rest for your souls. For my yoke is easy and my burden is light" (Matt. 11:28–30).

That's a great passage for artists who are weighed down with perfectionism, who have become weary trying to live up to their own expectations, who are heavy-laden with negative self-talk. Jesus says, "Come to Me just as you are, warts and all. Come to Me and be free, free from the pressure of your self-inflicted perfectionism." Notice that Jesus is not the slave-driving, impossible-to-please God that we make Him out to be. He is gentle and humble.

Sounds inviting, doesn't it? Compared with the demands we perfectionists put on ourselves, His yoke is easy and His load is light. He's there, ready and willing to help shoulder our burdens. So lay it all down at the foot of the cross and find your rest in Him.

Follow-Up Questions for Group Discussion

1. Do you see any signs of perfectionism in your life? Go through the following list and put a check by any of the tendencies you see in yourself.

    _____Minimizing the positive, maximizing the negative

    _____The dot syndrome (looking at a small flaw and ignoring the overall good)

    _____Black-and-white thinking (I'm either all bad or all good)

    _____Self-esteem based more on performance than on identity

    _____Setting unrealistically high expectations

    _____Negative self-talk

2. Do you think your team does a good job of celebrating when God uses the team in a special way?

3. How can you savor something you've done artistically that God has blessed, without becoming prideful about it?

4. When was the last time you attended an artistic event such as a concert, movie, or play or visited an art museum? How was the experience?

5. What would be a hypothetical example of an artist offering a "blemished lamb" for service in the church?

6. Are you convinced that it's important for art in the church to communicate clearly? What about art for art's sake?

7. In your mind, what is the difference between pursuing perfection and pursuing excellence?

8. How do you know if your artistic endeavors are anointed by the Holy Spirit?

9. What does it entail for the artists in your ministry to be prepared spiritually to minister in the church?

10. Why do you think it scares some people to talk about excellence in the church?

Personal Action Steps

1. Schedule an artistic outing, such as going to a concert or play.

2. Find the verse in the Bible that speaks most convincingly to you about God's love for you personally. Meditate on that verse and memorize it.

3. Develop and implement an ongoing plan to help you further develop your artistic skills. Decide to whom you can be accountable regarding this.

4. Take steps to improve the ability of your art to communicate clearly.

5. Decide what you can do to better prepare yourself spiritually to minister as a Christian artist.

Let the Lord Love You

I cringe every time you cut yourself down
You hide your pain like it doesn't count
So when I hear you laugh are you cryin' deep inside
'Cause you fall below the standards in your mind
Though you'd never deny our God's a loving God
You feel He turns away when you make mistakes
But our heavenly Father nurtures His own
To Him you matter more than you'll ever know

So let the Lord love you
Let His voice be heard above the rest
Hold on to what you know is true
And let the Lord love you

We may search for truth, but we listen more to lies
Play them over and over in our minds
Till we're left with some distorted point of view
That cripples who we are and all we do
There are times you've gotta fight for all you're worth
Stand up to the voices from the past
And as you draw close to Him the more moments you'll have
When His love overwhelms and you know it's true

That the Lord, He loves you
So let His voice be heard above the rest
Hold on to what you know is true
And let the Lord love you
You gotta let the Lord love you[9]

Rory Noland

Artistic growth is, more than it is anything else, a refining of the sense of truthfulness. The stupid believe that to be truthful is easy; only the artist, the great artist, knows how difficult it is.

Willa Cather, *The Song of the Lark*

Five

Handling Criticism

*J*ustin is the sound technician at Southport Community Church. He puts in a lot of hours volunteering at the church. For most every service or major event, he's the first one there and the last one to leave. He sets up the sound equipment for the service, mixes drama, band, and vocals, and runs the lights. During the week he maintains the church's sound and lighting gear, and he's been doing all this for well over ten years. The church doesn't pay him and he's okay with that, even though he could easily spend more than forty hours a week there. He knows how rare it is for a church to hire a technical director. So he teaches physical education at the grade school every day and then runs over to the church by late afternoon. He enjoys what he does at church, but lately he's been at odds with Sam, the new programming director. Sam's got all sorts of new ideas that put Justin on tilt every time they talk.

When they first met, Sam gave Justin a long list of changes he wanted to make. First of all, he wanted to lengthen rehearsal time, which meant that Justin would have to be at the church even earlier. Justin was already stressed out from all the hours he was putting in. He couldn't help but think, *What's wrong with the way we were doing things before?* Sam wanted new monitors, he wanted to move the speakers in the sanctuary, he wanted to mic the drums differently, and he wanted to go stereo with all the keyboards. Justin thought, *Who does this guy think he is to come in here and change everything?*

One of the changes that has been especially difficult for Justin has been the evaluation meeting he's now forced to attend very early every Monday morning. The key leaders involved in putting the service together meet with the pastor at a local restaurant and critique the previous day's service. This is hard for Justin. Every time anything negative comes up about the sound or the lighting, he gets very defensive. One time the pastor asked why his lapel mic sounded as if it were on the verge of feedback during the sermon, and Justin snapped back, saying, "Well, if I had some decent equipment to work with, we wouldn't have this problem." No one knew what to say. The conversation moved on, but Justin wasn't really listening during the rest of the meeting. He was lost in a series of negative and defensive thoughts: *They have no idea how hard I work. . . . I'm doing the best I can. . . . They're lucky to have me. . . . No one else would put up with all this. . . . I don't get paid to do this. . . .*

Sam has made several suggestions about the band mix and the vocal sound that haven't set real well with Justin. One time Sam was onstage and asked for less reverb on the group vocals and more "warmth." This made Justin angry. *I know what I'm doing. I don't need anybody to tell me how to run sound,* he thought. But he complied, and even he had to admit that less reverb gave the overall sound more clarity. To add insult to injury, several people complimented Justin on the mix as they left church that morning. Many people said they could hear the lyrics better. Justin appreciated their innocent encouragement, but he still didn't like the idea of that new guy Sam telling him how to do his job.

The communication between the two men has seemed like a tug-of-war. Every time Sam makes a suggestion, Justin asks why and then grudgingly complies. As a result, there is tension at every sound check, every meeting, and every service. People feel as if they have to walk on eggshells when they're around Justin, because he takes even the slightest bit of criticism so personally. He seems angry all the time.

To make things worse, the two men clashed over a moral issue that came to the surface in Justin's life. Justin and his fiancée, who wasn't a believer, had been living together for several months. When Sam confronted him about it, Justin at first denied it. Sam persisted, and Justin accused him of being judgmental, pointing out that the decision to live together was a financial one.

The straw that broke the camel's back, however, may have occurred last week. More singers than usual were to perform during the service. As microphones were being handed out ten minutes before the service was to start, someone discovered two bad microphone cords—and no spares. Justin had been meaning to buy some new cords, but he just hadn't gotten around to it. He had dropped the ball. When Sam anxiously questioned him about it, Justin became defensive and angry, finally telling Sam, "If you want mic cords, get 'em yourself!"

During the service Justin could hardly concentrate. He was seething inside. He was angry at Sam, he was angry at everyone onstage, and he was angry at the church. His thoughts outpaced his emotions. *What right does this newcomer have to make such outrageous demands all the time? And where does he get off, telling me how to do my job? Doesn't he think I know what I'm doing? If it wasn't for me, this service wouldn't even be happening. I deserve to be treated better than this.* The anger burned hotter and hotter until Justin couldn't take it anymore. He got up and left, right in the middle of the opening song. He turned the board off and everything went dead. There was a loud boom throughout the auditorium, and the entire congregation turned and watched Justin storm out of the booth, down the hall, and out the door.

After the service, Sam tried several times to call Justin at home, but Justin was screening his calls and never picked up the phone. In his own way he was trying to punish Sam. He had everyone's attention now and he wanted to make his point. He sat home alone, sulking in front of the TV.

Questions for Group Discussion

1. Why do you think Justin reacted negatively to every suggestion Sam made?

2. Why do you think Justin took everything so personally?

3. What would you suggest Justin do to patch up his relationship with Sam?

4. What should Sam do next to try to patch things up with Justin?

5. Do you think Sam was right in confronting Justin about living with his fiancée?

6. Is there any way the tension between Justin and Sam could have been avoided? What could they have done differently that would have enabled them to work together more harmoniously?

7. How does a defensive spirit affect rehearsals?

8. How do you think an artist should handle criticism?

9. What happens to an artist when he or she is not open to constructive criticism?

10. What is the best way to give feedback to an artist?

The Dangers of Defensiveness

Sometimes those of us with artistic temperaments get defensive when we're criticized. We can be overly sensitive, and we let the least little thing hurt us. Sometimes we're offended even when no offense was intended, and we take things more personally than they were meant to be taken. We may have a defensive spirit due to pride, fear, insecurity, or a dysfunctional upbringing, but whatever the reason, it can really stifle a person relationally and spiritually. And it can have devastating effects on your ministry and on the team with which you serve. Very often the person who's overly defensive doesn't realize it. You may think this is not a problem for you, but believe me, if you're a sensitive artist, the potential is always there for you to take something more personally than it was meant to be taken. Artists can also be the most stubborn of all people. We want to do things our way, and when anybody challenges that, we get angry.

Scenarios like the one I described with Justin and Sam are all too common, especially among artists. I've seen instrumentalists get defensive about intonation: "*I'm* certainly not out of tune. My instrument was pitched at 440 at the factory, and it never goes out of tune." I've witnessed vocalists getting defensive when they're having difficulty learning a part. I've observed defensiveness in the actor or actress who responds to a well-meaning suggestion by snidely saying, "I was just doing what the director told me to do." I've seen writers and other creative types get defensive about their work, as if to say, "How dare you criticize what I wrote. This came from God; I'm not changing a thing. It's fine just the way it is!" With some of us artists it's like this: "You can criticize anything you want, but don't you dare criticize my work!"

A defensive spirit can hurt you and your art. We can't grow as artists until we deal with this character issue, which can be such a blind spot for us artists. Let's start by looking at some of the dangers of defensiveness.

Defensiveness Alienates Us from Others

Being defensive cuts you off from other people. It leads to bitterness and resentment. It stifles communication. It alienates. People who are always quick to defend themselves are not very approachable. When others feel as if they have to walk on eggshells around you, you end up alienated from others, and that can be very lonely. I've often seen situations in which everyone feels as if they have to be extra sensitive around a certain individual, and they start avoiding that person because it can be very draining to have to deal with a defensive spirit. If you always feel as if you're hurting someone, you tend to avoid them after a while. Sometimes we get defensive to avoid getting hurt. We can't stand rejection or the thought that someone might not like us. Yet inevitably the very thing we're trying to avoid happens. People reject someone who's chronically defensive. The irony here is that the overly sensitive person eventually becomes insensitive to others because they're so self-absorbed. What starts out as a defense mechanism against being hurt turns out to inflict an even greater hurt: loneliness and alienation. This isn't good for the artist who's trying to experience community or trying to build meaningful relationships in his or her life.

Defensiveness Keeps Us from the Truth

Honesty is a sign of integrity. The person who recognizes truth and speaks honestly is a person of high moral character. Being defensive, on the other hand, is a serious character flaw. It keeps you from the truth about yourself and the world around you. People tend to shy away from being honest with overly sensitive people, because they don't want to hurt them. I have walked away kicking myself numerous times after talking to someone who's being defensive with me, because I either said too much or too little. I stretched the truth a bit to make the person feel better, or I held something back because I was afraid of hurting the person. What I should have said was no doubt more needful, but I let the person's hypersensitivity keep me from being totally honest.

Because I lead a team of artists, I take my responsibility to shepherd them very seriously. There are times when I need to speak honestly to someone about his or her work or about certain character issues in his or her life. Whenever I have anything especially difficult to share with someone, I go into it with the attitude that the truth helps us be better people. Most people want me to be honest with them, but I occasionally run across an artist who can't handle constructive criticism of any kind. They don't want to hear the truth. How sad; they don't realize how liberating the truth can be.

We choose defensiveness to protect ourselves from self-doubt. Yet the very thing we're trying to prevent happens. People who put up walls to protect themselves from the truth encounter more self-doubt than those who face their weaknesses squarely and grow from them. In an effort to protect our self-esteem, we open ourselves up to something more damaging than a bruised ego, and that's deception. Believe me, being deceived about your abilities is far worse than knowing and accepting your strengths and weaknesses.

Defensiveness Keeps Us from Being All We Can Be

Being defensive keeps us from being the artists we can be. It stifles us artistically and creatively because listening to feedback, critique, or suggestions is one of the ways we improve. We can learn so much by being open to feedback. As a music director at a church, I've been burned numerous times by songwriters who requested my honest feedback about songs they wrote. For some reason I get demo tapes sent to me from writers all across the country. On occasion, after trying to be sensitive and affirming, I'll make a few suggestions and a songwriter will get angry and defensive. The writer didn't want my feedback. What the person really wanted was for me to say that we'll use his or her music at our church. It definitely makes me wary of giving feedback to the next writer who comes along.

When we allow ourselves to be defensive, we stop growing as people and as artists. Sometimes we get defensive because we feel threatened. We think we have to protect ourselves and our art. But the very thing we're trying to protect suffers the most from our defensiveness. That's because we cut ourselves off from that which can help us flourish as artists: constructive feedback.

Taking Offense

Because many artists are sensitive people, our egos bruise easily. Sometimes too easily. We're good at picking up signals from people, things that others might not even notice. Because we're going to pick up a lot of things like that, we need to be careful that we don't pick up something that's not really there. Our intuition is not infallible. Don't be easily provoked (1 Cor. 13:5). Proverbs 3:30 warns us not to take offense when none was intended. Proverbs 11:27 says, "He who seeks good finds goodwill, but evil comes to him who searches for it." Don't go looking for trouble. Don't walk around with a chip on your shoulder. Ecclesiastes warns us not to take everything people say so personally that we become easily offended (7:21). Don't make a big deal out of a comment that was not intended to be a big deal. Don't blow someone's feedback out of proportion.

When the elders of Israel approached Samuel and asked him to appoint a king over them, he was offended. He took it as an indictment against his leadership. He took it as a slap in the face, because he was old and his sons were doing a poor job of leading the nation. The Lord, however, told Samuel not to take it personally: "Listen to all that the people are saying to you; it is not you they have rejected, but they have rejected me as their king" (1 Sam. 8:7). In other words, God said to him, "Don't make a mountain out of a molehill, Samuel. This isn't about you, so don't take it personally."

We artists don't hold a monopoly on becoming easily offended, but we sure own a major franchise in the business. Often without ample evidence, we can become convinced that someone is trying to undermine us. It's not always true. The problem might be a simple misunderstanding, or perhaps we're being overly sensitive. The nation of Israel went to the brink of civil war because of a simple misunderstanding (Josh. 22). In the end cooler heads prevailed, and when they sat down and talked, they realized it was much ado about nothing.

When in doubt, check it out. If you're taking offense because of something you heard secondhand, go to the person and ask about what was said. If you're taking something personally but are not sure it was meant to be taken that way, check it out. I don't know how often I've been offended and have gone to the person only to find that I took what was said more personally than was ever intended, that I misunderstood what was said, or that I misinterpreted something the person did. So be careful not to take offense if none was intended.

Keeping Up the Facade

Many of us work hard at keeping up the impression that we have it all together. This is a trap that a lot of performers fall into because we always have to put on our best face when we're onstage. When we audition, we have to look our best and do our best. When we perform, we want to be "on" and put on the best show we can. We have to appear confident, even if we're not. So we learn to put up a facade to sell ourselves. This facade, this self-generated confidence, then causes us to be defensive toward anyone with constructive criticism.

Likewise, if anyone tries to point out one of our character flaws, no matter how loving the person tries to be, we gear up to defend ourselves. We must appear to have it all together. "How dare he suggest that I have a problem in that area!" we fume. We go to such great lengths to keep up the facade that we cut ourselves off from the one thing that will help us grow spiritually, and that's humility.

By the way, this is one of the biggest differences between performing and ministry. I've seen many professional entertainers try to approach ministry the same way they've always approached performing. Performance is entertainment. You have to own the stage. You have to appear self-confident and enthusiastic. It doesn't matter if you're going through a deep personal crisis. The show must go on. You have to put it all behind you and step onstage and wow everybody one more time. Ministry, on the other hand, is not entertainment. Instead of pretense, there is authenticity—we need to be real onstage. Instead of working hard to whip up confidence, we need to be humble. Ministry demands that we allow the Holy Spirit to own the stage.

Responding to Feedback

I understand where defensiveness comes from. An artist can be extremely vulnerable. If you're a performer, you stand onstage (sometimes all alone) pouring your heart out and giving complete strangers a glimpse into your soul. To be vulnerable is a price every performer pays. If you're a creative person, you too are vulnerable. You pour your heart and soul into creating something, and you hold it protectively in your hands. When it comes time to show it to the world, you open your hands up slowly, hoping no one will kill your brainchild before it has a chance to become something. Because art is such a personal thing, it's difficult for us to separate ourselves from our work.

Another reason we feel vulnerable is because we are constantly being evaluated. We evaluate ourselves, wondering how our audience liked what we did. As a result, whether we perform or create, we can often feel as if our work is always "out there" for people to evaluate. Sometimes it feels as if whether we're gifted at all depends on how people respond to our latest endeavor. "You're only as good as your latest outing," is not true, but sometimes that's how it feels. Artists often feel as if their validity is at stake whenever they step out on the stage. And it doesn't help that critiquing the arts is, more often than not, very subjective. One very respected person may love something we do, and another well-respected individual may hate it. So how do you overcome all this and respond to feedback without being defensive? How can you be sensitive but not overly sensitive?

Greet Feedback As Your Friend

First of all, consider constructive criticism to be always in your best interest in the long run. The Bible says that it's foolish not to be open to feedback (Prov. 1:7). David was an artist who realized the value of constructive criticism. In Psalm 141:5 he says, "Let a righteous man strike me—it is a kindness; let him rebuke me—it is oil on my head. My head will not refuse it." Greet feedback as your friend. Have a teachable spirit. Be open to critique. Realize that it can be God's agent to bring growth into your life—spiritual growth as well as artistic growth.

Someone who is honest with us truly loves us. Proverbs 27:5–6 says, "Better is open rebuke than hidden love. Wounds from a friend can be trusted, but an enemy multiplies kisses." I know a musician who's chronically defensive. Everyone walks on eggshells around this person and is very careful about what they say. It's like the elephant in the room. It's there, it's creating a huge problem, but no one wants to talk about it. Everybody knows there's a problem except the person with the problem. Don't we love others enough to tell them that they are only hurting themselves with their constant defensiveness? There is often some degree of genuine love and concern behind most constructive criticism. That's why feedback can be greeted as a friend, not an enemy.

There is a character in the Bible who has been a quiet example of this for me. His name is Apollos, and his story is recorded in Acts 18:24–28. It seems Apollos was a gifted teacher and leader, but his theology was a little off center. Two people, Priscilla and Aquila (one of the great wife-and-husband teams in Scripture), pulled Apollos aside and confronted him about his theology. We don't know exactly what was said, but we do know that Apollos was faced with a choice. Either he was going to listen to truth and gain from it, or he was going to take offense and ignore the truth. It's obvious that Apollos was open to the truth and greeted feedback as beneficial, because after he listened to Priscilla and Aquila, his ministry flourished. "He was a great help to those who by grace had believed. For he vigorously refuted the Jews in public debate, proving from the Scriptures that Jesus was the Christ" (vv. 27–28). Apollos went on to do great things for God because he was open to constructive criticism.

Apollos knew that it is better to hear the truth, even though it might be hard to hear, than to be soothed by a lie that makes us feel good. I shudder to think what major impact for the kingdom would have been lost had Apollos been defensive and refused to listen to honest feedback. I also cringe when I think about what a setback it would have been for the early church if there hadn't been people like Priscilla and Aquila around. Those two loved the bride of Christ, and Apollos, so much that they were willing to risk a confrontation for the ultimate good of all involved.

My fellow artists, we don't have to be defensive when someone offers us suggestions about our work. If you're a performer, be open to suggestions that can make you a better performer. If you're a creative person, don't be narrow-minded about constructive criticism. Don't hesitate to solicit honest evaluations from friends. "In abundance of counselors there is victory" (Prov. 11:14 NASB). Greet feedback as a friend, not an enemy. The real enemy is our own defensiveness.

Respond with Grace

Even if we're convinced that constructive criticism is good for us, it can still be difficult to know how to respond to suggestions or criticism with grace instead of anger. James 1:19 shows us how to do that: "Everyone should be quick to listen, slow to speak and slow to become angry."

Be quick to listen. Instead of being quick to justify yourself, listen first. Listen without being threatened. Listen as a beloved child of God, secure in His love, someone whom God loves intensely. You are a person God cares deeply about, not someone who has to have his or her giftedness or worth validated every time something negative is hinted at. Listen to what's being said, without blowing it up to be bigger than it is. Sometimes we're too busy being defensive to really listen. Negative feedback triggers all sorts of negative self-talk. That's what kept happening to Justin in our opening scenario. He couldn't hear accurately because of all those defensive voices in his head.

Be slow to speak. Don't be so quick to defend yourself. When someone offers us feedback, our first response should not be a defensive one. Our first response should be to ask ourselves, *Is any of this true?* Proverbs 18:17 says, "The first to present his case seems right, till another comes forward and questions him." We shouldn't be quick to defend ourselves, because someone could come along and corroborate the criticism. When someone offers constructive criticism in a loving way, we need to express appreciation for his or her courage, concern, and love. It's not easy to speak the truth. Even if you may doubt the person's care and concern, you're usually not in the best position to judge the person's motives.

It's a very wise person who cultivates an environment of honesty surrounding everything he or she does. I'd hate to get to the end of my life knowing that I was deceived about certain things about myself simply because I wasn't open to the truth, because I was too quick to defend myself. Neil T. Anderson says that "if you are in the wrong, you don't *have* a defense ... if you are right, you don't *need* a defense" (emphasis in original).[1]

Be slow to become angry. Take a step back. Cool down. Sometimes we get angry and defensive and take things in ways they were never intended to be taken. If you're hurt by someone, it's your responsibility to confront him or her about it as Matthew 18 instructs. Letting anger fester and stew is never a God-glorifying option. Chances are, if you're quick to hear and slow to speak, you'll be slow to anger.

Be Discerning

When you invite constructive criticism, you may get conflicting opinions that'll make your head spin. How do you know what's from God and what isn't? In Proverbs 15:31 we learn that "he who listens to a life-giving rebuke will be at home among the wise." If you are open to constructive criticism, it'll make you wiser. You will grow in your ability to understand what's from God and what isn't.

You should listen to feedback, but you don't have to take everything you hear as being the absolute truth. "A simple man believes anything, but a prudent man gives thought to his steps" (Prov. 14:15). This is especially important for those artists who find themselves in situations in which many people (sometimes too many people) are putting in their two cents' worth. In film, for example, a script might get edited and rewritten by dozens of people along the way, to the point where the finished movie only faintly resembles the original screenplay. For those of us who are under the microscope of many who constantly offer us feedback, it's essential that we be discerning. Not all feedback is given with sensitivity, but we can still learn from it. This is important because you're always going to run into the tactless individual who speaks without thinking. We need to learn to listen to what those people are saying and overlook how they're saying it. Not all feedback is given with good intentions, but you can take what is helpful and leave the rest. Even if the criticism wasn't offered in love, you can turn it into something beneficial by asking yourself, *What can I learn from this criticism that can make me a better artist?* That's a sure way to make constructive criticism work for you instead of against you.

Sometimes creative people can get married to an idea or a line and can't let go of it, even though it's hurting the overall piece. For example, we songwriters can become too attached to a lyric line. It may be our favorite line in the song, but if someone points out that the line doesn't work, our inflexibility can cause us to lose our objectivity. A friend of mine, Judson Poling, is a writer, and on the subject of receiving feedback I once heard him say, "All my little darlings must die." Don't be so obsessed with an idea or a line that you can't hear constructive criticism.

Have a Teachable Spirit

When you begin to be open to feedback, another very healthy thing happens: you swallow your pride and realize that no matter what age you are, you always have something to learn. You realize you can always improve. Every critique has some kernel of truth. Take what's true and let the rest fall by the wayside. When you have trouble identifying the truth or validity of someone's feedback, run it by someone who knows you well. See what he or she thinks about the criticism. Ask what parts of it are true. Ask how you can grow in the area that the constructive criticism may reveal as a weakness. In so doing, you'll learn what feedback to take seriously and what you can basically ignore. You'll be secure enough to say to yourself, *Yeah, that's true. I could really grow in that area* or *I'm grateful for feedback, but I don't think that fits with what others have told me about my work.* The result can be a very healthy response to feedback. Although not all feedback is from God, He can definitely speak to us through others. We never know when God might be the one who's trying to speak to us and help us grow.

For some reason I used to think that if someone has to give me constructive criticism, I must not be very good at what I do. Somebody would point out something he or she didn't like in one of my songs, and I'd be thinking, *Oh no! There's something wrong with this song. I must not be a good writer.* I have since learned that even the best writers solicit feedback, and they're constantly rewriting and reworking their material. They have a teachable spirit.

Learn How to Fail Graciously

It's okay to fail. No one succeeds every time. You and I will make mistakes, so we need to learn how to fail graciously. We need to own up to our mistakes, not run away from them or pass responsibility on to someone else. No one's expecting perfection (except maybe us), so we don't need to defend ourselves every time we fail. When we mess up, let's swallow our pride, admit it, learn from it, and move on. Just because we fail doesn't mean we're failures. And you and I will never know success unless we fail. We need to learn to say, "Yeah, I blew it. I didn't do it on purpose. It doesn't mean I'm a bad person. It doesn't mean God loves me any less. It doesn't mean my friends are going to love me any less, and it doesn't mean others on the team are going to love me any less. It simply means I've got some work to do to improve for next time."

Verdi wrote fifteen operas that bombed before he wrote *Rigoletto*, which he didn't write until he was thirty-eight years old. From that point on he was famous the world over as one of Italy's best opera composers. He didn't consider himself a failure just because he failed. He didn't give up. When you and I learn to fail graciously, we can learn from our mistakes and then go on to become better artists. If your mistake is due to a lack of preparation, build more preparation time into your schedule. If you need to brush up on some technique, do it. If you need to go back for a few lessons, do it. If you're having a mental block with lyrics, memorize those words until you're sick and tired of them ... and then memorize them some more. If you had some rough spots in rehearsal, work them out before the next service or performance. Learn all you can from your mistakes.

How Easy Are You to Work With?

The stereotype with artists is that we're difficult to work with because we don't take suggestions very well. Is this true at all of you? Would people say you are easy to work with or difficult to work with? I've worked with difficult musicians before. It's no fun. When I make a suggestion, they'll say something snide like, "I was playing what you wrote" or something caustic like, "You told me to play it that way last time." Even if I try to explain that I've changed my mind, defensive people still have a tough time being gracious or flexible.

One of my favorite pianists to work with is a friend of mine named Brian Clark. Brian works in the field of advertising and serves faithfully at our church. The most common thing I hear from others about Brian is that he is so easy to work with. In all the years I've worked with him, that's been my experience, too. Brian is a hundred times the piano player I'll ever be, yet he is always open to doing things another way and graciously listens to any suggestions I make. I don't think Brian has a defensive bone in his body. Because of his demanding job, he doesn't have time to play as much professionally. Yet he's so talented—the consummate pro—he could if he wanted to. He's not only an excellent musician but is extremely flexible to changes—even last-minute changes. He doesn't get all bent out of shape when a nonmusician, such as one of our drama directors, makes suggestions about how he should play

behind a drama scene. He doesn't belittle the vocalists for wanting
to take liberties with tempo. Indeed, Brian is a dream to work with.

Giving Feedback

My hope is that we would all become more open to constructive
criticism, but what about those giving the feedback? Can they learn
how to give feedback better? I'm talking about pastors, program
directors, friends, and spouses who give feedback to artists. Is there a
way to critique the art without destroying the artist? Many of us evaluate our church services to improve the quality, and that's essential if
we're going to grow in excellence, but we've got to do it in a way that
truly edifies. The longevity and the joy level of our musicians and
creative contributors depends on how well we do this thing called
constructive criticism. I've seen musicians shaken so badly by a poorly
communicated critique that they wanted never to go onstage again.
I've seen drama people, dancers, and other artists near tears because
of criticism that was communicated without sensitivity. I've also
known writers who completely lost their desire to write because of
ongoing feedback they received that was not constructive but hurtful and damaging. No one really means for this to happen, and I think
it's more a matter of ignorance than anything else.

What makes criticism constructive is the way it's delivered. If it's
not offered in a loving way, it can do more harm than good. The
truth must be spoken in love (Eph. 4:15). Constructive criticism
must be truthful. Don't lie about the quality of someone's work.
Be honest. Don't say something you don't mean. But speak the
truth with love. Say it with tenderness and sensitivity. Say it in a
way that builds the artist up. You can criticize one performance or
one aspect of a person's work constructively without tearing down
that person as an artist. Trust is a major ingredient here, and it needs
to be developed over time. Artists need to feel that the people giving them feedback believe in them and have their best interest in
mind. Feedback that's given and received in an environment of love
and trust is extremely valuable and God-honoring. "A word aptly
spoken is like apples of gold in settings of silver" (Prov. 25:11).

I believe that every artistic community should have its own ground rules for critiquing. These things need to be brought out into the open and discussed if you're trying to build a community of artists. I have a few suggestions, and following is a list that I've shared with some of my friends who give me feedback.

Give Your Overall Reaction First

Let's say I'm a gifted carpenter and I build a quality piece of furniture, such as a table, and I bring it to you for your opinion. Let's say you think it's an excellent piece of work, but you don't say that at first. You might even think that this is the best table you've ever seen. It might be so obvious to you that it is excellent work that you assume I know it, and you don't say anything right away because you're too busy admiring my table. Then you notice a small flaw at the base of one of the table legs—nothing major, and it certainly doesn't detract from the beauty of the table. You might even be proud of yourself for finding a little flaw that most people wouldn't notice in such a fine piece of work. You say something about it, so the first words out of your mouth are a negative reaction to a minor detail. Since I'm eager to hear your opinion, I'm immediately drawn to that little flaw you're pointing out. You might be thinking, *Wow, what a great piece of work*. But because the first thing you said was about that little flaw, it's no longer a little flaw to me. I conclude that the flaw was so big that it ruined the entire table. Remember, to the artist who's excited about what he or she is working on and seeks your opinion, your first words represent your *overall* reaction. The flaw at the base of the table was not your overall reaction; it wasn't even your first reaction. Your overall reaction was that you were very impressed with the table, but you never said that. If your overall reaction is positive, communicate that and then go on to the negative. The negative is usually easier for the artist to take if he or she knows you generally like the work in question.

This holds true when evaluating a ministry experience. How do you really critique a worship service? Should you critique worship? It's okay to critique the band and vocalists, but the bottom line is whether worship happened or not. Were people brought into the presence of

God? Did we worship in Spirit and in truth? That's what is most important. Don't miss the big picture. Answer those kinds of questions first, then move on to ways you can improve the band and vocalists.

Try to Say Something Positive

When giving feedback, always start by saying something positive. Even if your overall reaction to a performance or a piece is negative, try to find something positive to say. Artists need encouragement. Give them feedback in a way that shows your love and respect. Treat them with dignity. Don't make something up just to have something positive to say. Be honest.

I have to practice what I preach when I preside over auditions at church. No matter how bad the audition goes, the first thing out of my mouth has to be something truthful and positive. Tell artists what you enjoyed about their audition before you tell them what bothered you. Mention their strengths before you discuss their weaknesses. Even if the only positive thing you can say is, "Thanks for taking time out of your busy schedule to come and audition," say it with love and sincerity. Don't jump into the negative without saying something positive.

Acknowledge Effort and Hard Work

Express appreciation for any extra effort that was put forth. It's demoralizing to work especially hard and feel as if no one noticed. Most people have no idea how many hours an artist has invested in a performance or in a work. If the performance doesn't turn out as well as everyone would have liked, it feels as if all that hard work was in vain. That can be a very discouraging experience for an artist. Even if something didn't work or fell apart completely, express appreciation for any extra preparation or rehearsal. No one means to fail, and working in the arts takes a great amount of effort. Be sure to honor the effort even if it falls short.

Nehemiah didn't take all the credit for rebuilding the wall in Jerusalem. In chapter 3 of his narration, he mentions by name seventy-five people who labored diligently throughout the project. He even recorded for posterity the role they played, and described exactly what they did. A wise leader will always acknowledge effort and hard work.

Avoid Hyperbole

Avoid extreme statements. Whether they're positive or negative, they do more harm than good. For example, "That's the best song we've ever done!" or "She's our top vocalist!" I feel sorry for anyone who has to perform right after something or someone has been crowned "the best ever." One time we were playing a song at church and the band was very noticeably out of sync for about eight measures. Later that week someone told me that our little journey into polyrhythms made the person feel very uncomfortable sitting out in the congregation. I was told that it was the worst experience the person had ever had musically at our church. Needless to say, this was an extreme statement, and it made me feel terrible. I take full responsibility for the music I lead. I arranged it. I rehearsed it. I was part of performing it. No one messed up on purpose, yet I felt responsible for this person's "worst experience" with the music at our church. I suggest we all avoid hyperbole when giving feedback to artists. Extreme statements usually draw extreme reactions.

Avoid Negative Comparisons

When we don't like something, it's tempting to emphasize that by comparing it to something that's, in an artistic sense, obviously unfashionable or mediocre. At the music school where I studied composition, it was quite common to call something "warmed-over Tchaikovsky" if you didn't like it. That drove the point home that someone's music was passé. In the past, certain names in pop music conjured up the same kind of scorn and ridicule, names such as Barry Manilow or the Bee Gees.

We need to avoid making those kinds of negative comparisons, because they can be very hurtful to an artist. One time someone compared a musical number that I had arranged to something that sounded like the singing group Up With People. No offense to those of you who are fans of Up With People, but he didn't intend this to be a compliment, and in all honesty I felt put down. We use negative comparisons like those to make a point, but they do more harm than good. There's always a better way to get the point across than resorting to negative comparisons. Avoid them.

Forgiving Those Who Have Hurt You

Have you ever been hurt by someone's harsh criticism? Have you ever fallen victim to someone whose insensitive and negative words about your art still haunt you? Artists who are chronically defensive are usually harboring bitterness and resentment toward people in their past who have said disparaging things about them and their work. We've discussed earlier that when you've been hurt, the scriptural thing to do is to go to the individual who hurt you and talk about it. I know that's not always possible. Maybe the incident happened long ago, and the person who stung you with their words has moved out of state or you've lost contact with him or her. Perhaps the person has even passed away. Whatever the circumstances, somewhere along the line you need to forgive that person. I say this more for your sake than for the person's sake. Harboring bitterness and resentment can do more damage to you than negative words ever did. I know people who are in bondage to bitterness because they auditioned for something and didn't make it. It might have happened years ago but it still hurts. Every time they think about it, they feel tense, because that memory triggers one of the greatest fears every artist faces: the fear of not being good enough. They can't free themselves from the tyranny of those negative words until they extend forgiveness.

You can't control what people are going to say about your work, but you can control how you're going to respond. Scripture says that no matter who it is, no matter what that person said, if we have anything against anyone, we need to forgive that person just as God has forgiven us (Col. 3:12–13). If it's hard to forgive, ask the Lord to help you. Tell Him you want to forgive the person who wounded you with negative words. Ask the Lord to free you from the hold this negative opinion has had on you. If you absolutely can't bring yourself to say that prayer yet, ask the Lord to work in your life to get you to the point where you can say that prayer with all sincerity. Forgiving the person who hurt you can set you free from those negative words that hold you back as an artist. It's a major step in the process of undoing the hurt. Let the power of forgiveness restore your heart and soul.

Being Open to the Truth

Are you open to the truth about your giftedness? When I came on full-time staff at Willow Creek, there were a few musicians who I could not in all honesty affirm as having musical ability. I conferred with some of my colleagues to make sure I wasn't missing something and found that they agreed with me. I invited this handful of musicians to re-audition, because I wanted to give them every opportunity to succeed, but the auditions further confirmed my opinion that they didn't have what it takes to be in our music ministry. So we had some difficult conversations. First of all, I thanked these dear servants for their ministry to the church and for the important role they had played, but then I told them that I didn't see them as having the abilities we needed for the next leg of the race. Understandably, this was hard to hear, and there were lots of angry tears. (Before I go on, let me reiterate how important it is to be serving in an area for which you're well suited. If I put somebody in a position they're not cut out for, I'm depriving that person of experiencing true fulfillment somewhere else in the church, someplace that's in line with his or her giftedness.) A few years later I received a note from one of the women we had let go. This is what she said:

> When you told me that I didn't have the ability I needed to sing at church, I hated you. I had been singing in church all my life, and no one had ever told me that I couldn't sing. Your words were some of the most difficult words I had ever heard, but they forced me to face the possibility that maybe I wasn't a singer after all. So for the first time in my life, I got down on my knees and asked the Lord to show me what he wanted me to do with my gifts and abilities. He led me back to school

and into counseling. Today I opened my own counseling practice and I owe it all to you. Thank you!

Not all situations like that have such happy endings, but this sister had a life-changing experience because her willingness to be open to the truth about herself caused her to seek out God's wisdom for her life. The truth, no matter how hard it is to hear, will always set you free (John 8:32).

I'd like to share a more personal story with you. The reason I know something about being defensive is because I've struggled with it. I was in my early twenties when someone in my ministry lovingly pulled me aside and said, "Brother, we all feel like we have to walk on eggshells around you. You get so defensive whenever anyone says anything remotely negative." Well, at first I was shocked. I had no idea I was coming across that way, and I felt bad. To think that people were withholding valuable feedback from me, and maybe just outright avoiding me, because I was a defensive person really shook me.

I spent the next week meeting with all the people with whom I worked closely in my ministry, and I apologized. I was so sorry that I had alienated them and had not listened to their input. I promised that from that day on I was going to be open to any and all constructive criticism. I gave them the freedom to speak truth to me. I then invited them to point out any shred of defensiveness that they might see in me.

That person who pulled me aside and pointed out my defensiveness is someone to whom I owe a great deal. I hate to think of where I'd be now had he not risked our friendship and spoken the truth in love. I certainly don't think I would be in ministry today had that friend not confronted me. Several years later when, as a songwriter, I entered into a relationship with a publisher, a woman in the business expressed appreciation and surprise at how open I was to feedback. "You'll go far as a writer," she said. If she only knew how I used to be.

I certainly can't take credit for any growth in this area. God's the one who's been working all these years to keep this defensive spirit of mine in check. Praise Him. Much of that growth was initiated by my friend, who had the courage to confront me about my defensiveness. I am forever grateful to this brother who acted coura-geously out of love for me.

Being Defensive About Sin

One last area we should discuss is our defensiveness about sin. If there is an area of habitual sin or willful disobedience in your life, I hope you will be open to the truth when confronted by a brother or sister. Living in denial only makes it harder on yourself, because no one can help you if you don't think there's a problem or if you're lying about it.

God is not pleased when we live in denial concerning sin: "You say, 'I am innocent; he is not angry with me.' But I will pass judgment on you because you say, 'I have not sinned.'" (Jer. 2:35). Living in denial can be exhausting and draining. David tried to cover up his sin with Bathsheba, but when Nathan finally confronted him about it, to David's credit he caved in. He probably said something like, "Yes, no more living in denial. I have sinned against the Lord" (2 Sam. 12:13). He repented and got right with God. But listen to how agonizing it was for him to try to live in denial: "When I kept silent, my bones wasted away through my groaning all day long. For day and night your hand was heavy upon me; my strength was sapped as in the heat of summer" (Ps. 32:3–4).

I once spent two hours with a man who kept denying he had a serious problem with lust until he finally broke down and confessed to being involved with pornography, prostitution, and phone sex. It took us two hours to cut through the denial and the deception about his sin. If there's a sin problem in your life, if you fall, don't go into hiding. Bring it to the light (Eph. 5:11). Take ownership of your sin, and experience forgiveness and healing. Trying to cover up your sin is a waste of time and energy, because Scripture teaches that "your sin will find you out"(Num. 32:23). Remember, it takes more energy to cover up sin than it does to confess it.

In closing I'd like to ask you, What stands in your way when it comes to being open to the truth about yourself? If being defensive is a problem for you, what's behind the problem? It's usually pride. Pride nearly kept Naaman from being healed (2 Kings 5:1–14). He couldn't be helped until he was able to swallow his pride. Pride keeps us on the defensive, too. It keeps us in the dark about the truth. Don't let pride rule your spirit. Humble yourself before God and before others, and put an end to being defensive. Greet constructive criticism with an open mind. We artists need to be open to the truth about ourselves if we're going to grow spiritually, relationally, emotionally, and artistically.

Follow-Up Questions for Group Discussion

1. What causes an artist to be defensive?

2. Why is defensiveness such a blind spot for artists?

3. Can you think of someone who takes criticism well or responds to suggestions with grace? What do you notice about the way this person handles those kinds of things?

4. Have you known any defensive people in your life? How did their defensiveness affect you?

5. Have you ever felt offended by someone and found out later that they didn't mean to hurt you? What did you learn from that?

6. What should artists do if they disagree with someone's review of their work?

7. What prevents most people from being quick to hear, slow to speak, and slow to anger?

8. Why are artists afraid to fail?

9. As a team, come up with your own list of ground rules for critiquing. Post them somewhere for all to see.

10. Does your team have an "elephant in the room"? Are there any problems that are big and obvious, such as defensiveness, but no one dares to talk about them? How can your team enter into a healthy discussion about those kinds of issues?

Personal Action Steps

1. Rate yourself in your ability to take suggestions and be open to constructive criticism. Do you take offense easily, do you rarely give it a second thought, or do you fall somewhere in between?

2. Think about how others would rate you in your ability to take suggestions and be open to constructive criticism. Ask those close to you if they feel comfortable speaking truth to you.

3. The next time you perform or create, invite feedback from three people. Make sure you don't avoid getting feedback from people you know might be tough on you. Remember, you want to use this as an opportunity to practice responding to feedback with grace.

4. If you have received any constructive criticism recently, take time now to write down the lessons you can learn from it.

5. If you think people might describe you as difficult to work with, decide what you can do differently to make it easier for others to work with you.

Open to the Truth About Myself

It can be hard for me
To confront what's deep inside
All those weaknesses
I desperately deny
But when I face them honestly
I find it easier to be
Open to the truth about myself
Open to the truth about myself

I could surround myself
With what I want to hear
But I need friends who tell me
What I need to know
Friends who shoot straight with me
'Cause they know I'm tryin' hard to be
Open to the truth about myself
Open to the truth about myself

I never could understand
How the truth could set me free
'Til I came face to face
With the truth about me

I'll always be grateful
For those who care enough
To risk our relationship
And speak the truth in love
So even when it brings me pain
I hope I always will remain
Open to the truth about myself
Open to the truth about myself

Rory Noland

It is because you focus on the prize
   of worldly goods, which every sharing lessens
   that Envy pumps the bellows for your sighs.

But if, in true love for the Highest Sphere,
   your longing were turned upward, then your hearts
   would never be consumed by such a fear;

for the more there are there, who say "ours"—not "mine"—
   by that much is each richer, and the brighter
   within that cloister burns the Love Divine.

                           Dante Alighieri, Divine Comedy

Six

Jealousy and Envy

*B*renda loves to dance. She's been dancing since she started walking, and she can do it all, from ballet to tap to modern dance. During her stellar career she has danced with some prestigious dance companies and toured all over the world. She's semiretired now, raising a family and teaching at a dance studio near her home.

In recent years Brenda has developed a passion for dance in the church. She feels that God has given her a vision for how dance can be used during worship. She's been a little frustrated, though, because it seems as if getting dance accepted in her church has been an uphill battle. When she first brought it up, the pastor was very cautious. He brought her idea to the church's board of elders, and they interviewed Brenda several times. They took six months to decide it was okay, but they set down some pretty strict guidelines. They wanted to see everything she would do before the service, and they wanted to have a say in what she would wear. That seemed fair enough to Brenda. Besides, she was just elated that they had said yes. But she never heard about it again, from either the board of elders or the pastor. Special worship services came and went. Christmas and Easter came and went, and still no word from anybody at church about using dance. She didn't know what was going on. Had she said something that offended someone? Was there something about her they didn't like? What did they have against dance?

Then something strange happened. Brenda was sitting in church when the pastor got up and introduced a handsome young couple, Bob and Carol, who had just started coming to the church. As soon as Brenda saw Carol, her intuition told her that Carol was a dancer. She was right. The pastor told the congregation that Bob was a dentist and that Carol was a professional dancer. *Oh, good,* Brenda thought, *another dancer in the church.* Then the pastor said, "I know we've never included dance as part of worship, but that's changing as of today, and Carol is going to facilitate worship this morning with a dance." He went on to share Scripture verses regarding worshipful dance—verses that Brenda had gathered in her presentation to the elders. In fact, she heard him say some of the same things she had been saying for almost two years. Carol danced and it was beautiful. The congregation was deeply moved and gave her a standing ovation. Brenda had a strange mix of emotions. She was glad that dance was finally given a chance at church, but she was a little jealous of all the accolades heaped upon this newcomer.

The next few months were very confusing for Brenda. Carol performed at church every week. The church members couldn't stop talking about her. They wanted her to start a dance ministry. In fact, the pastor called Brenda to see if she wanted to be a part of it. Brenda declined, making up some story about being too busy at home and at work. Meanwhile, Carol's popularity continued to spread. She even got invited to dance at other churches.

Brenda tried to talk her husband into visiting other churches, but he didn't want to leave their church. Their children also didn't want to leave. She felt stuck. She never introduced herself to Carol, never spoke to her. At church Brenda would always avoid her. She envied Carol. She envied her success. She envied all the attention Carol got. Carol and her husband became good friends with the pastor and his wife. *Oh, that's it,* Brenda rationalized. *She gets to dance because she's buddy-buddy with the pastor's wife. It's all politics, isn't it?*

Brenda started working in the nursery so she could get out of going to church and seeing Carol dance. But even in the nursery she couldn't get away from Carol's success. After the service, when people came to pick up their kids, they raved about the service and about Carol. "Don't you dance too, Brenda?" some would ask. "You should get up there with Carol."

"Oh, no, I'm too busy," Brenda would reply politely. "Besides, I've quit dancing." The latter wasn't entirely true, but she sure felt like quitting.

On a few occasions people asked Brenda what she thought of the new dance ministry. In a rather patronizing tone she would point out some technical flaws that "only people who know anything about dance" would notice. She would later regret those disparaging remarks, but they've continued to leak out from time to time.

Deep inside, Brenda is angry with the church, herself, and God. She doesn't know what to do with all these bitter feelings. She knows Christians are not supposed to be envious, so she never lets on to anyone how much emotional turmoil she's in. She can't bring herself to be happy for Carol. She doesn't like Carol. Brenda can't rejoice that the church finally has a thriving dance ministry. She continues to withdraw with her feelings and thoughts. She wishes she could run away.

Questions for Group Discussion

1. What would you do if you were Brenda?

2. Is Brenda's anger understandable to you?

3. Do you think the pastor handled this situation with Brenda very well? If not, how should he have handled it?

4. Do you think Brenda did the right thing by declining to be involved with the dance ministry under Carol's leadership? Why or why not?

5. Is Carol to blame for what's happening to Brenda?

6. What lessons might God want Brenda to learn through this?

7. What lessons might God want the pastor to learn from this?

8. What lessons might God want Carol to learn through this?

9. What lessons might God want the congregation to learn as a result of all this?

10. How common is jealousy and envy among artists in the church? Do you think it's a major problem or a minor one?

Thou Shalt Not Covet

Have you ever envied the talents of another artist? Have you ever been jealous of someone else's success? If you're an artist, you need to know how to deal with jealousy and envy, because there will always be someone more talented, more successful, more in vogue, more attractive, or more prominent in ministry than you.

The words *jealousy* and *envy* are virtually synonymous in our everyday language. We often use them interchangeably, but I've run across a few explanations that point out differences between the two. One idea is that jealousy involves a triangle of relationships (such as a husband, his wife, and another man), while envy is between only two people. Another theory is that envy occurs over something you want that somebody else has, while jealousy occurs in trying to protect what you already have against a rival. This latter distinction comes closer to what the dictionary says. According to the dictionary, the word *jealousy* has a sense of rivalry attached to it, like the jealousy our friend Brenda felt for all the attention Carol was getting. The word *envy* indicates a desire for something that someone else has, such as talent or abilities.[1] For our discussion I'm going to lump jealousy and envy together, since they're so closely related anyway.

Jealousy and envy are serious sins in the eyes of God. They are "acts of the sinful nature" (Gal. 5:19–21), and God is grieved when we allow bitterness and resentment to take root in our hearts. He was angry at Miriam for being jealous of her brother Moses and dealt seriously with her by striking her with leprosy and removing her from fellowship for seven days (Num. 12:9–15). So don't think that God takes this sin lightly.

Jealousy and envy carry enough explosive power to undermine unity and split any group. That's why Paul confronted the Corinthians about the jealousy that was tearing them apart (1 Cor. 3:3; 2 Cor. 12:20). He considered the sin of jealousy to be as serious as carousing, drunkenness, and sexual promiscuity (Rom. 13:13). James tells us that wherever there's jealousy, "there you find disorder and every evil practice" (3:16). Unfortunately jealousy and envy are more common among artists in the church than we care to admit. In the midst of our serving the Lord together, there is always the potential for jealousy and envy. In fact, the very first murder was committed because of jealousy between two brothers who were trying to serve God (Gen. 4).

There are plenty of examples of jealousy and envy in the Bible, such as Isaac and Ishmael (Gen. 21) or Jacob and Esau (Gen. 25). Rachel was deathly jealous of Leah because Leah had children and Rachel didn't (Gen. 30:1). Joseph's brothers were seduced by jealousy and sold him into slavery (Gen. 37). Miriam and Aaron were jealous of Moses and his standing with God (Num. 12). Saul was jealous of David (1 Sam. 18:8). The Prodigal Son's brother was jealous of all the attention his father showered on his wayward son (Luke 15:25–32). Matthew says that the reason the religious leaders crucified Jesus was because they envied him (27:18).

Jealousy and Envy Among Artists

Anybody who's been in the arts for any length of time knows that jealousy and envy run rampant among artists. We compare our talent with the talents of others, our work with theirs, our lack of success with their achievements. We feel threatened by the talent of others. The less secure we are, the more suspicious we are of other artists. We want to know who's sitting at the head table, who's friends with whom, and who's getting the breaks. We don't want to feel left out, and we don't want to be left behind, so we scratch and claw for what we feel is rightfully ours, whether it be a position, a role, a commission, or a prize. In short, the haves and the have-nots have been feuding since the dawn of time.

History tells us that the artistic community has struggled with jealousy and envy for centuries. The infamous rivalry between Leonardo da Vinci and Michelangelo instantly comes to mind. Henri Nouwen writes very graphically about backstage hostility in his book *Reaching Out*.

> Recently an actor told me stories about his professional world which seemed symbolic of much of our contemporary situation. While rehearsing the most moving scenes of love, tenderness and intimate relationships, the actors were so jealous of each other and so full of apprehension about their chances

to "make it," that the back stage scene was one of hatred, harshness and mutual suspicion. Those who kissed each other on the stage were tempted to hit each other behind it, and those who portrayed the most profound human emotions of love in the footlights displayed the most trivial and hostile rivalries as soon as the footlights had dimmed.[2]

My favorite story, though, involves the Italian Renaissance painter Giovanni da San Giovanni (1592–1636). He arrived in Rome to make a living as an artist, but there were bitter rivalries among the artists at Rome in those days. Giovanni received a commission to paint a fresco for Cardinal Bentivoglio and set out to work on it at once. After the first day of working on his new masterpiece, he went home. When he came back the next day, he found dirt and mold all over the painting. Giovanni thought there was something wrong with the plaster he was using, so he kept trying different mixtures and combinations. But the results were still the same. Every day he'd arrive at his studio and find the previous day's work ruined. This went on for five days, until it dawned on him that this might be the work of vandals. So he decided to sleep in his studio one night, and sure enough, about midnight the perpetrators quietly broke into the studio. As the villains climbed the ladder to the scaffolding, Giovanni pushed the ladder over, sending them crashing to the floor. They turned out to be two jealous French painters in town.

Anger and Contempt

Most Christians don't know how to handle jealousy and envy. I first started teaching about this because I saw in myself and in other Christian artists an inability to deal with jealousy and envy in a healthy or mature way. We know it's wrong to covet; it's one of the Ten Commandments (Ex. 20:17). But instead of bringing our sin out into the open and talking about it, we try to hide it. It's embarrassing and it feels petty. To come out and say, "I'm jealous of Suzy" is to admit that Suzy is better than me. So not only are my feelings of jealousy and envy out on the table but so is my inferiority.

Jealousy and envy are not always blatant. They're often subtle. In fact, many times the problem can be difficult to detect on the surface, because it lurks deep in our hearts. Deep inside we're actually angry. We're angry that we're getting "dissed." We're mad because somebody has something that we want. We feel as if we've been treated wrongly. We know it's unchristian to hate somebody, so we try to deal with our envy by sweeping it under the rug and pretending it's not there. The problem is that it comes out in many different ways. It surfaces whenever we complain out loud or to ourselves, "Why does so-and-so get to sing the solo all the time instead of me?" Sometimes we disguise our jealousy and envy with seemingly good intentions, such as, "Why does that person get to be up front all the time instead of someone else, like Bill or Bob?" That makes it sound as if we're really concerned for Bill or Bob, but what we really mean is, "Why does that person get to be up front all the time instead of me?" We may even be keeping score: "Let's see, that's five times in the last two months that Suzy has played the lead part, and I've only played it once."

We may also try to subtly sabotage others' ministries, perhaps by bad-mouthing them behind their backs. When we resort to that, we're on dangerous ground because we're setting ourselves up against God, who raises up servants and puts them in roles He wants them to play (Ps. 75:7). The Lord does not approve of us undermining people He's anointed for ministry (1 Chron. 16:22). If we're not for them, we're against them. Whether she realized it or not, Brenda's disparaging remarks were meant to undermine Carol. She also resisted Carol passively by not throwing her support behind the new dance ministry.

If we don't deal with our jealousy, we will eventually end up contemptuous of the person we envy. Dallas Willard points out that contempt is even worse than anger: "In anger I want to hurt you. In contempt, I don't care whether you are hurt or not. Or at least so I say. You are not worth consideration one way or the other. We can be angry at someone without denying their worth, but contempt makes it easier for us to hurt them or see them further degraded."[3]

What may have started out as a small frustration has now escalated into full-scale bitterness and hatred. Indeed, "stirring up anger produces strife" (Prov. 30:33). We end up not caring at all about what happens to the other person. He or she doesn't matter anymore. When that happens, we can't bring ourselves to root for the fellow artist, because instead of wishing the person success, deep inside we're wishing that he or she will fail. So we can't "rejoice with those who rejoice" (Rom. 12:15), or do so genuinely. Dante writes of one whose vindictiveness was so intense, he couldn't stand the thought of good things happening to someone else.

> The fires of envy raged so in my blood
> that I turned livid if I chanced to see
> another man rejoice in his own good.[4]

Dealing with the Green-Eyed Monster

One way (the wrong way) to deal with our anger and frustration is to turn against ourselves and devalue our own talents and abilities. "I'm not as good as so-and-so," we might say. "He's talented and I'm not. He's a winner and I'm a loser." We might try to make ourselves look better than someone else by putting the person down or building ourselves up; we might gossip about or slander another artist or try to manipulate conversation so people notice our talents and abilities instead of, or as well as, the other person's. We may even harbor some anger and resentment toward God because He's allowed that person to be in the spotlight instead of us.

Yet Galatians 5:26 tells us not to envy one another, and 1 Peter 2:1 instructs us to put all envy aside. How do you do that? You can't just tell yourself to stop being envious. Jealousy and envy produce strong feelings of animosity that don't go away that easily. Proverbs 27:4 says, "Anger is cruel and fury overwhelming, but who can stand before jealousy?" It is not an easy thing to rid our hearts of jealousy and envy, yet the Lord wants to work in our hearts and get us to love each other instead of compete against each other. Let's talk about some ways we can cooperate with Him to bring that about.

Confess It As Sin

The first step to being free from jealousy and envy is to confess it as sin. Confess your anger and contempt as sin. Don't hide it.

Don't justify it. Confess it. James 3:14 says that "if you harbor bitter envy and selfish ambition in your hearts, do not boast about it or deny the truth." God knows your every thought and He has seen it all. He's not going to be surprised by your confession. Ask Him to help you deal with your feelings of jealousy and envy toward your brother or sister.

Sometimes people ask me if I think they should admit their feelings to the person who is the object of their jealousy and envy. I would say yes, if you think the person can handle your vulnerability. It can actually bring the two of you closer together. I've known situations in which one person goes to another and admits to being jealous and envious and finds out that the other person has some jealousy and envy toward the first one. Confessing this sin can free you from its grip on your heart and can deepen the sense of community you share with your fellow artists.

Appreciate Your God-Given Talent

Be thankful for whatever talent the Lord has given you. First Peter 4:10 says that each of us has received a special talent or ability from God. *The New Living Bible* has this rendition of Romans 12:6: "God has given each of us the ability to do certain things well." What is it that God has given you to do well? Be grateful for that. While we're busy envying someone else's talents, we forget about what God has given us. Just because other people have talents and abilities doesn't mean that you don't. Stop viewing yourself as one of the have-nots. It's not true. In God's eyes there are no have-nots. I know a pianist who was discouraged because his songwriting wasn't taking off the way he wanted it to. He said he didn't want to be known as "just a piano player." It's a shame because he is an excellent piano player. I know people who would give their eyeteeth to do what he can do. It seems as though we always want to be something we're not, and are seldom happy being who we are. If you can perform or create to any degree, you can do something that the average human being cannot do. My fellow artists, always remember that other people would just love to be able to do what you do. Don't let the Evil One convince you that you're untalented or worthless. You're less apt to envy someone else if you're content with what God has given you, so put this book down right now and thank God for whatever talent—large or small—He's given you.

Give Credit Where Credit Is Due

Instead of giving others credit for performing or creating well, we rationalize their success by grumbling that it's because they have connections and we don't. They get all the breaks and we're victims of the system. We might even criticize them behind their back to try to ruin their reputation or spoil their success. We don't give them any credit for working hard and earning their success. "They don't deserve it," we mutter to ourselves. "It's just not fair."

When I'm seduced by envy, I can't seem to give other songwriters their due. I refuse to admit that their work is better than mine. There must be another reason for their success. They have an "in" with someone, or people like them more than me, or even God likes them more than me. It's all sour grapes. Hence we arrive at the darkest side of envy. It's not only that we envy what others have but that we don't want them to have it instead of us. We resent them and their blessing.

I have gained a great deal of freedom by facing the reality that others can and will write something better than I can. We need to recognize the talents of others and give them credit for writing or performing as well as, if not better than, us. If a fellow artist writes or performs something well, tip your hat to that person and say, "Well done, friend. You deserve to be recognized for your hard work and success."

The Real Issue Is Faithfulness

There once was an old patron of the arts who was leaving town for a while, so he gathered his little colony of artists together for a going-away party. To one artist he gave five talents, to another he issued two talents, and to yet another he entrusted one talent. After they drove their benefactor to the airport, the artists all went their separate ways (as artists often do). Several months later the old patron returned, all rested and suntanned. The artist who was given five talents eagerly met him at the gate. "Master, you entrusted me with five talents and look, I've gained five more talents," he enthused.

"Well done," said the patron. "I am full of joy. You were faithful and I'll give you even more."

The artist who was given two talents ran down the concourse shouting, "Master, you entrusted me with two talents and look, I've gained two more talents."

"Well done," said the old man. "I am overjoyed. You were faithful and I'll give you even more."

The artist who was given one talent was waiting by the baggage claim. "Master," he sheepishly started, "I didn't want you to get mad at me. I'm pretty sensitive, you know, and I don't handle rejection very well, and it's so hard being an artist in this cold, cruel world. I wasn't really good enough to make it big-time, because you only gave me one talent, so I didn't do anything with my talent. I hid it. Here, you can have it back." The artist opened his hand and looked straight down at his shoes. The talent was as new and undeveloped as the day he got it.

The old man was silent. Then he responded in a soft voice, "My dear friend, you have squandered a fortune. I gave you something that was meant to be used. The issue was not how much I gave but what you did with what you had."

I'm sure you recognize this as the parable of the talents from Matthew 25. This parable reminds us that our talents and abilities are not our own. They belong to God. However, there is something that used to bother me about this passage. For years I've wondered why one person was given five talents, another two, and another only one. It doesn't seem fair, does it? Shouldn't they all have been given the same amount? I struggled with this until I realized that our God is a righteous God. Everything He does is right and He is full of wisdom. In other words, He knows what He's doing. The man in the parable entrusted each servant "according to his ability" (v. 15). Romans 12:6 also seems to suggest that gifts and abilities are given out not equally but in proportions. I can't tell you why one person is given five talents, another two, and some of us only one. Life is like that, it seems. But the real issue is not who gets what but whether I'm going to be faithful and obedient with what I've been given. God is not asking me to be faithful with someone else's talents. He's asking me to be faithful with what He's given me.

Remember when Jesus told Peter to feed His sheep? For a man who had denied Jesus and run away, this was a moment of healing, in which the Lord reaffirmed that He was going to use Peter in a mighty way. Yet I detect a little bit of jealousy on Peter's part when he refers to John and says in effect, "Well, yeah, that's great. I get to feed sheep, but what about John? What does he get to do?" Jesus answers lovingly but firmly, saying, "What is that to you? You must follow me" (John 21:22). In other words, "Don't worry about others, Peter. You just be faithful with what I give you to do."

In the same way, some teachers write books and have a worldwide following. Others teach a Sunday school class. One is not better or more important in God's eyes. The issue is not how famous you and I are or how prominent in ministry we are, but whether we are faithful and obedient with what God's given us. It's a stewardship issue. The parable of the talents says that if we're faithful with what God's given us, He will give us more.

The Danger of Comparing

Comparing ourselves with others is extremely dangerous. There is nothing to be gained and everything to lose from comparing ourselves with others. We end up looking either better than we really are or worse than we really are. First Corinthians 12:15–16 warns about the danger of comparing, which is the root of all jealousy and envy: "If the foot should say, 'Because I am not a hand, I do not belong to the body,' it would not for that reason cease to be part of the body. And if the ear should say, 'Because I am not an eye, I do not belong to the body,' it would not for that reason cease to be part of the body."

Gordon MacDonald writes that "the soul cannot be healthy when one compares himself or herself to others. The soul dies a bit every time it is involved in a lifestyle that competes. It gives way to the destructive forces of rivalry, envy, and jealousy."[5]

We need to discover our talents apart from the talents of others. We need to discover who God made us to be, and celebrate our uniqueness. Being different doesn't mean we're better or worse than anybody else; it just means we're different. It means we have different gifts and different callings. So I can be secure about who God made me to be and what He's called me to do. He's not asking me to be someone else (or someone more talented); He's asking me to be me and to stop comparing myself with others. We need to discover the role God has for us and fulfill it with enthusiasm. We will be more content by being what God has called us to be than by trying to be someone else.

Some men approached John the Baptist and asked him how he felt about the large crowds that Jesus was attracting. In fact, some people who had at one time been following John were now following Jesus. Was John jealous of all the attention Jesus was getting? No, because first of all, John knew that he himself was not the Messiah. "I am not the Christ," he said, "but am sent ahead of him" (John 3:28). John had no illusions about his place in the world. He was at peace about who he was and what God was calling him to do. He knew what he was about and he knew what he wasn't about. He saw himself as the friend of the Bridegroom. Jesus is the Bridegroom. John rejoices for the Bridegroom. He's genuinely happy for Him. He stands by the Bridegroom and doesn't draw attention to himself. That's why John was content to be what God made him to be, and content to do what God called him to do.

I know artists who are angry at God because He didn't give them as much talent as He gave other artists. They resent the fact that they're not as successful or as famous as other artists whom they envy, so they blame God. Their jealousy has turned to anger directed at God Himself. Romans 9:20 says, "Who are you, O man, to talk back to God? 'Shall what is formed say to him who formed it, "Why did you make me like this?"'" It must feel like a slap in the face to God when we question why He didn't give us someone else's talents. It must grieve Him when we wrongly conclude that He doesn't love us as much as He loves the person whose talents we covet. Just because God chose to give those talents to someone else doesn't mean He loves us any less. It merely means He wants us to play a different role in His kingdom.

Instead of wishing you were someone else, pray that you become all the artist God wants you to be. James strongly denounces jealousy and envy, and notice where prayer fits into the picture: "What causes fights and quarrels among you? Don't they come from your desires that battle within you? You want something but don't get it. You kill and covet, but you cannot have what you want. You quarrel and fight. You do not have, because you do not ask God. When you ask, you do not receive, because you ask with wrong motives, that you may spend what you get on your pleasures" (4:1–3).

There are millions of frustrated artists who would give anything to be fulfilled artistically. Unfortunately jealousy and envy have set in and caused all sorts of conflict like James describes. These artists either don't pray or gave up praying in spite of the fact that God wants to give us the desire of our hearts (Ps. 37:4). He wants us to blossom as artists. James says in effect, "Don't stop asking. Make sure your motives are right and keep praying." I don't know how often I've prayed, "Lord, help me to do what it takes to be a better songwriter or a better composer." I'd rather put my energy into prayer than into nurturing feelings of jealousy and envy, which only lead to trouble.

Turning Envy into Worship

There's a story about a bandleader who was lining up musicians for a big gig downtown. He went out and got together this excellent jazz trio and offered them union-scale pay for an evening of great jazz. Everything went off without a hitch. They sounded fantastic. Then the bandleader decided it would be nice to have a few horn players for the last set, so he got on the phone and just happened to find that a few of his friends were available, and they agreed to come over and play. When the night was over, the bandleader handed out the paychecks, and everybody got the same amount. The horn players got the same amount as the trio who had been the original hire and had played most of the night. As you can imagine, this didn't sit too well with the trio. They were visibly upset. They grumbled because they had borne "the burden of the work and the heat of the stage lights," and they were paid the same amount as those who had been hired for the last set and had only put in an hour of work. Very unfair. But the bandleader said, "Didn't I pay you what we agreed upon? I haven't cheated you out of anything. Can't I do what I want with my money? Or are you envious because I am generous?"

Obviously this is an adaptation of the parable about the workers in the vineyard, which Jesus taught in Matthew 20. The bandleader's last line is straight from verse 15: "Or are you envious because I am generous?" Whenever I read that line, I realize that sometimes my concept of what's fair is too limiting for a gracious God like ours. I want God to distribute gifts and talents as I would if I were God. But perish the thought. God is much more giving than I'll ever be, because He's God.

Now my envy can be turned to worship. I can acknowledge God's sovereignty in the way He distributes talents and abilities. I can worship His goodness for giving me more talent than I deserve. I can worship the Giver instead of the gift. God gifted each one of us according to His perfect will (1 Cor. 12:11). Instead of being jealous of other artists, I can thank God for how He's gifted them. I can praise Him not only for how He has gifted them but also for how He has gifted me. When we look at it that way, we can draw inspiration from the talents of others. Instead of being threatened by them, we can say, "Lord, I praise you for how you've gifted so-and-so. She's a great artist. Her commitment to excellence makes me want to be the best artist I can be."

David must have been extremely disappointed when he found out that he wasn't going to get to build the temple. God wasn't telling David to wait. He was saying no. Talk about having your dreams dashed. I admire David because he didn't give in to jealousy and envy. Instead he worshiped God with thanksgiving in his heart. After receiving the bad news, he said, "Who am I, O Sovereign LORD, and what is my family, that you have brought me this far?" (2 Sam. 7:18). Instead of focusing on what he didn't have, he focused on what he did have.

The writer of Psalm 73 also turned envy into worship. In the first part of the psalm, he's contrasting the life of a nonbeliever with that of a believer. He says that he almost got tricked into thinking that nonbelievers were better off. He felt himself starting to envy their prosperity, but he caught himself before it was too late (vv. 2–3). The turning point occurs when he comes into the sanctuary of God (v. 17). Being in the presence of God always gives us a fresh perspective. The psalmist realizes that the things he covets don't compare with knowing God. They don't hold a candle to what he has in the Lord. In verse 25 he says, "Whom have I in heaven but you? And earth has nothing I desire besides you." He makes an amazing discovery at the end, when he says, "As for me, it is good to be near God. I have made the Sovereign LORD my refuge; I will tell of all your deeds" (v. 28). He turned any envy he might have felt into worship.

Develop Relationships Instead of Rivalries

We tend to alienate ourselves from the people we envy. We hide from them. We avoid them. We may be angry at them or resent them. We may even hate them. I'd like to suggest that we reverse these tendencies and do everything we can to develop relationships with them. Get together with them. Invite them over. The more we get to know them, the less threatening they become. When we spend time with people, we start seeing them as partners or friends instead of competitors. Ask them how you can be praying for them. Pray regularly for them and for their success. Before you know it, your envy will be replaced by genuine love. That's why 1 Corinthians 13:4 (NASB) says that love is not jealous. You can't remain jealous of your fellow artists if you're compassionately praying for them and building relationships with them.

Jonathan had every reason to be jealous of David. If Jonathan had any aspirations of succeeding his father, Saul, to the throne, they were snuffed out when God anointed David to be king. Jonathan knew that God's hand was on David's life. Instead of being David's adversary, Jonathan chose to be his friend. Their souls were knit together in one of the deepest friendships recorded in Scripture (1 Sam. 18:1).

Developing friendships instead of rivalries has really worked for me. The people whose gifts overlap mine and who are more talented than me are some of my best friends. At the outset there was the potential for envy to become deeply embedded in my spirit. It would rear its ugly head and drive me to my knees, sobbing in shame. That's when I got the idea, to put it crudely, that "if you can't beat 'em, join 'em." I think it honors God if we try to develop any kind of friendship with those we envy. Instead of constantly withdrawing, we need to move toward them in love. God wants us to work together, not against each other. Instead of competing with each other, we can learn a lot from each other. We can be brothers and sisters instead of competitors.

No Longer Threatened by the Talent of Others

It is a sign of character when we are no longer threatened by the talents or abilities of others. It comes from being secure about who we are as individual and unique artists and from trusting God's work in our lives. The success of a fellow artist can't steal anything away from you. Somehow we think that we lose something when someone else is flourishing, but we don't. God's blessing doesn't get used up. There is plenty to go around for all of us. When somebody else is paid a compliment, it doesn't take anything away from you.

Numbers 11 records the story of two men who were prophesying mightily before the people of Israel. Joshua took offense for Moses. He wanted these men stopped because they were taking the limelight away from Moses. He goes to Moses and basically says in verse 28, "Do something, Moses. Stop these guys." But Moses was a wise man who was not threatened by the gifts of others. In the very next verse he says to Joshua, "Are you jealous for my sake? I wish that all the LORD's people were prophets and that the LORD would put his Spirit on them!" Moses realized that he didn't have a monopoly on the gift of prophecy. He was secure in his giftedness and in his calling. He saw a need for more prophets, and he cared more for the kingdom of God than for his own glory. We should have the same attitude, because we need more artists to be about the Lord's work. There is plenty of room for more artists in Christendom. The more the merrier.

If You Do Well

The verse that has helped me the most in dealing with feelings of jealousy and envy comes from Genesis 4. It grows out of the story of two brothers, Cain and Abel. Cain was a farmer and Abel was a shepherd. They both brought an offering to the Lord, but God rejected Cain's offering. We don't know exactly why, but we do know that God wasn't trying to be obtuse. He wasn't jerking Cain around. Both men knew what God expected. Abel did well in bringing God the best he possibly could, but Cain didn't. The Bible doesn't say that God was mad at Cain. In fact, God was willing to give him a second chance, but Cain was jealous of his brother and angry at God.

God tried to reason with Cain, but he wouldn't listen. God's words put Cain (and us) at a crossroads: "If you do well, surely you will be accepted. And if you do not do well, sin is crouching at the door; and its desire is for you, but you must master it" (Gen. 4:7 NASB, mg). History would be totally different if Cain had stopped right there and replied, "Lord, you're right. I want to do well in your eyes. Help me to do better next time." But he didn't. The next verse says that Cain told his brother what had happened. Cain probably moped around, brooding over his anger, grumbling about how unfair life is. I'm sure his side of the story painted God as unreasonable and overly demanding. I'm sure he played the victim, as we all do in these kinds of situations, and blamed God. At no point did he humble himself and repent. Instead Cain's jealousy led to murder. Sin really was crouching at his door.

God included stories like this in the Bible so we can learn from other people's mistakes. When I'm tempted by jealousy or envy, I hear God saying to me, "Don't worry about what's going on with your brother. If you do well, you will be accepted." If I've learned anything from this story, it's that the appropriate response to God in a situation like Cain's is, "Lord, help me to do well. Help me to do better with the talent You gave me. Help me to grow spiritually and artistically so when I offer You something, You're delighted to accept it and use it."

If You've Got It, Don't Flaunt It

What if you're the object of someone else's jealousy and envy? If you sense that's the case, can I suggest that you be sensitive to the person who's struggling with envy toward you? I know you can't control how others respond to you, and their jealousy is not your fault. It's a response they choose to make, but you can alienate them further by being insensitive. You don't need to censor everything you say or be disingenuous, just be mindful of their struggle. Remember, you never want to cause a brother or sister to stumble (1 Cor. 8:13). First Peter 5:3 warns us not to misuse our gifts and lord it over others, so be careful not to flaunt your talents and abilities around others.

God hates pride and arrogance. "Haughty eyes" are an abomination to Him (Prov. 6:16–17). The Pharisees were people who flaunted their position and abilities. They would stand up in front of a crowd and pray out loud, "God, I thank you that I am not like other men—robbers, evildoers, adulterers—or even like this tax collector. I fast twice a week and give a tenth of all I get" (Luke 18:11–12). The lowly and despised tax collector, on the other hand, stood in the corner with his head down, far away from the center of attention, and beating his fists against his chest, he prayed, "God, have mercy on me, a sinner" (v. 13). Jesus favored the tax collector over the Pharisee. He said, "I tell you that this man, rather than the other, went home justified before God. For everyone who exalts himself will be humbled, and he who humbles himself will be exalted" (v. 14).

Joseph was his father's favorite son. His brothers were already jealous of Joseph, so it didn't help things when their father gave Joseph a multicolored robe that he had made especially for him. Joseph's relationship with his brothers was further strained when he predicted that someday they would all be bowing down in submission to him (Gen. 37:6–11). No wonder they didn't like him. He was so cocky. They were already feeling that their father didn't care about them, and this young upstart kept rubbing it in. I know he couldn't help being the object of his father's favor, but I wonder how different Joseph's relationship with his brothers would have been if he had shown more discretion. If you have been greatly blessed, please don't flaunt it before other artists.

Also, if someone comes to you and confesses to harboring jealousy and envy toward you, it would help that person a great deal if you accepted his or her apology with love and understanding. Realize how difficult it is to confess the sin of jealousy to the one you envy. If you shame the person for feeling envious, or get all defensive about it, you will alienate the person even further. If you also struggle with jealousy and envy, it would be a relief for the person to hear that he or she is not alone. Promise to pray for each other. Ask if there's anything you're doing that causes the person to stumble.

Greg Ferguson is a good friend of mine, and, as far as I'm concerned, Greg has world-class talent. He's one of the best songwriters I know. He can write on demand. His lyrics are logical and natural, his melodies are memorable, and his harmonies are sophisticated and interesting. He's also one of the best singers—and one of the best communicators—I've ever worked with. He's a professional jingle singer heard on TV and radio spots all across the country, and he serves tirelessly and sacrificially at our church. If anybody had any right to flaunt his or her talent, it would be Greg. Yet he is one of the nicest, most humble people I've ever met. People don't expect someone who's so talented to be such a nice guy. He isn't very vocal about his achievements professionally. Most people are unaware when his radio spots "go national." He doesn't throw his weight around at rehearsal, and he treats the other vocalists at church as his equals. It's refreshing to know someone who's got it but doesn't flaunt it. It reminds me that people who really do have it don't need to flaunt it.

In conclusion, jealousy and envy are very strong emotions. They tend to dominate and lead us to do regrettable things. In the case of Cain and Abel, jealousy led to murder. That's why God says that we must master this beast called jealousy and envy before it masters us.

Follow-Up Questions for Group Discussion

1. What would make it difficult for artists to talk about any feelings of jealousy and envy they might have toward another artist?

2. Do you think that the Christian community does an adequate job of addressing the problem of jealousy and envy? Why or why not?

3. Have you ever seen a relationship strained or terminated by jealousy and envy?

4. When do you think a person's jealousy and envy are serious enough for the person to do something about it?

5. What do you think prevents us from being content with the talents we've been given?

6. In what ways could healthy competition benefit an artistic community?

7. When is competition bad for an artistic community?

8. What happens when we compare ourselves with others?

9. How can people with similar gifts and talents really be friends?

10. How does praying for someone affect your relationship with that person?

Personal Action Steps

1. Write down the names of any people in your life toward whom you have feelings of jealousy and envy.

2. Confess your sin of jealousy and envy to God and ask Him for His help in dealing with this sin.

3. Think about how you can turn your jealousy and envy into worship.

4. Describe the negative results of comparing yourself with others.

5. Choose someone in your life to whom you can be accountable for how you handle feelings of jealousy and envy.

I'm Amazed

I'm amazed at all You've done for me
Who am I that You'd bless me so
I stand in awe of all Your wondrous deeds
You've dealt with me so graciously

Broken by all the times I've failed
And the days I've hung my head in shame
Time and again I'm driven to my knees
And I find Your great compassion there for me

I'm amazed at all You've done for me
Who am I that You'd bless me so
I stand in awe of all Your wondrous deeds
You've dealt with me so graciously

You've blessed me with more than I deserve
Mercy and love at every turn
All that You give flows out of who You are
And I thank You Lord from the bottom of my heart

I'm amazed at all You've done for me
Who am I that You'd bless me so
I stand in awe of all Your wondrous deeds
You've dealt with me so graciously[6]

Rory Noland

But when the melancholy fit shall fall
    Sudden from heaven like a weeping cloud,
That fosters the droop-headed flowers all,
    And hides the green hill in an April shroud;
Then glut thy sorrow on a morning rose,
    Or on the rainbow of the salt sand-wave,
      Or on the wealth of globed peonies;
Or if thy mistress some rich anger shows,
    Emprison her soft hand, and let her rave,
      And feed deep, deep upon her peerless eyes.

She dwells with Beauty— Beauty that must die;
    And Joy, whose hand is ever at his lips
Bidding adieu; and aching Pleasure nigh,
    Turning to poison while the bee-mouth sips:
Ay, in the very temple of delight
    Veiled Melancholy has her sovran shrine,
      Though seen of none save him whose strenuous tongue
    Can burst Joy's grape against his palate fine:
His soul shall taste the sadness of her might,
    And be among her cloudy trophies hung.

John Keats, from "Ode on Melancholy"

Seven

Managing Your Emotions

Dan is what most people call a real artist. He's a twenty-year-old student at the Chicago Art Institute and hopes someday to make a living being an artist. As long as he can remember, he's always wanted to be an artist. His favorite medium is pencil, and he carries around a pocket-size sketchbook everywhere he goes. He's always busy and he's extremely dedicated to his work, sometimes going without food or sleep if he's on a roll with a project. Some people say he's obsessed. He calls it being focused. He knows what he wants and he knows what it takes to get there.

Dan doesn't have a lot of time for a social life or any extracurricular activities. The only other thing he allows time for besides art is a weekly Bible study group. The group has been going for a little over a year, but Dan is starting to wonder if he should continue in it. The main reason is that Dan feels so "out of it" in the group sometimes. Dan is more emotional than most guys and wears those emotions on his sleeve. Some people would call him moody; others have labeled him as passionate. Still others have said that Dan is painfully honest, to a fault. As you can imagine, Dan feels very abnormal sometimes and often feels like a bad Christian.

Take last week's meeting, for example, at the home of Ted and Nancy Jones. Ted and Nancy were high school sweethearts. He was an all-state football standout and Nancy was a cheerleader. Ted had asked each group member to come to the meeting having selected a psalm that best describes where his or her life is at right now. Ted is in seminary studying to be a pastor. He selected Psalm 1:1 and read it as if he were about to give a sermon: "Blessed is

199

the man who does not walk in the counsel of the wicked or stand in the way of sinners or sit in the seat of mockers." He had just finished a term paper on that passage, so it was fresh in his mind. Nancy went next and wanted to celebrate how God had been blessing her and Ted financially lately. She enthusiastically read Psalm 100:5: "The LORD is good and his love endures forever; his faithfulness continues through all generations." Adele Peterson was next. She's a legal secretary, and Ted and Nancy were trying to match her up with Dan. She was struggling in a new job and shared a passage about trusting God, Psalm 37:4–5: "Delight yourself in the LORD and he will give you the desires of your heart. Commit your way to the LORD; trust in him and he will do this."

Then it was Dan's turn. Dan has been a little down lately. He's not really sure why. It's hard to put a finger on it. He just hasn't been feeling very enthused about anything these past few days. It could have something to do with the argument he'd had last week with his dad, or the fact that the rent on his apartment is a week overdue, or perhaps he's just tired of the cold, gray Chicago winters that linger too long into spring.

Anyway, when it was Dan's turn to share, he had trouble putting his thoughts together and spoke mostly in incomplete sentences that rambled. He tried to share his struggles with feeling accepted by the group, but the more he talked, the more frustrated he felt inside. He had trouble putting into words exactly what he was feeling. The words always came more easily after he had time to think about it, like during the middle of the night when he was painting or drawing. He finally cut himself off midsentence and read Psalm 88, starting with verse 13: "I cry to you for help, O LORD; in the morning my prayer comes before you. Why, O LORD, do you reject me and hide your face from me? From my youth I have been afflicted and close to death; I have suffered your terrors and am in despair. Your wrath has swept over me; your terrors have destroyed me. All day long they surround me like a flood; they have completely engulfed me. You have taken my companions and loved ones from me; the darkness is my closest friend."

A hush fell over the room, and there was an uneasy silence when Dan finished. Then Ted cleared his throat. "Why, Dan, with all the blessings God has given, I was hoping you would read something uplifting, like one of the praise psalms. Psalm 150, perhaps?"

Dan didn't know what to say. He was kicking himself for sharing as much as he had, yet it was just the tip of the iceberg. Nancy tried to break the tension with humor. "Dan, don't be so doom and gloom. Take some Prozac, buddy, and lighten up," she kidded. Adele giggled. There was good-natured laughter and chuckles all around the room, except from where Dan sat. He couldn't remember much else about the meeting after that. He tried to engage himself but his mind was elsewhere. He really wasn't listening anymore. He had withdrawn inside himself and was grappling with emotions he didn't know what to do with. He soon left, using the excuse that he had to get up early the next morning.

Dan drove home that night feeling very misunderstood. He was barraged with all sorts of emotions. *That's the last time I share anything personal again,* he thought. *They all think I'm depressed all the time. I don't know why I have to be up all the time anyway. Can't I be honest about how I feel? I don't know why I'm wasting my time with this group. I don't fit in with them at all. They all seem so much more together than me. They don't struggle. At least not like I do. They probably don't want me in the group anymore, and that's just fine with me. Who needs them anyway? They're all so shallow. . . . I'll show them. They'll be sorry someday when I'm an accomplished artist. . . . I'll bet they're sitting around talking about me right now. They're probably going to ask me to leave the group. I'm sure they have a lot more fun when I'm not there anyway. Maybe there is something wrong with me. And another thing—they never ask how my work is going. They never come to any of my showings at the gallery or at school. And they didn't invite me to their Christmas party last year. They even forgot my birthday. . . .*

Questions for Group Discussion

1. How would you like to have seen the small group react to Dan's emotional honesty?

2. Why does Dan often feel like a bad Christian?

3. Do you think Dan had good reason to be down, or was he just being moody?

4. Dan's other choice would have been to suppress his feelings and share something a lot safer. Do you think that would have been a good idea? Why or why not?

5. How much of what Dan was feeling on the way home was based on reality?

6. Have you ever had an experience like the one Dan had? What makes experiences like this difficult?

7. Do people with artistic temperaments tend to be more negative or moody?

8. What challenges await people who wear their emotions on their sleeve?

9. How do you react to someone who's negative or critical all the time?

10. How can you tell if you're being controlled by your emotions? When is that not healthy?

Emotions: Friend or Foe?

People with artistic temperaments tend to be more emotional. We are more in touch with our feelings than most people. That's a wonderful privilege. I feel bad for people who are out of touch with their emotions. They miss out on some of life's most meaningful moments. Some people are more reserved because outward displays of emotion were discouraged as they were growing up. Others are just too busy to feel anything. Whatever the reason, it's their loss. People with artistic temperaments are very lucky to be able to experience the emotional side of life.

What's your opinion about emotions? Are emotions bad or good? As I was growing up, I somehow got the message that it wasn't proper for a man to show any emotion. Men weren't supposed to cry or be overly exuberant. They were to be "stable," meaning emotionless. I suppressed a lot of feelings as a result. When I became a Christian, though, the door cracked open a bit on my emotions. It seemed as though emotions were okay with God. After all, Jesus wept (Luke 19:41; John 11:35) and so did Paul (Acts 20:19). Ecclesiastes also tells us there is a "a time to weep and a time to laugh" (3:4). Then when I got married, the door cracked open even farther as my ever patient wife gently prodded me to engage emotionally with her. In the process, I discovered emotions I never knew I had before. But the greatest emotional emancipator occurred when I became a father. Being there when both my boys were born was just the starting point of all the intense feelings I've had, and probably always will have, for them. As a result of this emotional evolution, I've changed over the years. I'm enjoying more emotional freedom in my life than ever before.

This emotional freedom can quickly turn to bondage if we're not careful, though. When people talk about the tortured artist, they're usually referring to the propensity we artists sometimes have to be controlled by our emotions. The great Italian opera composer Giacomo Puccini is known to have said that he always carried "a great sack of melancholy."[1] I often get calls from pastors because the music director they're thinking about hiring has put me down as a reference. One question I get with alarming frequency goes something like this: "Is this person moody?" Pastors want to know if their music person is going to bring everybody else down because he or she has the blues all the time. That's a valid concern. My hope is that we would be free to be who God made us to be as emotional human beings but not be constantly haunted by the dark side of our emotions; to be healthy emotionally instead of emotionally unstable; to be free to feel but not a slave to feelings.

Emotional disorders of people with creative temperaments have been well documented and well publicized. Friend, if you struggle at all with your emotions, you're in good company. At the age of twenty-two, Michelangelo wrote in a letter to his father, "Do not wonder if I have sometimes written irritable letters, for I often suffer great distresses of mind and temper."[2] Berlioz, Tchaikovsky, and Rachmaninoff all experienced severe depression. Robert Schumann and Hugo Wolf were manic-depressive. Vincent van Gogh was driven to suicide. He was thirty-seven.

Songwriter Jimmy Webb says this about the artist's frequent bouts with depression:

> The true poet understands this strange mood shift all too well—walking out the front door onto the porch on a glorious spring morning, serenaded by the liquid songs of birds, only to find that the day has taken on a darkly sinister aspect and that there is a uranium slug suddenly buried in the pit of the stomach—all made worse by the fact the victim knows all too well that the cause lies within. . . . The effort involved in holding this monster at bay creates other vulnerabilities: the temptation to self-medicate along with the addictions that may follow, as well as related professional failures that may destroy a person's faith in their own future.[3]

I need to say right at the beginning here that if you're suffering from serious emotional problems, you really should seek professional help from a pastor or Christian counselor. There's nothing wrong with getting professional help in this area. I know a man whose wife displays all the classic signs of clinical depression but who feels it's unchristian to see a counselor or get medication. Instead he constantly chides her for her lack of faith and drags her to one healing service after another. Meanwhile she grows more despondent every day and bitter toward her husband for not being attentive to her needs. If she had a broken leg, he'd take her to the best doctor he could find. But for some reason, in his mind depression is a no-no for Christians. Clinical depression is serious and warrants professional and sometimes medical attention. Often it is the result of a chemical imbalance in the brain and can be treated medically. If you're deeply depressed over a long period of time or are suffering with a serious emotional condition, please seek professional help. Really, it's okay to do that.

Having said that, let me say that just because you don't need professional help doesn't mean that you will never deal with out-of-control emotions. There is no such thing as a person who doesn't have feelings. We may be suppressing them or may not know how to communicate them, but we are all emotional people. Some people are obviously more emotional than others, but even the person who is least emotional needs to learn how to deal with his or her feelings.

Is It Okay to Be Sad?

Some Christians have no room in their theology for negative emotions such as anger, disappointment, and sadness. They think Christians are supposed to be up all the time, and consider it a bad witness to be down. You wouldn't want the unsaved neighbors to see you depressed, would you? Being down doesn't fit the picture some believers have of what a true Christian should be. So we suppress our feelings, thinking God (and the neighbors) can't handle it when we're down. Our tendency is to alleviate any pain and suffering in our lives at all cost, to look for the quick fix.

Yet Jesus said, "Blessed are those who mourn" (Matt. 5:4). We need to embrace pain and suffering instead of trying to avoid it. Life is a struggle for all, and non-Christians are watching us to see how we deal with it. If they never see us down or sad, they will conclude that Christians don't deal with their emotions—they suppress them. I think God has proven that he can handle our darkest emotions. Just look at some of the Old Testament prophets. Elijah was so low, he wanted to die (1 Kings 19:4). Jeremiah was so despondent, he cursed the day he was born (Jer. 20:14–15). There's even an entire book of the Bible called Lamentations. God can handle it if we're sad.

David was an emotional guy. He didn't suppress his feelings, not even the negative ones. He held nothing back from God. A case in point is Psalm 88:13–18 (which Dan quoted in our opening scenario). Would David feel at home in your church? Do we have a place for people who need mercy and grace? Or is church only for those who have "arrived"? Do we have room for people who are fainthearted (1 Thess. 5:14; Isa. 35:4)? You know what I mean—people who are going through difficult times. Everyone does at one time or another. Do we reach out to them, or do we demand that they get it together? Do we love them, or do we view them as projects—people we hope to fix? Do we "mourn with those who mourn" (Rom. 12:15), or do we send them away with the Ten Steps to Becoming a Happier, More Victorious Christian? Do we have room in our hearts for someone who is strong with emotion but has trouble managing that emotion? Why are we so afraid of authentic emotions? Why is it illegal to be sad? Why can't we listen to someone who's disappointed with God? If the church is going to embrace people with artistic temperaments, we've got to stop sending them underground with their feelings.

If we expect people to be up all the time, we make no room in our thinking for what Saint John of the Cross calls "the dark night of the soul." This dark night is a rare but very legitimate spiritual desert. It's a dry period, a very sad time. Richard Foster sees this as something God uses for various reasons, one of which is to break us of a faith that's based mostly on our feelings. During this dark night of the soul, Foster writes, we "may have a sense of dryness, aloneness, even lostness. Any overdependence on the emotional life is stripped away. The notion, often heard today, that such experiences should be avoided and that we always should live in peace and comfort, joy, and celebration only betrays the fact that much contemporary experience is surface slush. The dark night is one of the ways God brings us into a hush, a stillness so that he may work an inner transformation upon the soul."[4]

One thing we need to ask before going on is, Do you ever enjoy being sad? Some people actually like being down. Or more precisely, they enjoy the attention they get when they're down. People talk to them more. As a result, they feel more special. It's a shame, but the only time they feel loved might be when they have an emotional problem, so they may overly dramatize their problems to get attention. Some people can even get addicted to sadness because it puts them in touch with their feelings and they feel more alive when they have something to be sad about. If this describes you, please stop. This is not healthy for you or your friends. Any attention you're getting is coerced, and any community you experience is self-centered. All the energy that you're putting into manipulating others to fill your emotional needs would be better spent pursuing intimacy with God and true community with others. When that happens, you will experience the joy of the Lord, and it'll indeed be your strength (Neh. 8:10).

When Our Emotions Get the Worst of Us

One indication that a person is being controlled by his or her emotions is chronic negativity. Negative people often feel alienated from others, and it's sad to say but they usually are. We tend to avoid negative people. They're moody. They're "downers" and they're draining. Negative people are often pessimistic. They resist change and stand in the way of new and progressive ideas. They lack enthusiasm and have very little life in them. They often take themselves much too seriously. They wallow in self-pity. They're not much fun to be around, no matter how talented they are. Negative people are often very critical. Proverbs 15:4 says that "a soothing tongue is a tree of life, but perversion in it crushes the spirit" (NASB). People who are constantly critical tend to wound others with their words and crush others' spirits. All this tends to make us want to avoid negative, overly critical people.

Negative people also tend to be cynical. They always assume the worst and they have a bleak outlook on life. The glass is always half empty, nothing ever works as it should, and tomorrow's going to be another lousy day. Their knee-jerk reaction is to assume the worst. They assume that others don't like them and are trying to put them down. Dan assumed that his friends didn't want him in their small group anymore. He assumed the worst: they didn't like him, they had more fun without him, and they were going to kick him out of the group. We've all done that at some point. We hear one side of a story and get carried away with all sorts of negative emotions without knowing all the facts. We choose to believe the worst instead of believing the best. I've experienced this as a leader at church. People have a problem with something I've done concerning them, and they come to the conclusion that I don't like them, I'm out to hurt them, or I'm trying to kick them off the team. They're often surprised and embarrassed to learn later that their negative assumptions were totally off base. Proverbs 12:16 says that "a fool shows his annoyance at once, but a prudent man overlooks an insult." In other words, a prudent person doesn't jump to a negative conclusion without the facts. A wise person is not easily provoked to negativity. Many times our negative reactions turn out to be foolish because they're not grounded in reality.

The person who mismanages his or her anger also does what I would call piling on. When something bad happens, we keep rehashing it over and over until it becomes a highly charged emotional issue. It gets added to the memories we've stored up of all the other times we've been hurt. After a while we have accumulated a huge amount of bitterness, and we carry this baggage around wherever we go. When our emotions are triggered—the negative emotions tied to these unresolved issues, our "stuff," can be triggered by the most innocent of comments—we start piling on even more negativity. With me it usually begins with the phrase "And another thing . . ." Then I launch into something that happened a long time ago that I realize I'm still carrying a grudge about. In our opening scenario Dan does the same thing. He piles the disappointment of the night onto some of his other frustrations: his friends don't support him as an artist, they don't invite him over for Christmas, and so on. Because he has a negative frame of mind, Dan piles the latest hurt onto all the others and jumps to conclusions that are based more on his feelings than on reality.

Since they're driven by how they feel, people who don't know how to manage their emotions also tend to feel alienated from God. They base their standing with God on how well they feel their lives are going. If everything's going well, God must like them. If things aren't going well, God must be mad at them. If anything good happens to them, they don't want to get too excited, because they're waiting for the other shoe to drop. As a result, they end up with a distorted view of God. They perceive that God is not really big enough to handle their problems or doesn't care. God only loves them if they feel loved. God's not somebody they can have a relationship with. He's there to make their life happy or miserable, and if they don't feel His presence, they conclude He must not be there.

Managing Our Emotions

Proverbs 25:28 says, "Like a city whose walls are broken down is a man who lacks self-control." The person who doesn't know how to manage his or her emotions is defenseless against negative feelings. Similarly,

Proverbs 16:32 says that the person who manages his or her emotions well is better than someone who captures an entire city. It's easier to conquer a city than to conquer negative emotions. In fact, I think managing our emotions is one of the most difficult challenges facing those of us with artistic temperaments. It's not easy for emotional people to avoid being controlled by their feelings. When I'm hurt, it usually triggers a chain reaction of emotions that seem beyond my control. Then without thinking, like one of Pavlov's dogs, I say or do something I later regret and end up in an even bigger mess. If only I had kept my wits about me and not given in to the emotion of the moment. If only I had used my head instead of acting on cue according to those negative emotions. It's not easy to manage your emotions.

The good news is that God wants to help us manage our emotions. If we're willing, He wants to give us a new heart and a new spirit (Ezek. 36:26). It's not going to happen overnight, and it's not going to happen without some effort on our part. We have to be proactive about it. Remember, I'm not talking about suppressing your emotions. That's not the answer. I'm talking about managing them so they don't manage you. Again, the goal is to be free with our emotions, not controlled by them.

Proactive About the Truth

It's difficult for negative people to change. They've probably been that way their entire lives. Remember, Proverbs says it's easier to capture a city than it is to take charge of your emotions. That's why the person who tends to be negative should make every effort to dwell on "whatever is true, whatever is noble, whatever is right, whatever is pure, whatever is lovely, whatever is admirable" (Phil. 4:8). To dwell on whatever is true means more than just thinking about it once in a while. It means that we vigilantly speak truth to ourselves and to others, that we make a concerted effort to look for the reality of God's truth in every situation. A commitment to truth telling is a sign of character. You might want to pray every day something similar to what David prayed in Psalm 51:8. Ask, "Lord, help me to hear joy and gladness today instead of doom and gloom."

Our feelings always need to be examined in light of the truth. Dan immediately jumped to the conclusion that his friends didn't want him in the group, but he didn't know that for a fact. So was it true, or was he living in a false reality created by his own negative thinking? The only way to find out whether something is true is to come out and ask. Just because you feel a certain way doesn't mean something's true. Perhaps you truly feel that way, but it still might be a lie. Next time you catch yourself jumping to a negative conclusion, ask yourself if the information that led you there is true. Instead of assuming the worst, try assuming the best about people. First Corinthians 13:7 says that love "bears all things, believes all things, hopes all things, endures all things" (NASB). Love believes the best. We've got to stop forming opinions and drawing conclusions without knowing the whole story. Next time you catch yourself assuming the worst, ask yourself, *Am I basing my reaction on truth or on speculation?* Make a commitment to believe the best about people and how they interact with you.

Proactive About Worshiping God

To avoid being controlled by our feelings, I suggest we channel them into worship. We need to make a commitment to worship the Lord regularly. Worship is an intensely emotional experience. Some of you have been expecting me to tell you to deny your emotions for the sake of your mental health. You're just waiting for me to say, "Let's be good little Christians and not get all wrapped up in emotion." Instead I'd like to invite you to cut loose and experience the fullness of worship. Lose your emotions in worship. Get emotional about God.

My favorite definition of worship comes from William Temple: "Worship is the submission of all our nature to God. It is the quickening of conscience by His holiness; the nourishment of mind with His truth; the purifying of imagination by His beauty; the opening of the heart to His love; the surrender of will to His purpose—and all of this gathered up in adoration, the most selfless emotion of which our nature is capable and therefore the chief remedy for that self-centeredness which is our original sin and the source of all actual sin."[5]

You could feast on every line of that quote and glean all sorts of great insights. I've been carrying this quote around in my Bible for quite some time now, and I read it often. Each time I gain something new from it. Temple says that worship is "the most selfless emotion of which our nature is capable." When we connect with God in heartfelt worship, we realize that this life is not all about us. It's about the Lord. When we feel weak, one of the best things we can do is worship God. Worship brings us into His presence, where there is deep joy and true pleasure (Ps. 16:11; 21:6). Worship causes us to take our eyes off ourselves and focus and meditate on Him (Ps. 77:6).

Worship is not primarily or exclusively an emotional experience, but emotion is an essential part of true worship. We must engage our minds *and* our emotions. That should come as good news to those of us who are intensely emotional. It's okay to have feelings. That's why we need to spend time worshiping God, not just in church but also personally, on our own. John Piper explains the role of truth and emotion as it relates to worship: "Truth without emotion produces dead orthodoxy and a church full (or half full) of artificial admirers (like people who write generic anniversary cards for a living). Emotion without truth produces empty frenzy and cultivates shallow people who refuse the disciplines of rigorous thought. But true worship comes from people who are deeply emotional and who love deep and sound doctrine. Strong affections from God rooted in truth are the bone and marrow of biblical worship."[6]

When your church gathers for worship, are you there ready and willing to engage fully with God? Or are you "somewhere else" during corporate worship, distracted by personal concerns or the events of the day? Do you come ready to be loved by God, or are you there to criticize the music, the drama, or the sermon? Do you regularly get alone with the Lord and worship Him? Do you ever meditate or journal on His attributes? When we worship, we come away changed. When we bathe our emotions in deep worship, it cleanses our souls. That's why C. S. Lewis called worship "inner health made audible."[7]

I would recommend a steady diet of praise music to help keep all of us on track emotionally. In the midst of persecution and adversity, Paul and Silas worshiped from their jail cell (Acts 16:25).

When Saul was struggling, he would have David play the harp for him. First Samuel 16:23 says that the music ministered to Saul and refreshed him. Indeed, worship music can refresh and restore us. It can lift our spirits and reconnect us to God. Try it. Play some worship tapes while you drive, when you're at home, or at work. I guarantee it'll lift your spirits.

Living in the Psalms

Ecclesiastes 8:1 says that God's word can settle into someone who's angry or sad and cause their "face to beam" (NASB). I believe every artist should live in the Psalms. It'll help your face beam with peace and joy. Many of the Psalms were written by someone with an artistic temperament. David had that sensitivity that many of us have. He had that desire to create and express that many of us have. And he walked so close to God that God referred to David as "a man after my own heart" (Acts 13:22).

We need to live in the Psalms because they are some of the most emotional writings in the Bible. David is a model of emotional freedom. He freely expresses his emotions, from one extreme to the other—sometimes in the span of one psalm. In some of the Psalms (such as Pss. 3, 6, 13, 59, 62, 86, 109, 142) we see extreme emotional mood swings, from the depths of despair to the ecstasy of God's glory. This is reality. It gives us an example to follow from someone who is very similar to us in many ways. Listen to these examples from the book of Psalms:

> "I am worn out from groaning; all night long I flood my bed with weeping and drench my couch with tears" (Ps. 6:6).
> "Be merciful to me, O LORD, for I am in distress" (Ps. 31:9).
> "I am about to fall, and my pain is ever with me. I confess my iniquity; I am troubled by my sin" (Ps. 38:17–18).
> "List my tears on your scroll" (Ps. 56:8).
> "I will sing of your strength, in the morning I will sing of your love" (Ps. 59:16).
> "Shout with joy to God, all the earth!" (Ps. 66:1).

"When the LORD brought back the captives to Zion, we were
like men who dreamed. Our mouths were filled with laughter, our tongues with songs of joy. Then it was said among
the nations, 'The LORD has done great things for them.' The
LORD has done great things for us, and we are filled with
joy" (Ps. 126:1–3).

We artists must live in the Psalms because they can recalibrate
our concept of God. I am a different person after saturating my mind
with the Psalms, because I come away with a more accurate picture
of God. My problems might not go away, but they usually look different in light of who God is. I need an accurate view of God more
than I need my problems solved. It's too easy to lose sight of what
God is really like and who He really is, and a distorted view of God
quickly gives way to a distorted, negative view of life. Because they
are worshipful, the Psalms give us an accurate concept of who God
is. They reveal His attributes to us. When you read a psalm, try to
pick out an attribute of God that means a lot to you.

For the longest time I couldn't relate to the word *magnify* during worship. I could relate to *bless, exalt,* and *extol,* but *magnify* had
me stumped. What does it mean to magnify the Lord? Then it hit
me that when problems come into my life, I usually magnify them
to the point where they're bigger than God is. We artists have a tendency to magnify everything in our lives—our problems, ourselves,
and even our art—to be bigger than God. Now when I see "magnify the Lord" in the Psalms or hear it in worship, it has a way of
reminding me about who God is. It sharpens my easily cloudable
vision of God. Listen to David's view of our Lord:

"You are God my Savior, and my hope is in you all day long"
(Ps. 25:5).
"The voice of the LORD is powerful; the voice of the LORD is
majestic.... And in his temple all cry, 'Glory!'" (Ps. 29:4, 9).
"By the word of the LORD were the heavens made, their starry
host by the breath of his mouth.... Let all the earth fear
the LORD; let all the people of the world revere him...."

Blessed is the nation whose God is the LORD" (Ps. 33:6, 8, 12).

"The LORD is close to the brokenhearted and saves those who are crushed in spirit" (Ps. 34:18).

"Your love, O LORD, reaches to the heavens, your faithfulness to the skies" (Ps. 36:5).

"Our God is a God who saves" (Ps. 68:20).

"Who, O God, is like you?" (Ps. 71:19).

"Great are the works of the LORD; they are pondered by all who delight in them" (Ps. 111:2).

"The LORD will fulfill his purpose for me" (Ps. 138:8).

We artists need to live in the Psalms because they're not only emotional, they're not only accurate portrayals of who God is, but they show an intensely emotional and sensitive human being (like us) struggling with the difficulties of life and struggling with the reality of God. Art at its best shows real people dealing with real issues. David didn't gloss over his feelings, even the negative ones. He brought them before an omniscient and omnipresent God. He took his frustration, his disappointment, and his pain to God and came away a new man. Listen to some of these examples:

"Turn to me and be gracious to me, for I am lonely and afflicted. The troubles of my heart have multiplied; free me from my anguish" (Ps. 25:16–17).

"God sets the lonely in families" (Ps. 68:6).

"When anxiety was great within me, your consolation brought joy to my soul" (Ps. 94:19).

Be Angry, But Don't Sin

You can't control how you feel about something, but you can control how you're going to respond to it. That's why the Bible says, "In your anger do not sin" (Eph. 4:26). Remember, we sin because we choose to sin. You may not be able to avoid getting angry, but you can choose not to retaliate or lash out verbally. You may not be able to avoid feeling negative, but you can choose not to attack someone with critical remarks. We don't need to suppress our feelings; we just can't let them cause us to sin. It is a sign of character to do the right thing even when you don't feel like it.

When I became a father, I learned from firsthand experience that disciplining my two sons out of anger did much more harm than good. That's why Paul tells fathers not to provoke their children to anger (Eph. 6:4 RSV). In my anger I said hurtful things that ended up being more sinful than whatever my sons did to set me off in the first place. It's better to tell them I'm angry but not let that anger cause me to sin. It's healthier for me to withdraw momentarily and give myself time to choose how I'm going to respond.

Don't Take Yourself Too Seriously

The artist who has lost his or her sense of humor can be the most miserable person around. Sometimes we can be too serious for our own good. Joy is one of the fruits of the Spirit, and laughter is indeed good for the soul. Have you ever wondered if God has a sense of humor? Well, wonder no more. One visit to the zoo will tell you that God has a sense of humor and that He must have had a lot of fun creating the world. Have you ever seen a platypus? How about an ostrich or a baboon? Did you know that the male sea horse is the one who gives birth? You can't tell me God doesn't have a sense of humor.

Jesus used plenty of humor in His teaching. I'll bet the disciples laughed about trying to get the speck of sawdust out of their brother's eye while carrying around a plank in their own eye. If you think about it, that's really a funny picture. Or the one about a camel going through the eye of a needle. It's old hat to us now, but I'll bet they sat around and laughed over that one for days. Have you seen the picture of Jesus in which He's laughing? Are you okay with that, or is your picture of Jesus one of complete seriousness all the time, in which He never cracks a smile, never shows any joy? Christians who are too religious to have any fun or too serious to enjoy life are missing out. Ecclesiastes 7:16 says, "Do not be overrighteous, neither be overwise—why destroy yourself?" In other words, don't be such a stuffed shirt. Don't be so rigid and take everything so seriously. Besides, it is more theologically correct to smile than it is to frown.

I have a tendency to take myself way too seriously. In His eternal wisdom God gave me a wife who likes to laugh. Sue has a great sense of humor. It's one of the things that first attracted me to her. I love being around her, because she laughs easily. She'd tell you it's one of the keys to having a successful marriage. I'd agree. Laughter is important at our house. I know firsthand what Scripture means when it says that "a cheerful heart is good medicine" (Prov. 17:22).

There's an individual in my life who struggles with being negative. I'm his accountability partner, so he'll often ask me, "How am I doing with my negativity?" I like to ask him what he's done for fun lately, because doing things that are enjoyable helps to curb a negative attitude. By the way, being accountable to someone about these things is always a good idea.

Dealing with Disappointment

I'd like to move on to something that all artists have dealt with at one time or another: disappointment. Anyone who has ever ventured to succeed in the arts has run up against this rude spoilsport. How do you handle being disappointed? Do you let anger turn to bitterness? Do you turn your anger inward and become depressed? Do you give up trying to be an artist?

This may come as a rude awakening, but I should tell you that you may never experience ultimate fulfillment as an artist in this life. I hate to say this, but the life of an artist is extremely hard, and a career in the arts is a risk any way you look at it. You may have ambitions for a successful career, but you may never get discovered. Some people are fortunate enough to make a living in the arts. Others are not. You may even be more talented than those who make it, but you never got the breaks they did. Maybe they knew the right people and made the right connections. You worked hard but things just didn't happen for you. Your career as an artist may fall short of your dreams and expectations. If that's the case, how are you going to handle it?

I spent a great deal of time earlier in this book touting the virtues of using your talents in your local church. What if that turns out to be a very disappointing experience also? What should you do if you experience rejection in the church? What if the church doesn't use you the way you wish they would? What if using your talents in your church turns out to be an unfulfilling experience? Does that mean you shouldn't do it?

What about the virtuoso organist who attends a church with no pipe organ? Or a drummer who goes to a traditional church? Or the serious writer who wants to do more than write copy for the church bulletin? Or the visual artist who wants to do more than make banners at Easter? Or the actor who wants to sink teeth into a meaty role for church? What about the dancer who's fighting resistance to dance in church? What if you're one of many flute players and the church orchestra has but a few openings? What if you write songs but they never get played at church? Negotiating these tensions can be a real challenge. The way we handle these kinds of issues will reflect our maturity and character.

I know that the church doesn't exist solely for the sake of the arts. It has a higher calling, and it is not a performing arts organization. But as a music director at a church, I still agonize over situations like the ones I just described. I've come to realize that every church has a narrow scope of musical style compared with the full range of styles available to us today. In other words, every church can't possibly accommodate all the different styles of music and art that exist. The style of music we use at Willow Creek is what I would call contemporary Christian music. Pop music is the general label given to the style that best suits our target audience. Even though there's a lot of variety within that genre—rock, jazz, country, rhythm and blues, and so on—it still doesn't accommodate all the different types of musicians that have come our way. For example, the bona fide opera singer and the purely classical pianist might not feel at home in our ministry. What should I do? There's got to be a lot of frustrated musicians out in our congregation. Am I responsible for the fulfillment of every musician at Willow Creek? Is that reasonable? Is it even possible?

Finding Your Sweet Spot

Anybody who plays tennis knows that when you serve, the best place to make contact with the ball is in the sweet spot of the racket. When the ball hits that sweet spot, it jumps off the racket and shoots over the net. To carry this analogy over to the church and the arts, it would be nice if all artists could serve in their sweet spot all the time. However, it doesn't always work out that way. Many of us don't always serve in our sweet spot as artists. Our talents don't get used to their fullest all the time.

My own experience reflects this theory. I can write songs and arrange music with a limited degree of success, but what I probably do best is more along the lines of serious composition. At one time I wanted to get into film scoring, and I'm still a big fan of film scores. I listen to all types of music, but when I want to listen to something for personal pleasure, it's usually a classical piece or some film score. Yet here I am, working in a church where, by design, pop music is the main food on the menu. Don't get me wrong. I love pop music. I love all good music. But pop music is not the only music I listen to, and it may not be the kind of music I do best.

For the longest time I doubted my calling because I didn't know what to do with my frustration as an artist. I asked the Lord to move me out of the church so I could be more fulfilled artistically. That never happened. As often as I prayed, I never sensed the go-ahead from God to leave the ministry.

Then something happened that made me realize I was right where God wanted me all along. One year at Willow Creek we did a Holy Week musical called *The Choice*. Along with contributing as a songwriter, I wrote some orchestral underscoring for the scene in which Jesus is taken down from the cross, and for another scene at the tomb on the morning of the Resurrection. It was like doing a film score, as I was given the freedom to stretch myself creatively. I was in my sweet spot. Finally! We repeated *The Choice* two other years, and thousands of people have seen it. Many have come to Christ as a result of it. It was the most fulfilling thing I've ever done artistically as well as from a ministry standpoint. I have since looked back on those years when I pleaded with God to let me leave full-time church work, and I'm glad He didn't answer my prayer, because I realize that my heart has always been in ministry. Today I wouldn't trade places with the most successful film score composer in Hollywood. I wouldn't trade my experience with *The Choice* for anything in the world—not even a Grammy-winning film score. What I was given the privilege of doing was not only gratifying artistically; it mattered for eternity. I was allowed to do something spiritually significant with my art. If it only happens once in my lifetime that I experience that kind of fulfillment artistically and spiritually, that one time was well worth it.

What or Who Is Standing in the Way?

How about you? Do you feel fulfilled as an artist? What has your experience been like as an artist in the local church? Is your church able to use you in your sweet spot all the time, sometimes, once in a while, or never at all?

To make a more personal application, let's ask the following question: What is standing in the way of you being fulfilled as an artist in the church? Is it a circumstance beyond your control? Are you in a church in which the arts are underutilized? Are you a rock drummer in a traditional church? Or a dancer who's been told that your church will probably never have a dance ministry? If that's the case, you have two options to prayerfully consider. One option is to leave that church and serve at a church that will allow you to use your artistic talents. If you choose this route, make sure God is definitely calling you to another church and leave your former church with style and grace. Don't burn bridges if you leave. Don't use your departure as an opportunity for some parting shots about how no one appreciates you there. If God is truly calling you away, let that be your reason for leaving, and do it with class.

Your second option is to stay. God may have you there for a reason. Maybe your church is on the verge of some major break-throughs in the arts, and He wants to use you to bring about some much needed change. If that's the case, be patient and be fervent in prayer. Though surrounded by hostile enemies, the people of Israel were on the verge of major victory when Joshua said to them, "Consecrate yourselves, for tomorrow the LORD will do amazing things among you" (Josh. 3:5). If God is on the verge of doing wonders in your church, quitting is not an option for you. Hang in there. Your toil is not in vain in the Lord (1 Cor. 15:58). You're paving the way not only for yourself but for all the future artists in your church as well.

What else is standing in the way of you being fulfilled as an artist in the church? If it's not a circumstance, is it a person? Is there a leader who doesn't call on you to perform or create as much as you'd like? Do you feel overlooked by that leader? Is there a personality clash there? If there's a person standing in the way, I suggest you meet with that person and share your frustration. He or she might be unaware of your situation. You might discover that the reason that person has not been using you has nothing to do with you at all. Maybe the opportunities haven't presented themselves. Maybe the person wasn't aware of your availability. Maybe he or she tried to call you but you were out of town.

On the other hand, the leader's reason for not using you might have everything to do with you. There might be something you're doing that's not going over well with the congregation, or something about your performance or communication skills that need a little work. Be open to what the leader has to say. You might learn something very valuable. Be humble. Have a teachable spirit. Remember, part of being a good steward of the talents God has given you means developing those talents to the best of your ability. Don't let pride stand in the way. Try to get to the bottom of why you're not being used as much as you'd like. During certain lulls in my songwriting, I've had to swallow my pride and ask, "Why aren't we using this song of mine?" The honest answers I've received have helped me grow as a writer. Tell your leader that you want to serve your church in the best way you possibly can. Ask your leader to help you know how to do that.

What If God Is Saying, "Wait"?

Suppose you've done everything I've suggested so far. You've prayed and you're sure you're at the church to which God has called you. You've talked through your frustration and are doing everything you can to be usable to God and the church. Let me ask the question no one wants to ask: What if God is standing in the way of you being used right now? God is the one who raises up people to serve (Ps. 75:7). He's the one who ultimately gives you a platform. Nothing and no one can stand in His way (Acts 11:17). First Peter 5:6 says that He exalts us "at the proper time" (NASB). Is it possible that now is not the proper time for you? Many artists out in the world have been spoiled by early success. They lit up the night and then burned out fast. They weren't ready for fame and fortune. Their early success proved to be creatively stifling in the long run. If it's not in God's timing, it's not the proper time. Habakkuk reminds us that God's best is always worth waiting for: "The revelation awaits an appointed time; it speaks of the end and will not prove false. Though it linger, wait for it; it will certainly come and will not delay" (2:3).

I know this may not be what you want to hear, but is it possible that the Lord wants you to wait? I have gone through numerous periods of disappointment and frustration as an artist. I have had my hopes dashed many times. I have known from firsthand experience what the writer of Proverbs is describing when he says, "Hope deferred makes the heart sick, but a longing fulfilled is a tree of life" (13:12). Any time you can't do what you long to do as an artist, it's very frustrating. It makes your heart feel sick. Many of us have lofty dreams, and it's hard when those dreams come crashing down around us. On the other hand, when your dreams come true—when you get to do what God has gifted you to do—it's very life-giving.

It is not in our nature to wait, but it's very often part of God's plan. God told Joshua and the people of Israel that He was going to do something great in their midst and that they would subdue Jericho (Josh. 3:5; 6:2). But it involved a wild plan. For six days they were to march around Jericho once a day without saying a word, and then come home. Now the first day, it might have been a real hoot to get all dressed up and march around Jericho, but I'm sure by the third or fourth day it got a little old. I'm sure some of them must have thought, *What are we waiting for? We know God's in this, so why do we have to wait another day?* Knowing artistic types, I'll bet the musicians were getting impatient and wondering, *Man, when do I get to blow my horn?* (Now we know the real reason they were all told they couldn't talk during the march—it was to keep them from complaining.) On the seventh day they marched around the city seven times (prolonging the inevitable even longer), until Joshua gave them the command to blow the trumpets and shout. We all know what happened next. The walls came a-tumblin' down.

Waiting seems to be part of God's plan. Have you ever wondered why? Why did Noah and his family have to wait it out for so long in that stinking ark? Why did the nation of Israel have to wander for forty years in the wilderness? Why did Abraham and Sarah have to wait until they became senior citizens to have a baby? Why three whole days in the tomb before the Resurrection? After all, God is God. He certainly could have caused these things to happen sooner. God even wrote the principle of waiting into the laws of nature. We have to endure winter to get to summer. We have to worry through the growing season to get to the harvest. We have to be patient for nine months until the baby is born. Important things are happening during the waiting period whether we can see them or not, but it doesn't make the waiting any easier.

The Benefits of Waiting

What are the benefits of waiting? Isaiah 40:31 says that "those who wait for the Lord will gain new strength; they will mount up with wings like eagles, they will run and not get tired, they will walk and not become weary" (NASB). Waiting produces strength to endure and courage to carry on. While we wait, God brings spiritual growth into our lives. That maturity prepares us to receive God's blessing. God acts on behalf of those who wait for Him (Isa. 64:4). He's not trying to be a spoilsport when He tells us to wait. The growth and maturity He gives while we wait is as much a blessing as is that for which we're waiting. While we wait, we grow in three areas:

1. We grow in faith.
2. We grow in patience.
3. We grow in contentment.

Growing in Faith

If we let it, waiting helps us grow in faith, because it challenges us to trust the Lord. Because God is a perfect and righteous God, we can trust that the way He deals with us is for the best. So are we going to trust the plans He has for us? Can we trust that those plans are indeed for our welfare and not for our calamity, that they are to give us a future and a hope (Jer. 29:11)?

As we wait, God's will also becomes more clear to us. We can submit to His lordship and eventually accept His will as right. I say eventually because I hate it when Christians say, "It must be God's will" and sound all cheery about it, when deep inside they're so angry they could spit. Why do we think we have to put a happy face on everything when we're disappointed? We're not fooling God and we're certainly not fooling our friends. We're only fooling our-selves. Getting over disappointment takes time. If we're struggling with God's will, let's come out and say it. Only then can we grow in faith. Only then will we realize that God's timing is for the best. Only then will we be able to honestly say, "Not as I will, but as you will" (Matt. 26:39). If you're struggling with disappointment, put what little faith you can muster in God. He is faithful, and He will give you the strength you need (Isa. 41:10). Authentic submission to God's will is a sign of character. It's part of the work God does in our hearts during those times when He's telling us to wait.

I can cooperate with God's plan to develop faith in me by running to God instead of running away from Him. Some Christians handle disappointment by shaking their fist at God and turning away. Others are more subtle. They just slowly drift away from Him. They stop pray-ing, stop reading the Word, and stop going to church. Even if you're sad or angry, don't think that God doesn't want to embrace you. He wants you to come to Him even more. If you're burdened with disappointment, remember that He is compassionate when we are weak. He cares when we are hurting. "A bruised reed he will not break, and a smoldering wick he will not snuff out" (Isa. 42:3). If you're down, draw near to God and He will draw near to you (James 4:8).

Growing in Patience

If we let it, waiting also helps us grow in patience. Most Christians are leery about praying for patience. "Whatever you do, don't pray for patience," I've heard people say. "If you do, God's going to send all sorts of horrible things into your life to make you more patient." Really, I'm not sure God has to go that far out of His way to teach us patience. Life already presents numerous opportunities to learn patience. A simple trip to the grocery store, for example—driving there, fighting traffic, finding a place to park, trying to remember everything you need, finding everything you need, waiting in the checkout line, and getting back home—is enough to challenge anyone's patience. No, I'm talking about something deeper here. I'm talking about perseverance. I'm talking about reaching a point where we stop wanting everything right now. I'm talking about having peace about God's timing. I'm talking about being convinced that "in all things God works for the good of those who love him, who have been called according to his purpose" (Rom. 8:28). Willingness to delay gratification is a sign of character, and it too is something God accomplishes in us when He tells us to wait.

I can cooperate with God's plan to make me a more patient person, by affirming my trust in His timing. "God is not a man, that he should lie. . . . Does he speak and then not act? Does he promise and not fulfill?" (Num. 23:19). If God reveals that He's going to do something, it's going to happen. He doesn't rush things but He doesn't delay either. Even when it doesn't feel right to us, God's timing is always perfect.

Growing in Contentment

Finally, waiting helps us grow in the area of contentment, if we let it. People who are content have peace in spite of their circumstances. They maintain their equilibrium through the ups and downs of life. Paul emerged from the adversities of life and found contentment. According to 2 Corinthians 11, he endured imprisonment, physical abuse, danger, and starvation. Yet he learned to be content in all things (Phil. 4:11). No wonder he said that "godliness with contentment is great gain" (1 Tim. 6:6). Paul was content because he was at peace with himself and with God.

People who are discontented forget how much God has done for them (1 Tim. 6:7–8). Paul saw this happening to the church at Galatia, and he cried out to them, "Where then is that sense of blessing you had?" (Gal. 4:15 NASB). They had lost sight of how good God had been to them and had become ungrateful. Contentment has been a rare commodity for human beings throughout history. The human race would be spared a great deal of pain if we could learn how to be content. For those of us who have an authentic relationship with Jesus Christ, contentment helps us put what we want in light of what we have. We find we no longer demand that all our problems be solved. We no longer need to have our way all the time. We're content whether we get what we want or not. In fact, we realize we don't deserve what we already have, let alone anything more. Our contentment doesn't depend on outward things or circumstances. It's a reflection of a soul that's filled with gratitude. The ability to be content with what you have is a sign of character (1 Tim. 6:8; Heb. 13:5).

Is it mere coincidence how often artists, specifically musicians, are exhorted in the Bible to worship with joy and thanksgiving? The people who struggle most with being negative and moody are commanded to "sing for joy" (Ps. 5:11; 132:9), "sing joyful songs" (1 Chron. 15:16), come before the Lord with "joyful songs" (Ps. 100:2), and shout joyfully in song (Ps. 95:1–2). We are to admonish one another with psalms, hymns, and spiritual songs, singing with thankfulness in our hearts to God (Col. 3:16; Eph. 5:19–20). Psalm 87:7 says that "as they make music they will sing, 'All my springs of joy are in you'" (NASB). James asks, "Is anyone happy? Let him sing songs of praise" (5:13). We are to lead others in joy-filled worship and thanksgiving (2 Chron. 20:21; Ps. 42:4; 43:4). In fact, the first organized choir in the Bible was formed to lead others in giving thanks

(1 Chron. 16:7–36), and when you read Nehemiah 12, you get the impression that the only thing in the choir's repertoire were hymns of thanksgiving. No wonder their joy was so loud that it "could be heard far away" (v. 43). Jesus desires for us to be filled with joy: "I have told you this so that my joy may be in you and that your joy may be complete" (John 15:11). Joy is also one of the fruits of the Spirit that we're exhorted to cultivate (Gal. 5:22), and Paul says that God's will is for us to rejoice, pray, and give thanks (1 Thess. 5:16–18).

I can cooperate with God's plan to make me more content, by practicing being thankful. "Give thanks in all circumstances," Scripture says (1 Thess. 5:18). I know that's not always easy. Don't be hypocritical about it. But even in those times when it's hard to find anything to be thankful about, start by trying to think of at least one thing you can be thankful for. We're so quick to forget how much God has done for us. Next time your worship leader invites the congregation to worship with thanksgiving, you sing at the top of your lungs. My fellow artists, let's never lose our sense of blessing. Let's be proactive about having an attitude of gratitude.

Be Careful How You Measure Success

You could sign a major record deal, make a lot of money, and be famous the world over and still not be a success in God's eyes. On the other hand, you may never know success as an artist and still be successful as a person. That's because God looks at the inside. He's not impressed with outward appearance; He looks at the heart (1 Sam. 16:7). So be careful how you measure success.

Recently I was talking with a friend who was sharing his disappointment over the fact that he's never been able to make a living doing music. He always dreamed about being a professional musician but had to settle instead for a job in the computer field. We talked about some struggles he's going through, and I mainly asked questions and just listened. At the end of our conversation my friend said something that I think must have pleased God. He said, "You know, when I really think about it, I guess I have every reason to be content. I have a good job, a great wife, a wonderful family, a thriving small group, and I get to play my horn regularly at church." What my friend is too humble to say, but what I can say for him, is that he is a success in God's eyes even though he never made it in music. He walks with Christ and is trying to grow in his relationship with Him. God is using him powerfully at church as he plays and leads a small group, and I was thrilled to hear that he derives a great deal of contentment from being involved in our music ministry.

Character is more important to God than worldly success. You will derive more contentment from being the person God wants you to be than from being successful in the eyes of the world. Don't harbor a negative or critical spirit. Let the Lord work in your heart and teach you to manage your emotions in a healthy way. Remember, the Bible says it's easier to capture a city than to rule your emotions.

Free to Be Human

I'd like to end this chapter with some words of encouragement for those artists who are working and still waiting for God to use their art the way they long for Him to do. This is from a chapter called "Free to be Human" found in Franky Schaeffer's book *Addicted to Mediocrity:*

> And now a word to my fellow artists and those employed or hoping to be employed in some professional capacity in the arts, fields of expression and communications, and also to those who, while living in different professions, have artistic and creative urges and interests personally (therefore, I trust, everyone).
>
> "The world had many kings," said his contemporary Aretino, "But only one Michelangelo."
>
> Do not be discouraged. History is on your side. God has given you a talent. You are important to him and live in the court of God, not the court of men. You cannot wait for the Sanhedrin's approval.
>
> By expressing yourself as an artist and by exercising those talents God has given you, you are praising him. Whether what you express is "religious" or "secular," as a Christian you are praising him. Everything is his.

The church's attitude toward the arts, the narrow-mindedness of it, the demand for slogans and justification, the utilitarianism, the programs, the guilt-ridden view of all life is unchristian, unbiblical, ungodly and wrong. Do not let this suppress you, as a member of this generation of creative people, the way it has suppressed so many in the recent past. You must press on.

Remember that as a creative person, the important thing is to create. Who sees what you make, where it goes and what it does is a secondary consideration; the first is to exercise the talent God has given you.

You cannot expect too much too soon. It is the lifelong body of work that counts. It is that body of work whose expression means something and changes cultures in which we live in terms of bearing fruit. One individual work cannot say everything.

Your work will vary, one day to express something rather important to you personally and perhaps less important to the world around you, perhaps another time to wrestle with a weighty issue. There is no right or wrong method. There is no Christian or unchristian subject matter (except in the area of art work or expression that would deliberately have as its primary purpose to lead people away from truth).

You are tremendously free, you are the most free, for you have form on which to build your freedom, you know who you are, you know where your talent comes from, you know that you and your talent will live forever. You know that God has placed worth on you; you know creativity, unlike so many things in this fallen world, did not come from the Fall, but was something there with God before he created, with him when he created, and that he has given to man as his creature. It will be there in the new heavens and the new earth. Your creative talent, exercised and worked on in this life, is something you will take with you. Unlike money, or spiritual slogans, it is eternal.

Produce, produce, produce. Create, create, create. Work, work, work. This is what we must do as Christians in the arts, with or without the support of the church, we are to exercise our God-given talent, praise him through it, enjoy it, bear fruit in the age in which we live.

It is a worthwhile fight, and more than a fight it is an enjoyment of a good and gracious gift from our heavenly Father, freely given, to be enjoyed, practiced, and treasured.

When you get discouraged as a Christian in the arts, consider the heritage in which you stand. Bathe in the knowledge that for centuries Christians have practiced and nurtured the arts with faithfulness, and that you now carry this torch forward. Take courage from this. Take courage from the creativity and beauty of God's world around us. Take courage from the creativity of other people.

If any single group of people are in tune with God himself, certainly it is those Christians who enjoy, practice or simply appreciate creativity.[8]

Follow-Up Questions for Group Discussion

1. As you were growing up, were you allowed to express your emotions freely, or were you taught to suppress them?

2. Why do you think it's awkward for Christians when we encounter someone who's down or sad?

3. What should you do if you suspect someone is trying to get attention by creating his or her own emotional turmoil?

4. How do you feel when you're around someone who's constantly critical?

5. How can one person's negativity affect the church?

6. Why is it important to try to dwell on the truth? What kinds of things force us to dwell on God's truth?

7. What kind of effect does worshiping God have on us emotionally?

8. What does our concept of God have to do with how we look at life?

9. Do you agree that every artist should read the Psalms regularly? Why or why not?

10. How would it affect the church if we were all more content and filled with gratitude?

Personal Action Steps

1. If you are not happy about the emotional balance in your life right now, decide what you would like to see changed, and to whom you can be accountable for this change.

2. Make a commitment to read one of the Psalms every day for two weeks and journal about what you read.

3. Habakkuk 3:17–18 was written from the point of view of someone engaged in an agrarian profession. Rewrite the passage from an artist's standpoint.

4. Make a commitment to listen to worship music this week during the times you would normally watch television.

5. Choose one thing you can do this week to force you to dwell more on God's truth.

Praise God on High

Someday our pain will be no more
Someday our tears will fade away
Someday we'll see our Lord and Savior face to face

Someday we'll rest from all our burdens
Someday we'll see His smile
Someday He'll look us in the eyes
And say welcome home My child

Praise God on high
All that's wrong will be made right
How we long for the day
Every wounded soul will be made whole
So let's worship Him with a mighty voice
Like we're already with Him in Paradise
Praise God on high
Praise God

Someday we'll walk beside the Father
Someday we'll rest at His feet
Someday our trials will all be over
We'll be completely free

Praise God on high
All that's wrong will be made right
How we long for the day
Every wounded soul will be made whole
So let's worship Him with a mighty voice
Like we're already with Him in Paradise
Praise God on high
Praise God[9]

Rory Noland

O! now, who will behold

The royal captain of this ruin'd band

Walking from watch to watch, from tent to tent,

Let him cry "Praise and glory on his head!"

For forth he goes and visits all his host,

Bids them good-morrow with a modest smile,

And calls them brothers, friends, and countrymen.

Upon his royal face there is no note

How dread an army hath enrounded him;

Nor doth he dedicate one jot of colour

Unto the weary and all-watched night:

But freshly looks and overbears attaint

With cheerful semblance and sweet majesty;

That every wretch, pining and pale before,

Beholding him, plucks comfort from his looks.

A largess universal, like the sun

His liberal eye doth give to every one,

Thawing cold fear. Then mean and gentle all,

Behold, as may unworthiness define,

A little touch of Harry in the night.

William Shakespeare, Henry the Fifth

Eight

Leading Artists

Rick didn't sleep well last night. He tossed and turned most of the night and got only a few hours of sleep. Nights have been like this for Rick ever since he agreed to be the programming director at Christ Community Church about a year ago. At the time it seemed that God was definitely calling him into the ministry, but now Rick isn't so sure. Rick started playing piano at the church about three years ago, when the previous piano player left because he was too burned out. Rick became a mainstay on the music team. He could sing and play well, and he wrote some outstanding new worship choruses for the church. Because Rick was so gifted, he was able to attract some very fine talent to the music ministry. The people at church greatly appreciated Rick and his ministry. In fact, many newcomers admitted that it was the music that had first attracted them to the church. Rick enjoyed his work at the church much more than his job with the computer consulting firm he had started with a friend from high school. Doing music was much more fulfilling than meeting with clients. Eventually the church approached Rick about coming on staff full-time to lead the arts ministries, which meant that he would also be starting a drama ministry. Rick was very excited about the opportunity to combine his musical talent and his love for the arts with ministry and do something meaningful with his life. He prayed about it and said yes, even though it meant a substantial pay cut.

When Rick came on full-time staff, though, he quickly realized that he had been asked to lead an entire ministry, and he wasn't sure he was cut out to be a leader. It was sobering to discover that music ministry in the church was much more than leading worship. There were even non-music-related responsibilities that landed on his plate. There were meetings to attend, people to shepherd, teams to build, services to organize, and new conflicts every week that needed to be resolved. Church was much more fun when Rick wasn't on staff.

After a full year of church music ministry, Rick is feeling inadequate as a leader. He's discouraged that the ministry isn't going ahead the way everybody wanted. He can't seem to keep up with the demands for more programming elements at each service. The drama ministry he's been trying to start hasn't taken off yet. He knows he should be doing more to bring in new musical talent and build the ministry. He knows he should be doing more to shepherd his musicians. He knows he should be constantly finding new music. It's not that he doesn't want to do all these things, but he doesn't have the time to do all these things. And it's not that he hasn't tried, either. He regularly puts in sixty-five hours a week, but that doesn't seem to be enough. So what other conclusion is there except that he's simply not a good leader? He's not cut out for this job. He still enjoys playing the piano at church, but unless something changes drastically, he feels he just can't lead a ministry.

To make matters worse, some problems began to surface between Rick and the senior pastor. They haven't been getting along very well lately, which is a shock to Rick because they got along fine before Rick started working for the church. Rick's been called into the pastor's office several times this past year. Once it was because the music was too loud and "over the edge." Another time it was because Rick dropped the ball on a project the pastor assigned him. On yet another occasion the pastor expressed frustration that Rick hadn't started that new drama ministry yet. On numerous occasions he's questioned whether Rick is a good manager of his time. To Rick, it seems as if he only hears from the pastor when things aren't going well.

What hurts Rick the most, though, is that he doesn't have the time, the energy, or the enthusiasm to put into his music the way he did before. It bothers him that he doesn't have time to write anymore. That really hurts because he loves to write worship choruses. Being creative breathes life into his soul. He loves to write and he loves leading worship, but he doesn't like working for a church. It's not at all what he expected. He fantasizes about quitting and going back into the marketplace. "I'm just not cut out for church work," he tells his wife. "Maybe I should go back to computers and lead worship on a volunteer basis. Volunteering is much more fun than leading."

Questions for Group Discussion

1. Is it true that volunteering is more fun than leading?

2. If you were Rick, what would you do to develop a better working relationship with the senior pastor?

3. What changes do you think Rick needs to make in his job to allow him more time to write?

4. Can someone with an artistic temperament be a good leader? Why or why not?

5. What characterizes a great leader, in your opinion?

6. How can one learn to be a better manager of one's time?

7. How is it possible to meet all the demands and responsibilities of being a leader in the church these days?

8. What do you feel it takes to lead an arts-related ministry (such as the programming, music, drama, visual arts, dance, or production teams) in the church today?

9. What words of advice would you have for someone just starting out in church work?

10. If you're a leader, what do you struggle with most in that role?

The Tension Between Being a Leader and Being an Artist

Being a leader of a ministry and being an artist don't often go well together. In fact, if you ask me, I think they work against each other. The dual role of artist-leader creates constant conflict. Both of these functions are extremely demanding. There are many people who are full-time artists and many who are full-time leaders, so how do you do both and do them well? Also, each job is so different and calls for different skills. Many of us artists are somewhat introverted by nature, but you can't be a good leader and not be with people a lot. Some of us are a little more oriented toward our emotions than toward our intellect, but most of the examples of great leaders seem to be people who are thinkers, not feelers. It seems conventional for artists to be more "right-brained" and leaders to be more "left-brained." To complicate matters, many artists don't really see themselves as leaders. Books and seminars on leadership never address the artist who is also a leader. As a result, we have a leadership crisis in the arts department of a lot of churches these days. There is a lack of leadership because artists who find themselves in positions of leadership are experiencing an identity crisis due to this conflict between being an artist and being a leader.

Most of us aspired to be artists before we ever aspired to be leaders. To be totally honest, I resented being a leader for a long time because I felt it took time and energy away from doing music. I love to write music, but how can anyone find time to write, when being a leader (especially in the church) can be so time consuming? My dream job would be to live in the mountains and write music all day. Living in Chicago and working for a church is a far cry from that. There is this conflict many of us have between the demands of leadership and our love for the arts. In fact, for me the conflict was very serious. I was unhappy trying to do both, because I felt I was doing neither well. I came to resent being a leader and started to wonder if it was time to choose between the ministry and music, because I didn't see how I could continue to do both. I found myself wondering how many more songs I could have written if I weren't so encumbered by leadership responsibilities. After wrestling with this for a long time, I came to the conclusion that I was going to have to choose one or the other. Either I would go back to being a full-time musician, or I would forget about music and throw myself into leading my ministry. Here I was, well into my adult years and still struggling with what I wanted to be when I grew up. I finally said to the Lord, "Father, you're going to have to tell me which one to choose, because it's impossible to do both. I can't be an artist and a leader." I was honestly at the point where I didn't care anymore. I just wanted the Lord to show me what He wanted me to do.

When Our Own Giftedness Gets Lost

Can you relate to any of this? Do you ever feel a tension between the artist in you and the leader in you? Do you ever doubt your calling? Do you ever wonder if you're really in the right place? Or whether you're doing what God really wants you to do? Do you ever feel restless? Do you ever find yourself fantasizing about that dream job?

Some of you are doing a good job leading your ministry, but your own giftedness has become lost in the shuffle. Some of you are very gifted vocalists, instrumentalists, writers, dramatists, and visual artists, but because you're in charge of an active ministry, you don't have time for that anymore. Musicians know that if you want to stay sharp musically, you have to practice. But when you ask most music directors if they themselves ever practice and stay in shape musically, they laugh and say, "Who has the time?"

Some of us don't get to use our artistic gifts anymore. Irenaeus of Lyons, the second-century saint and theologian, said that "the glory of God is the fully alive human being." Some of us are not fully alive anymore because we are stifled artists. By necessity we've become more leader or more administrator than artist. We don't sing anymore. We don't play anymore. We don't write anymore. We don't dance anymore. We don't act anymore. We don't draw or paint anymore. Or if we do these things, we don't do them on a scale anywhere near what we used to. When many of us first became believers, our newfound faith found expression in the arts. For many of us, it was the first link between us and God. But not anymore. We're too busy for that. This is sad, because we really enjoy those kinds of things and we miss doing them. We are "God's workmanship, created in Christ Jesus to do good works, which God prepared in advance for us to do" (Eph. 2:10). Many of us were created to be artists. That's what God put us on the planet to do. If we don't get to be artists, we're not able to do those good works we were destined to do. If we continue to let this go unattended for too long, we will become frustrated artists who have become angry at the church for stifling our giftedness. The other danger is that we will become what Julie Cameron, in her book *The Artist's Way,* calls "shadow artists," people who give wings to everybody else's talent but their own. The end is the same. Our giftedness gets lost. There's this artist inside us that wants to come out but is being suppressed.

Who's Empowering You?

Several years ago when the tension between being an artist and being a leader was at its peak for me, I ran across a verse in Matthew that spoke deeply to my soul. In chapter 10 Jesus is sending the disciples out on their first ministry assignment, and the whole chapter contains His advice to them about how to conduct their ministry. Verse 1 says, "He called his twelve disciples to him and gave them authority to drive out evil spirits and to heal every disease and sickness."

I must admit that when I first read this verse, I was jealous of the disciples. The first thing Jesus did was to give them authority to minister. He empowered them. Can you imagine having Jesus empower you? Can you imagine hearing straight from the Savior what it is He wants you to do? My heart started to beat real fast as I was reading this, because I was longing to feel empowered to do whatever it was God wanted me to do. Would it be possible for God to empower me and give me authority so I could know once and for all what it is He really wanted me to be doing? Could this whole issue of whether I should lead a ministry or be an artist be settled for good? Could I know without any more doubt where God wanted me to be? The answer is yes. If Jesus was so careful to empower the disciples and make their calling clear, certainly He can do the same for you and me.

Being an Artist and a Leader

I spent the next few days praying and journaling. "Lord, please settle this once and for all. What are you giving me the authority to do? What are you empowering me to do? Do you want me to write or do you want me to lead?" I prayed and I prayed and an answer came, but it wasn't the answer I was looking for. I really sensed the Lord saying, "I want you to do both. I want you to write and to lead."

Even though it wasn't what I wanted to hear, it was a powerful moment for me. For the first time I really sensed that I didn't have to choose between being an artist and being a leader. The Lord had called me to do both. He wanted me to be an artist and a leader. The question then became, How do you do both?

This is what I'm still working on, but what I know so far is that the secret to doing both is that we've got to stop seeing ourselves as half artist, half leader. We are full-time artists and full-time leaders. I am convinced that the music director of tomorrow, and all future church leaders in the arts, will need to be fully both. How do you balance the tension between being an artist and being a leader? By throwing yourself into doing both.

Be a Full-Time Artist

First Timothy 4:14 says, "Do not neglect your gift." Don't give up on your art. Don't neglect your talent. Don't worry about whether you're talented enough. That's not the point. Whether your gift attracts large crowds or no crowds at all, it is not to be neglected. Be a full-time artist.

If you play, practice. Keep your chops in shape. Learn those jazz riffs you've always wanted to learn. Pull out some of the music you used to play in college and just play. Go back for a few lessons. Go see your favorite performer. Fall in love with music again. Have fun. Play for your own enjoyment.

If you sing, go back to that regular routine you used to have for warming up and vocalizing. Get your voice back in shape. Get some coaching by taking a few lessons. Go see a concert or an opera or a choral group. Learn a song in a style you've always wanted to sing. Learn a song that you'll never use in church, just for the fun of it.

If you write, write. Jot down every idea in an idea book. Don't evaluate every idea that comes along. Write for the fun of it. Write anything you want, just for the sake of writing. Write short stories. Write songs. Write that novel you've always wanted to write. Follow the muse. If you're a poet, invite a few friends over for an informal reading of your poems.

If you're a dancer, put on some music and dance. It doesn't matter if you're in shape or not. Get in touch again with what it means to dance. Or go see your favorite ballet company the next time they're in town.

If you're in drama, read a good play that you might not consider doing in church. Get some friends together and have a dramatic-reading party. Go see a play or musical.

Remember, you're a full-time leader and a full-time artist. This is not an either/or proposition. By God's grace, be fully alive as an artist.

Be a Full-Time Leader

We desperately need leadership in church programming ministries these days. I see a lot of artists shrink back from leadership because they don't consider themselves to be the leader type. We may not fit the stereotype of the leader who runs a business or heads a company. But God hasn't called us to lead a business. He's called us to lead artists. I've come to the conclusion that the best person to lead artists is someone who's an artist. Some of you are holding back from taking strong leadership because you're waiting for someone else to come along and tell you it's okay. Don't wait for the pastor or someone else you respect to say, "You're good at this. Do it." That would be nice if it happened but it rarely does. Don't wait for someone else to empower you. If you've been called to lead a ministry, Jesus has given you the authority to lead. Stop waiting for someone to validate you. If you wear the title of programming director or music director or drama director, take ownership. If you get paid to lead a ministry, please lead. Take initiative. Lead with boldness, knowing that God has placed you exactly where He wants you to be. He's the one calling you to lead. God has not given us a spirit of timidity, but a spirit of power, love, and discipline (2 Tim. 1:7). We must always reject passivity. You can't be a leader and be passive. Almost every mistake I've made in ministry, almost every bad decision I've ever made, was a result of being passive. We've got to step up and lead.

Why Does It Have to Be So Hard?

One reason I came to the wrong conclusion that I had to choose between being an artist or being a leader is because I was trying to avoid any hardship or difficulty in my life. I wanted life to be easy—no conflicts, please. And when it wasn't easy, I thought, *Certainly God wouldn't want me to do both. It's too hard.*

What is it about me that wants life to be easy? What is it about me that wants ministry to be easy? What is it about me that wants being an artist to be easy? Sometimes when things get difficult, I find myself thinking (actually whining), *Come on, I work hard. Give me a break, Lord. Can't something go smoothly just once?* It's as if deep inside I think I deserve an easy life, but that's just not realistic. Ask Moses if being a leader was ever difficult. Ask Nehemiah if rebuilding Jerusalem's wall was challenging. Ask Job if life ever got hard. Ask Jeremiah if doing God's will always went smoothly. Ask Paul if ministry ever got dangerous. The easy life is simply unrealistic, and it's not the life that Jesus is calling us to live. Why did Paul tell us not to give up (Gal. 6:9) if life was supposed to be easy? Jesus never said it would be easy. In fact, He said it would be hard:

> I am sending you out like sheep among wolves. Therefore be as shrewd as snakes and as innocent as doves. Be on your guard against men; they will hand you over to the local councils and flog you in their synagogues. On my account you will be brought before governors and kings as witnesses to them and to the Gentiles. But when they arrest you, do not worry about what to say or how to say it. At that time you will be given what to say, for it will not be you speaking, but the Spirit of your Father speaking through you. Brother will betray brother to death, and a father his child; children will rebel against their parents and have them put to death. All men will hate you because of me, but he who stands firm to the end will be saved. When you are persecuted in one place, flee to another. I tell you the truth, you will not finish going through the cities of Israel before the Son of Man comes. (Matthew 10:16–23)

Jesus told the disciples that ministry was going to be very rewarding but very difficult. He was brutally honest about the challenges of being in ministry. He warned them to expect conflict so severe that friends and family might turn against them. He warned them to expect opposition so intense that their very lives would be in danger. Let's face it: ministry is tough. We need to go into this thing with our eyes wide open, because ministry is extremely challenging.

Are you like me at all? Is there any part of you that wishes ministry were easy, or at least easier? I wish music ministry weren't so hard. I wish it weren't so hard to find the right music. I wish it weren't so hard to get players and vocalists. I wish it weren't so hard to work with people. I don't care whether you're in a big church or a smaller church; ministry is tough work. It's not a life of ease and comfort, no matter how much we wish it were. It's a life of difficulty, conflict, and hardship. In 2 Corinthians 4:8–10 Paul writes, "We are hard pressed on every side, but not crushed; perplexed, but not in despair; persecuted, but not abandoned; struck down, but not destroyed. We always carry around in our body the death of Jesus, so that the life of Jesus may also be revealed in our body."

Paul endured a lot more hardship in ministry than I'll probably ever see in a lifetime. He encountered physical danger and abuse. He survived attack after attack. His life was continually threatened during his ministry. I've had it easy compared with Paul. I've never been in any physical danger during the course of my ministry, but I can still relate to what Paul is saying. Many times I have struggled with ministry issues and felt greatly stressed and afflicted. At times I have also felt perplexed. There are so many things I don't understand, so many prayers that don't seem to get answered, so many issues I don't know how to solve. The ministry can be very perplexing. I have even felt persecuted. Sometimes because I'm in leadership and represent authority, I can be the object of someone else's resentment or anger. If someone has a problem with the music ministry, he or she usually has a problem with me. It's hard for people to separate the two. Or sometimes I make decisions that not everyone agrees with, and my character and motives come into question. I have also felt struck down, as Paul puts it. I have felt beaten down by people and beaten up by the church. I have come close to quitting. I have had my resignation letter all written. So this passage is not foreign to me. I think it's about time we face the reality that what we are trying to do is hard. It's not easy to build a ministry, and it's extremely difficult to build a fruitful ministry. We have so much going against us. That's why Jesus warned the disciples about the difficulties of ministry. Even He knows how hard it is.

In *Letters to a Young Poet* Rainer Maria Rilke writes, "People have, with the help of so many conventions, resolved everything the easy way, on the easiest side of easy. But it is clear that we must embrace struggle. Every living thing conforms to it. Everything in nature grows and struggles in its own way, establishing its own identity, insisting on it at all cost, against all resistance. We can be sure of very little, but the need to court struggle is surety that will not leave us. It is good to be lonely, for being alone is not easy. The fact that something is difficult must be one more reason to do it."[1]

Shrewd As Serpents

Jesus knows ministry is tough. He doesn't tell us to shut up and stop whining. He has some great advice and some words of encouragement. In Matthew 10:16 He tells us to "be as shrewd as snakes and as innocent as doves." C. S. Lewis puts it this way: "He wants a child's heart, but a grown-up's head."[2]

We need to be shrewd as serpents. In other words, we need to use our heads. If something's wrong in our ministry, we can't be moping around feeling sorry for ourselves or blaming others. We need to take responsibility and fix it. Don't wait for someone else to fix it. If something's not going well, think of a better plan. We can't sit back and complain and do nothing. Ask others for help and advice. Don't be too proud to hear suggestions from others. Scripture says that in an abundance of counselors there is victory (Prov. 24:6). Don't expect problems to go away by themselves. It's okay to problem solve and strategize. It's okay to have a battle plan. That's what it means to be shrewd as a serpent.

The key to reconciling the tension between being an artist and being a leader is shrewdness. One of the things that has helped me keep up with the demands of both has been to build some time into my schedule for creative endeavors. Willow Creek graciously allows me to pull out of meetings once every three weeks and work at home, arranging or writing. To some, that may sound like a radical move, but it has saved my job. For two weeks I'm aggressively involved with my leadership responsibilities—meetings, appointments, rehearsals, and so on. But once every three weeks I'm a musician again and happy as a lark. I'll often work in the middle of the night, driven by the freedom to be creative and enjoying every minute of it. It's especially hard to be artistic and creative in a rigid, nine-to-five environment. If you can build some flexibility into your schedule and free up some time for the artist in you, by all means do it.

Attention All Workaholics

We leaders also need to be shrewd about the pace of life we set for ourselves. When I was starting out in ministry, I read somewhere that the average stay of a music director in a church was two years. The reason was because of burnout. I don't know how true that average still is today, but I do see a lot of leaders in programming burning themselves out. Notice I said burning *themselves* out. They would tell you it was the church's fault, but quite frankly that's not always the case. Yes, church work is very demanding, but too many of us are workaholics to begin with (whether we care to admit it or not).

I have a friend who left a certain ministry because the pace was too hectic. It was unhealthy for him and his marriage. He went to work at another church in a small town, and a few years later he admitted that his workaholic tendencies had followed him to the new church as well. He thought he had rid himself of the problem, but the problem was him. Our lives are supposed to be witnesses for Christ. Our lives should be examples of the abundant life. We are to live them in such a way that they look attractive, even to an unbeliever (Heb. 13:7). The harried life of a workaholic doesn't look inviting to anyone. Who wants to live like that? God never intended for us to burn out in ministry. I can back that claim up from the life of Moses. In Exodus 18 we find Moses working literally day and night (v. 14). His father-in-law, Jethro, says in effect, "Moses, what you're doing is not good. You're going to burn yourself out" (vv. 17–18). Jethro's suggestion was for Moses to delegate more, to spread the work out among more people. That's good advice for us today as well.

Ministry and workaholism is a deadly mix. J. Oswald Sanders tells the story about a Scottish minister named Robert Murray McCheyne who died at the early age of twenty-nine. He neglected his health and completely burned himself out doing ministry. On his deathbed he uttered these words: "The Lord gave me a horse to ride and a message to deliver. Alas, I have killed the horse and I cannot deliver the message."[3]

I have workaholic tendencies. When I was single, I would work twelve-hour days at church every day of the week. Looking back, I would have to admit that too much of my self-esteem was wrapped up in my job. After I got married, I quickly realized I couldn't keep working twelve-hour days and stay happily married. After our children were born, I realized that I didn't want my two sons, whom I love dearly, to grow up hating the church because I wasn't at home enough. I didn't want them to end up hating all that I stand for, so I became accountable to my wife and some friends about my schedule. I drew up a forty-hour workweek and started telling my wife when she and the boys could expect me home. Today I work very hard but don't overwork, and my productivity is higher than when I was putting in seventy hours a week. God's Word says, "In vain you rise early and stay up late" (Ps. 127:2). I love my work and I praise God for giving me something important to do with my life, but being a workaholic doesn't impress or honor Him.

J. Oswald Sanders says that "while a leader is caring for church and mission, he must not neglect the family, which is his primary and personal responsibility."[4] Jesus wants us leaders to be shrewd even about our schedules. He wants us to use our heads. Don't burn out doing church work. That doesn't glorify God. Whether you work for a church or not, if your schedule is out of control, you're jeopardizing your family, your ministry, your witness, your effectiveness, and your longevity.

246 The Heart of the Artist

Innocent As Doves

Jesus also tells us to be innocent as doves. Ministry is tough on its own, but sometimes our own baggage—our dysfunctions, our sins, and our lack of character—create even more conflict. We all bring some baggage to this job, but we can't let it get in the way of our ministry. I know a music director who's carrying around a lot of anger from his childhood, and he can't seem to let go of it. This person is very impatient and snaps back at people a lot. In spite of constant relational conflict, he denies there's a problem and refuses to get help. Do you see any dysfunctions on your part that could hold your ministry back? If so, go for counseling and get them worked out. I know a worship leader who gets defensive whenever anyone brings up anything remotely negative about his playing. Do you have any bad habits that you need to die to? Do you know what your fatal flaws are? Do you know your weaknesses? Don't let them sabotage your ministry.

Encouragement from Jesus

Before the disciples went out on their little mission trip, Jesus encouraged them, and His words are for us too: "Do not be afraid of them. There is nothing concealed that will not be disclosed, or hidden that will not be made known. What I tell you in the dark, speak in the daylight; what is whispered in your ear, proclaim from the roofs. Do not be afraid of those who kill the body but cannot kill the soul. Rather, be afraid of the One who can destroy both soul and body in hell. Are not two sparrows sold for a penny? Yet not one of them will fall to the ground apart from the will of your Father. And even the very hairs of your head are all numbered. So don't be afraid; you are worth more than many sparrows" (Matt. 10:26–31).

First of all, Jesus says, "Do not be afraid" (v. 26). Are you afraid right now? Are you afraid of changes that are happening in your ministry these days? Are you afraid of failing? Are you afraid that you won't be a good leader? Are you afraid that you'll never be fulfilled as an artist in the church? Are you afraid of losing your job? Are you afraid you're not going to make enough to support a family or send your kids to college? God doesn't call us into ministry and then leave us all alone. He is there especially when we're afraid. He will reveal to us what He wants us to do next during those times of crisis.

Secondly, Jesus tells us to stay close to Him: "What I tell you in the dark, speak in the daylight; what is whispered in your ear, proclaim from the roofs" (v. 27). Being a leader doesn't mean that you get to do whatever you want with your ministry. It means you do whatever God wants with *His* ministry. How do you know what He wants unless you spend time with Him? Stay close to Jesus even during adversity so you can hear Him whisper in your ear. If you and I are going to work through the tensions of being an artist and a leader, it won't be by going to conferences. It'll be by listening to the Word of God and applying it to our lives. When I sensed the Lord telling me He wanted me to be an artist and a leader, I must confess I was disappointed because I couldn't see how it could be done. I was out of ideas. That's when I sensed the Lord saying, "Stay close to me. I'll show you how to do it. I'll help you figure this out."

Thirdly, accept the fact that you are precious to the Lord: "Are not two sparrows sold for a penny? Yet not one of them will fall to the ground apart from the will of your Father. And even the very hairs of your head are all numbered. So don't be afraid; you are worth more than many sparrows" (vv. 29–31). My fellow leader, you are precious to the Lord. He knows you intimately, down to the last hair on your head. He knows what you're feeling. He knows your discouragement and when you're tired and weary. He knows the tensions you live with and that ministry is hard. All the work you do for Him does not go unnoticed or unappreciated. Know that God delights in you and is pleased with you.

When Paul tells us leaders to "be steadfast, immovable, always abounding in the work of the Lord, knowing that your toil is not in vain in the Lord" (1 Cor. 15:58 NASB), it's not just a pep talk. It's yet another reminder that God loves us. Do you remember how Paul starts that verse out? He begins with, "Therefore, my *beloved brethren* . . ." He's talking to us. Do you think of yourself as beloved? God does. He loves you more than you'll ever know.

Leadership Styles That Don't Work Well with Artists

Most every book I've read about leadership fails to address the uniqueness of the artistic temperament. If you lead a team of artists, you need to know what does and doesn't work with them. Over the years I've observed some great leaders who worked well with artists and built significant programming ministries. However, I've also seen leaders who didn't know the first thing about working with artists, and they scared the artists off. The responsibility of leadership should never be taken lightly. Leaders need to remember that we will answer to God for how we shepherd the flock He's entrusted to us. Ecclesiastes 8:9 says that whatever hurt leaders heap upon those they lead will eventually return to them, so we would do well to talk about what it takes to lead a team of artists. Let's start by discussing certain leadership styles that don't work well with artists.

The Overly Demanding CEO

These are the type A personalities who are overly demanding, controlling, and insensitive. Their motto is, "It's my way or the highway." They run a tight ship and hold the reigns of authority very tightly. They have an opinion about everything and of course they're always right. They're impatient, aggressive, and very confident. They're rough and gruff with people. They don't like to get bogged down with details such as people's feelings. In fact, they don't care about anybody's feelings as long as the work gets done. People are a means to an end. CEO types are not very encouraging, and they have a hard time empathizing with people's feelings. They love to send memos out and when they do, they feel they're in touch with everybody. They roll their eyes if a sensitive soul ever expresses discouragement, and once a month they remind the troops to keep their nose to the grindstone. They love goals that force people to work harder than they ever have before. They don't listen very well. If you try to talk to them about a problem, they're more interested in presenting their solutions, or "action steps," than in really listening to what you're saying. All of this is fine in the fast-paced world of business, where the CEO has to mobilize an entire corporation toward a financial profit, but this style of leadership doesn't bring out the best in an artist. The CEO type usually thinks the person who leads artists is too soft with volunteers. They don't consider anyone with an artistic temperament to be a bona fide leader, because he or she is one of those artsy types who doesn't really know how to lead.

These leaders insist that everybody who works for them put in seventy hours a week. Or they insist that the drama team or choir double in size by next week. They don't care how you do it or who gets hurt along the way, just get it done.

I had a CEO type tell me once that I needed to be more demonstrative at rehearsals and that if things weren't going right, I should yell and throw something to get everybody's attention. In other words, I needed to throw a fit to get people to follow me. Needless to say, if I treated my musicians that way, people would be running for cover. I once saw on public television a show about Sir George Solti, and I was so impressed by how courteous he was to his musicians. He would stop conducting and say in his rich Hungarian accent, "Violins, would you be so kind as to do it this way," and he would hum a phrase, articulating what he was after. He obviously respected his fellow artists. "Would you be so kind?" is a far cry from throwing a fit. Maybe that's why Solti was one of the best conductors in the world. He was a leader who was also an artist, so he understood artists.

The Overbearing Coach

Overbearing coaches are pushy. They're intense about one thing only, and that's winning. Winning is everything and they want to win at all cost. They're focused on winning and they don't like excuses. They have tunnel vision. Their motto is, "No pain, no gain," so they inflict a lot of pain because it's good for you. They favor the person who's willing to give his or her all, and pretty much ignore everybody else. To these leaders, "giving your all" means living life on the edge, but it's often on the edge of insanity and on the verge of breakdown. If you're not giving 120 percent all the time, you're weak or you're a slacker in their minds. There is no room on their team for anybody who can't pull his or her own weight. They love to "separate the men from the boys." They see the artist as a second-class citizen who's weak and needs to be toughened up. In other words, they have no tolerance for the weak and hurting. You must always appear to be happy and positive when the overbearing coach is around. They're ecstatic if you win but merciless if you lose. They're pretty rigid and adhere to a strict code of discipline. They're fanatical about discipline. It is the key to success and the answer to all of life's problems. If you're having problems in your marriage, your family, or your job, it's because you're not disciplined enough. These leaders love goals that demand an extraordinary amount of commitment. They don't care about the individual; the team is all that counts. They stifle creativity. Being yourself, being who God made you to be, is not a high value for the coach, unless it helps the team win. They have a preconceived idea of what a team member should look like, and try to mold everyone into that ideal.

These are the leaders who bully volunteers and workers into submission. Or the leaders who have no regard for their people's schedules and push them to be involved far above and beyond what is healthy.

The apostle Paul was not pushy; he was passionate. He had a passion for people. He had a passion for the lost. He had a passion for the church. He said, "I face daily the pressure of my concern for all the churches. Who is weak, and I do not feel weak? Who is led into sin, and I do not inwardly burn?" (2 Cor. 11:28–29). Paul also had goals, but his primary goal was "love, which comes from a pure heart and a good conscience and a sincere faith" (1 Tim. 1:5). Paul, with his passion, his intense concern, his love for people, and his goals, was a far cry from the pushy, overbearing coach.

The Overly Protective Patron

These are leaders who coddle artists. They spoil them. They're the extreme opposite of the CEO and the coach. They see artists as so special and unique that they put them on a pedestal and do everything they can to protect them. They see artists as especially fragile and don't want to do anything to upset them. They pamper artists. They willingly walk on eggshells around artists and never say anything negative to them or about them. They champion the cause of the underdog, so they take up the cause of what they see as the neglected and misunderstood artist and make it their own. They see themselves as patrons of the arts rescuing those poor artists who can't help themselves. They're super gentle and always very sweet. They're great listeners and great empathizers. They often have blind spots to the shortcomings of the beleaguered artist they've adopted. In fact, they knowingly overlook blatant character flaws and even sin in the life of the artist. They keep saying, "Judge not," because they just want everybody to get along and love each other. They usually have the gift of mercy but lack discernment. They wouldn't dream of confronting an artist about character issues. In that way they're enablers, allowing, even encouraging, the artist to proceed through life with unhealthy sin patterns or character flaws. They would always put the needs of the individual above the cause of the team, especially if that individual were an artist.

An overly protective patron is the leader who is afraid to confront sin or character flaws in the life of his or her key vocalist. It's the music director who tolerates that obnoxious keyboard player because the director can't imagine the music program without the star musician. It's the drama director who pampers the prima donna because the artist is "so misunderstood."

The Silent Type

These are the leaders who give no feedback and no direction. You never know where you stand with them, and you never know what they're thinking. For some reason they're afraid to encourage artists because they don't want artists to get a big head. Or they assume that artists know they're good, so they don't need any more encouragement. As a result, no one knows where they stand with him or her. No one knows if they're doing a good job. The rub is that when you fail, the silence is broken. They either fire you or tell you what a terrible job you've been doing all along. They prefer working with people who are low maintenance, and you can never get close to them, because you never know how they feel about anything.

I'm talking about the pastor who hires a worship leader but doesn't give the person any feedback. The worship leader thinks he or she is doing an adequate job, until the person is fired two years later and finds out that the pastor had been unhappy with the leader all along. It's the music director who says nothing to his or her musicians about how they're doing. No feedback, no encouragement, no constructive criticism. Our volunteers deserve better than that. They need to know where they stand with us. They shouldn't be kept in suspense about their role or how we feel about them.

The Relationship Between Artist and Leader

At conferences and workshops I always get asked, "What do I do if I work for someone who's exactly like one of those leaders you just described?" What do you do if you work for, or serve under, an overly demanding CEO, an overbearing coach, an overly protective patron, or a silent type? If you serve in a church, your relationship with the ministry leader, the pastor, or whomever you report to is crucial. If you serve under somebody in a difficult situation, your first inclination is going to be to quit and go someplace else. If you end up leaving, make sure you're leaving for the right reasons. Make sure you're leaving because God really wants you to. Don't leave because of a personality conflict. Don't run away from your problems.

The hardest thing to do is to talk to the person with whom you have a conflict. But it's the right thing to do. It's the scriptural thing to do, as outlined in Matthew 18. It may take more than one conversation. That's okay. Progress is made whenever people talk. Some of you have been serving in difficult situations for so long, and you feel used and abused. Isn't it time you spoke up? Isn't it time you went in and gently and humbly talked about what's really going on inside? Don't put it off any longer. For your sake, for the sake of your ministry, and for the sake of all the other artists who come after you, talk about it. For some of you, that could be the most important thing you do this year.

I once talked with a young music director who works for an overbearing coach. This coach is a fine Christian, but he would say some of the most caustic things to this young man, who was feeling very hurt and betrayed. Their communication needed a lot of work because they were on two completely different wavelengths. The coach was also not very encouraging at all, and the young man had no idea whether he was doing a good job or not. The coach knew they had a communication problem. He too was frustrated with their working relationship. His style of leadership worked with everybody else on the team, so he thought the problem had to be with the music director. The music director felt the same way: *Everyone else seems to be okay with this; what's wrong with me?* Well, I have two sons and both of them are unique; sometimes they're exact opposites. They have different temperaments, different needs, different learning styles, and different communication styles. I can't treat them the same. I've found that I have to approach each of my boys differently. I even use different lingo for each of them. If you lead people, you must study them and learn how to deal with them as unique individuals.

Back to my music director friend. He worked up the courage to sit down with the coach, and they had a great conversation. Basically he just told the coach how he felt. There's nothing fancy about that; it just takes guts. The coach learned a lot from my friend that day, and I give this leader a lot of credit for listening and for being open to someone else's feelings. He showed a great deal of character and integrity in the way he responded to my friend. He had never thought that the things he was saying were hurtful, but when he put himself in the shoes of my friend, he realized how they could be taken that way. He also learned that encouragement is extremely important to an artist. He learned a great deal about leading artists because my friend had the courage to lovingly and gently open discussion on the issue. He didn't go in and lash out in anger. In fact, he tried not to be emotional as they talked, so they could stay focused on the issues instead of his feelings. He didn't give ultimatums. He assured his leader he was committed to their ministry. He didn't accuse him of being an overbearing coach and place all the blame on him. He went in very tender and humble, simply talking about how he felt and inviting his leader to speak freely about how he felt. They both handled a difficult situation with integrity.

Nurturing Artists

I long for the day when the greatest art is coming not out of the universities and such but out of the church, when the freshest, most powerful work is coming from Spirit-filled artists who have been

254   The Heart of the Artist

adopted by the local church. Wouldn't it be great if more local churches sponsored art festivals? Wouldn't it be great if more churches encouraged gallery-type showings of new artwork? How about churches having their own songwriters? Or their own composers-in-residence? Or their own dance companies? How about a church that provides regular theater presentations? Or a night of poetry reading by its own writers? Why couldn't the next generation of great filmmakers come out of local churches?

Those of us who dream about a golden era for the arts in the church know that we have a long way to go. In some churches we're working against a narrow-minded view of the arts, in others a strict utilitarian view. As a result, artists have left the church because they felt unaccepted and misunderstood. The local church can and should be a safe place for artists. However, we need to get serious about ministering to them. They will flourish and blossom if we nurture them. They will love the church and give back tenfold if only the church will take them in. If only the church would love and encourage artists, we'd see the arts unleashed in a powerful way.

Paul has a great passage in 1 Thessalonians 2, in which he takes the traditional mother/father roles and shows how they each contribute to a healthy community. Let's use this passage as a springboard for learning what it means to nurture artists.

Be Gentle and Sensitive

"We were gentle among you, like a mother caring for her little children" (v. 7). The first thing to remember about leading artists is to be gentle and sensitive. Gentleness is one of the fruits of the Spirit (Gal. 5:22–23). Jesus said, "Blessed are the gentle, for they shall inherit the earth" (Matt. 5:5 NASB). We need to be sensitive with artists, not because they're fragile but because they're vulnerable. When you're an artist, you constantly put yourself on the line. You're opening yourself up to public opinion every time you perform or create. When people see your work, there's no guarantee they're going to like it. You're out there, fully exposed and vulnerable. So leaders, be gentle with artists. You don't have to pamper them. You don't have to walk on eggshells around them. Just treat them as Jesus would.

How can you be more sensitive if that quality doesn't come easy to you? I have two suggestions. First of all, if you're trying to treat others as Christ would, look at them literally as He does. One time I spent several weeks reading through the Gospels, trying to discover Jesus' secret for dealing with people. There must have been something special about Jesus that made Mary want to sit at His feet, something about Jesus that made the woman at the well forget all about her tragic life and start witnessing to the very people who ostracized her, something about Jesus that made a despised tax collector and a forsaken prostitute follow Him wholeheartedly, something about Jesus that assured Jairus his sick daughter was going to be all right. I think it was the way Jesus looked at people, something about His eyes. He looked at them with love in His eyes.

Proverbs says that "bright eyes gladden the heart" (15:30 NASB). People like to feel special, and they can tell how you feel about them simply by how you look at them—or whether you look at them at all. Proverbs 16:15 says, "When a king's face brightens, it means life; his favor is like a rain cloud in spring." In other words, my fellow leaders, whether you're aware of it or not, how you feel about those you lead registers on your face. They can see it in your eyes. If those under you see your face light up when you see them, they will feel accepted. They will be drawn to you because the look of love and acceptance in your eyes gives them life. Looking at people with a positive countenance, with love in your eyes, is the first step toward becoming a more sensitive person. Try it sometime. Look at your spouse or your kids and try to communicate your love with just your eyes. Try it with the people you work with. Let your face glow with love and acceptance. Try it with the artists you serve with. You'll find yourself listening more intently. You'll find their faces surprisingly receptive. They'll feel that they have your full attention—and they do.

Secondly, learn to be more discerning about when to be tender and when to be firm. It's arrogant to say, "I'm not wired up that way" and not even try to grow in the area of sensitivity. Scripture tells us to be tenderhearted toward each other and to use tender words when the situation calls for it (Prov. 25:11; Col. 3:12–13; Eph. 4:32). First Thessalonians 5:14 (NASB) tells us to "admonish the unruly, encourage the fainthearted." Sometimes I get that turned around. I encourage someone who's being stubborn and unruly, and I'm hard on someone who's weak and fainthearted, someone who needs me to be tender. I've made this mistake with my wife, my kids, and the artists I work with. It's important to know when to be tender and when to be firm. Proverbs 25:11 says, "A word aptly spoken is like apples of gold in settings of silver." It takes discernment and a sensitivity to the Holy Spirit to have the right words at the right time, to know what to say and what not to say, but it's essential if you want to become a more sensitive leader. I find myself praying often, sometimes in the middle of a conversation, *Lord, do you want me to be gentle with this person or firm?*

One of the most common mistakes leaders make toward artists is being insensitive to their feelings. Ridiculing people's feelings or being oblivious to them undermines trust. Proverbs 25:20 likens an insensitive person to somebody who tries to sing happy songs to someone who's down. Instead of saying, "Don't worry, be happy" or "Come on, buck up," try listening. I mean really listening. If you want your artists to trust you, listen to their feelings. Let them share even their negative feelings. Let them talk about their weaknesses. Let them open up about their woundedness. Show them you care. You're not just their friend because of what they can contribute to your ministry. When they know they're accepted for who they are, warts and all, they'll blossom. Their feelings may be far afield from your own. That's okay. Don't be too quick to offer advice or solutions. Just listen. Be quick to hear and slow to speak (James 1:19). If you listen, you validate their feelings and you win their trust.

Love Them

Back to 1 Thessalonians 2: "We loved you so much that we were delighted to share with you not only the gospel of God but our lives as well, because you had become so dear to us" (v. 8). Paul was a leader who not only loved the church but loved the people in the church. They were very dear to him. Do the artists under you know how much you love them? Do they feel accepted by you? Paul says, "Accept one another, then, just as Christ accepted you" (Rom. 15:7

NASB). The best way you can show love to artists is to take an interest in their talents and take an interest in them as people. The best way to show love to creative artists is to ask them what they're currently working on. Ask them to play you that new song they're slaving over. Ask them to read you that new poem they're writing. Ask them to show you the painting they're working on. If you want to create a colony of artists who are alive with enthusiasm, create a safe place for them by loving them and taking a genuine interest in them and in their art. Don't love them just for what they can bring to your ministry. Love them for who they are.

Exhort Them

To exhort means to urge someone (1 Thess. 2:11–12 NASB). We need to urge our artists to achieve all they can for the glory of God, to fulfill their calling, to flourish in their giftedness. Listen to their ideas and their dreams and urge them onward. If you can't use something they do, urge them to do it outside the church, with your full support and blessing. Urge them to live up to their potential as artists and as ambassadors for Christ. See them as diamonds in the rough, and do what you can to help them shine. Cheer them on to new heights. Show them you believe in them, by giving them opportunities in which their gifts can be used by God. When somebody asks me to write something for a particular service, I'm immediately flattered. I think, *Wow, they believe I can do that.* It's great to feel that somebody believes in you as an artist.

Encourage Them

Encouragement is key (1 Thess. 2:11–12 NASB). Encourage your artists verbally. Encourage them in writing. Don't assume they know that something they did was good or exceptional. Even if they do, it's still nice to hear it. Don't withhold good from those to whom it is due (Prov. 3:27). Call your artists and give them feedback regarding their efforts. Let them know how you feel about their work. Don't be afraid that they will get cocky. Don't be silent. You don't have to tell them they're the greatest; just remind them that they're gifted and that God's using them in a mighty way. Artists really respond to encouragement. We appreciate the extra effort anybody makes to express gratitude to us. Encouragement is more than flippantly saying, "Nice job." That feels shallow after a while. To let a vocalist know, for example, that a song he or she sang went below the surface and touched your heart would greatly encourage that person—and to point out which lines of the song were especially meaningful to you would show that you were really listening and that you connected with the artist in a significant way.

Moses was a wise man who knew how to lead artists. In overseeing the building of the tabernacle, he employed a large number of artists. When the work was all done, "Moses inspected the work and saw that they had done it just as the LORD had commanded. So Moses blessed them" (Ex. 39:43). Moses personally examined all the work. He didn't send a memo. He met with the artists and inspected their handiwork. Then he blessed them. He encouraged them. He honored them and celebrated the contribution they had made. Again, encouragement goes a long way with artists.

The way we leaders respond to the failures of our artists will determine how safe our fellowship really is for them. If an artist falls short, be honest about his or her shortcomings, but reaffirm the artist's talent and future. Many artists go through self-doubt when they fail. They start feeling incompetent and wonder if they've lost their giftedness. Be there to tell them that one failure doesn't mean they can never be used again. They need to hear us say, "I still believe in you. You still have what it takes to be a great artist." We need to assure them that one failure doesn't mean the end of their ministry and that God will use them again. Don't be distant. Hearing nothing is far worse than hearing some constructive criticism. Not hearing anything from us just fosters more self-doubt. Remember, artists have good imaginations. If they don't hear anything, they usually start imagining the worst. Oftentimes we don't mean to be distant. We just forget to respond. Other times we're avoiding sharing honest feedback that might be negative. Either way silence is not golden. Be there when they fail, and urge them not to give up. Encourage them to keep trying. Help them to put their failure into perspective.

Implore Them

To implore means to beseech or charge (1 Thess. 2:11 NASB). It entails bringing truth and honesty to a person or situation. Be truthful with artists. We're not so fragile that we can't hear truth. We know the truth when we hear it. Truth is important. If our art is going to impact a world desperately seeking truth, we need to be open to the truth at all times. Being open to constructive criticism is part of the growing process for every artist. If you cultivate a safe place where artists are loved and encouraged, you have earned the right to speak truth. Never hold back your honest opinion about someone's art. Just make sure you speak the truth in love. You don't have to be brutal to be brutally honest. We want the truth. If it's done in a loving way, your honesty will help us to be better artists. It will help us to live up to our potential.

During a critique of one of my songs, a woman from a publishing company gently but firmly said to me, "This lyric line isn't your best. Based on what I've seen you do, I think you can do better." She was paying me a compliment but, at the same time, imploring me to do better. She did it in such a sensitive way that it made me want to come up with a better line just to prove I was as good as she thought I was. She brought out the best in me.

We leaders also need to speak truth about sin and how we should be living our lives as Christian artists. Implore your artists to live lives of godly integrity. Don't gloss over sin. Don't let it slide. Confront sin, with the goal of restoring the wayward artist to a right relationship with God and the church (Gal. 6:1). Confront character flaws and offer help in the form of a small group or one-on-one discipleship. Confront dysfunctional behavior and offer to help the artist find a good Christian counselor.

The Great Paradox of Leadership

We need to be sensitive and loving, and we need to exhort, encourage, and implore. This is what it takes to nurture artists. However, the great paradox about leading artists is that we need to be both giving and demanding.

Jesus modeled servant leadership. He was very giving. We need to serve those we lead. We need to love and cherish artists. We need to shepherd them. First Peter 5:2 says to "be shepherds of God's flock that is under your care." Proverbs 27:23 says to "know the condition of your flocks, give careful attention to your herds." Remember, ministry is people. God invites you and me to invest our lives in people. First Corinthians 3:11–14 encourages us to build our ministries on that which will last. You build a prevailing ministry by building into people. It would be a shame to get to the end of our lives and find that all we had to show for all our hard work was a few worship albums that the choir made, a few drama productions, or a few accolades for something we created. What about the people? Are the artists better off because they served under our leadership? Are they better off spiritually for having joined our teams? Don't just gather artists together and fail to build into them.

How do you invest in people? You build into them on a personal level. You spend time with them. You get to know them. You have lunch with them. You set up personal appointments. You get out of your office and hang out together. You call them on the phone and see how they're doing. You schedule artist retreats. You have relationships with the people in your ministry. This can be done one-on-one or in small groups. It takes a lot of commitment to be involved in any ministry, a lot of rehearsal and preparation time. People are not going to commit to something over the long haul unless they feel cared for.

This concept of investing your life in people is so close to my heart because I don't view my ministry at Willow Creek as being only to the congregation. My ministry is to the musicians on our team. My job is to try to meet their needs. Isn't that part of what we're supposed to be doing as a church—caring for people and trying to meet their needs? I have a burden for artists. I long to see them growing in Christ and becoming all they can be for Him. As a result, an important part of my job is to set artists up for meaningful ministry opportunities. I will contend till the day I die that there is no greater thrill in life than to be used of God. If you find something better, let me know. I just haven't found anything more fulfilling than the thrill of knowing that God has used me and my humble talents to impact another life.

I just love it when a vocalist gets off the stage and says, "Wow. I really sensed God using me during that song. I saw a man with tears streaming down his face as I sang about God's love." When God uses you, it is a very exhilarating and rewarding experience. We can experience that and provide meaningful ministry experiences for those under our leadership. In fact, that's one of the best things that church involvement has to offer. Getting a record deal and touring from city to city might look glamorous, but it has its disadvantages too. For one thing, it's hard to raise a family that way. And popping into town, doing a concert, and then leaving doesn't allow you to see what happened afterward to those you ministered to. On the other hand, when you minister to the same group of people week in and week out (such as your local church body), you see lives change over time. You know you're making a difference. And it's easier on your family as well.

The value of servanthood has now come full circle for me in a wonderful way. My fourteen-year-old son helps run sound and lighting for one of our grade school programs at church, called Promiseland. A few months ago we were driving home after the service, and I asked him how Promiseland went. After describing the whole program, from setup to teardown, he said, "It went well. I really feel God used me this weekend." For a young man his age to know the joy of being used of God is more than I could ask for.

We need to be giving but we also need to be demanding. Because artists tend to be more sensitive, we sometimes fail to be firm when we need to demand the best from those we lead. We want people to like us, so we don't ask too much of them. We don't like conflict, so we don't ruffle any feathers. That's weak leadership. It doesn't serve the artists or the church well at all. Besides, leadership is not a popularity contest. Most artists like to be in situations and rehearsals in which their best is demanded. Many of us have sat under the direction of dynamic drama directors, motivating music directors, or other inspiring leaders. They demanded that we live up to our potential. They were demanding because they were loving and they had our best interest at heart. We were flattered because they set the bar high and told us they believed in us. And we felt a tremendous sense of accomplishment for having achieved more than we thought we could. Likewise, it's okay for us to demand the best of artists, especially if it's in the context of a safe place where they know they're loved and cherished. We need to demand that our artists be the best they can be, not for our glory or theirs but for the glory of God. We need to demand that our artists give us their best whenever they perform or create. This is also what it means to pursue excellence, which is so sorely needed today in the church.

The secret to leading artists is to be giving and demanding. That's the sign of a good leader. It's a paradox. You can't have one without the other. If you're only giving and not the least bit demanding, you won't achieve excellence, because you're not inviting artists to do the very best they can, to the glory of God. You're not giving them a reason to feel good afterward about what they've done. If you're demanding but not the least bit loving, those wounded artists will quickly run away and look for a safe place elsewhere.

A True Leader of Artists

We have a deep sense of community among the artists at Willow Creek, and it's due to the leadership of our programming director, Nancy Beach. Nancy is a very gifted leader and has a deep passion for the arts. She's been a good friend for many years. One of the many things I've learned from Nancy is the value of celebration. She's our biggest cheerleader. When we do something well, she's right there, encouraging and thanking us individually or as a team. Sometimes it's a personal word. Sometimes it's a note or a phone call. Her enthusiasm and joy are contagious. More than once I've heard her shout for joy during a rehearsal when something worked well onstage. And she's great at throwing celebration parties. She knows how to honor artists and their work, and she does it in a way that gives God all the glory.

Another thing I've learned from Nancy is the value of a team. She is the consummate team builder. I have been on numerous retreats in which Nancy has led us in the most intriguing team-building exercises designed to deepen our friendships. She also comes up with great encouragement exercises that give each of us an opportunity to feel valued. The reason we in the programming department work so well together is because of the effort Nancy has put into building community among us artists. She's also taken us on memorable trips to stretch us artistically. My favorite was when the programming team (which was much smaller at the time) was riding in the church van, thinking we were going someplace nearby for a retreat, and Nancy turned off at the exit for O'Hare airport, pulled out a set of Mickey Mouse hats, and told us we were going to Disney World. We were stunned. But we had a great time in a setting that was rich in creativity. She's also taken us to New York for a weekend to see some Broadway shows and to stretch us artistically. Nancy knows how to encourage artists, and she knows how to build community among artists. She is a true leader of artists.

Follow-Up Questions for Group Discussion

1. Can you remember your favorite choir director or drama director, or some leader who inspired you to go further with your talent? What was it about this leader that inspired you so much?

2. What do you think is the most important ingredient needed to be a good leader of artists?

3. What ideas can you suggest to someone who's trying to balance the demands of being a leader and an artist?

4. What advice would you give to a leader who works sixty hours or more a week?

5. How can a leader help those they lead be the best artists they can be?

6. What can a leader do to help the artists they lead grow spiritually?

7. Can you think of any more leadership styles that don't work well with artists?

8. Which of the five keys for nurturing artists (being sensitive, loving them, exhorting them, encouraging them, imploring them)

do you respond to most favorably when you're under someone's leadership?

9. If you're a leader, what would you like to say at this time to
those you lead?

10. If you're under someone's leadership, is there anything you'd
like to say to your leader?

Personal Action Steps

1. If you're experiencing any tension between being an artist and
being a leader, find someone you can talk to about it.

2. Identify the areas of your life in which you need to assume
more leadership.

3. If you're a leader, try to rearrange your schedule so you can
spend more time with the artists you lead. (Why not start by
setting up some lunch appointments this week?)

4. Of the five keys for nurturing artists (being sensitive, loving
them, exhorting them, encouraging them, imploring them),
choose the one you need to focus on most this next year.

5. If you feel that you do not have a healthy relationship with your
leader, determine what you can do to improve that relationship.

Ever Devoted

I'm so tired of chasing worthless things
Seems they never satisfy
So disappointed, groping for more
I'm left more empty than before

I'm crying out to be more intimate
To walk more deeply with my Lord
Whatever's standing in the way
Isn't worth it anymore

There's no other way
I want to live my life
Than to live it
Devoted to the Lord
To belong to Him
Faithful to the end
Ever devoted
Devoted to the Lord

I'm through demanding all my problems be solved
Insist God meet my every need
I've got to die to my selfish ways
Lay myself down at His feet

There's no other way
I want to live my life
Than to live it
Devoted to the Lord
To belong to Him
Faithful to the end
Ever devoted
Devoted to the Lord[5]

Rory Noland

Ha, tempter! Methinks thou art too late! . . .
Thy power is not what it was! With God's help,
I shall escape thee now!

Nathaniel Hawthorne, The Scarlet Letter

Nine

The Artist and Sin

*B*rad was the most talented and successful worship leader that Oakville Community Church had ever had. In the five years Brad had been there, he took the music program from practically nothing to one of the biggest in the area. In fact, Oakville became known more for its music than anything else. The musicians there had a high degree of professionalism. Oakville's worship services were rich and meaningful, and its musicians recorded two CDs that were widely circulated across the country. Oakville's Christmas and Easter services were major events in the community, and Brad was sought after as a popular speaker for worship seminars and church music conferences. He was a great worship leader and a dynamic visionary; he was a real go-getter. He also had a winsome personality, and the people at Oakville just loved him. In five short years he had attained success, status, and popularity.

Just when Brad was at the apex of his ministry career, his entire world came crashing down around him when the news broke that he was having an affair with one of the women in his ministry. It had started out very innocently. Veronica was an excellent singer, and she and Brad started spending a lot of time together rehearsing. They soon realized there was a spark there and started to fan the flames of a passionate relationship. Veronica had never met anyone as encouraging and sensitive as Brad. She felt she had finally found a real soul mate. Her husband wasn't very supportive of her as a person or as a singer, and she began to look for, and even create, opportunities to spend time with Brad. A very similar thing was happening on Brad's side of the equation. His marriage had been slowly deteriorating as he threw himself into his job and his wife threw herself into raising three toddlers. After meeting Veronica, Brad felt that she was everything he had ever wanted, and was convinced that he had married the wrong person. His relationship with Veronica was so much easier than his relationship with his wife. They got along so much better, he thought.

Brad was starting to daydream and fantasize about Veronica a lot and couldn't wait to see her at rehearsal. They often rehearsed alone—just the two of them. When their rehearsals spilled over into the noon hour, it gave them a handy excuse to have lunch together. And Brad began working late at the office, rehearsing with Veronica. He knew the relationship was wrong. He would tell himself it had to end, but when he was with her, the physical and emotional attraction was so strong that he couldn't bring himself to end it. He knew he was jeopardizing his marriage and his career, but he was getting things from Veronica that he wasn't getting at home. A fellow staff member confronted Brad about how much time he was spending with Veronica, but Brad got defensive and denied anything was going on. Covering up the affair was exhausting, but it was the only way to keep seeing Veronica and still keep his job. Veronica also knew deep inside that this relationship was not right, but the pull was too strong for her too. She knew she was putting her own marriage at risk, but only if people found out. She and Brad talked about moving away together and starting over with a clean slate.

This went on for months. Their relationship got more and more involved. Finally Brad's wife, and subsequently Veronica's husband, found out. The whole church found out, too. Brad confessed to the affair in front of the whole church. He was humiliated and broken. He admitted the deception. He even confessed to a few other dark areas of his life, such as his addiction to pornography. That caught everybody by surprise.

The kids in the youth choir took it the hardest. Many of them felt angry, betrayed, and disillusioned. It was all shocking, ugly, tragic, and so very sad. Brad was asked to resign his position immediately and was advised to seek counseling. The church split into factions, and people argued over how the whole thing was handled. Some even left the church as a result. There were those who blamed the church because they felt Brad was overworked, so the church, in their minds, was the cause of the affair. Some thought Brad should be retained and that the church should love him back into fellowship. Others thought he should be banned from ministry forever. Still others resented Veronica and thought she should have been asked to leave instead of Brad. It was all very sticky.

Brad's wife divorced him and won custody of the children. He lost his job, his ministry, his wife, his family, and his reputation. He moved away, was never heard from again, and never saw Veronica again. And he never again worked in church music ministry. Veronica and her husband also divorced. She tried to stay at the church, but the shame she felt made it extremely uncomfortable for her to be there. It was hard to face people at church, and it was especially hard to see Brad's wife and kids. She thought of running away with Brad. She almost did, but their relationship had started to turn sour after everything hit the fan. Anger and resentment had begun to take its toll on their relationship as well. That spark that had once been between Brad and Veronica had turned into a devastating fire that engulfed and ravaged their lives. Neither was ever the same again.

Questions for Group Discussion

1. What bad decisions did Brad make that contributed to his fall?

2. What bad decisions did Veronica make?

3. Besides their bad decisions, what else contributed to this affair?

4. Brad bought into several lies about sin. What were some of those lies?

5. In what ways was Veronica deceived about her sin?

6. What were the consequences of this affair?

7. How could the affair have been avoided?

8. Would you feel comfortable confronting someone if you saw him or her involved with sin? Why or why not?

9. Do you agree with how the church handled this situation? If not, how should the church have handled it?

10. How prevalent do you think the problem of pornography is today among Christian men?

The Artist's Susceptibility to Sin

Chances are pretty high that this scenario about Brad and Veronica sounds familiar to you. You may have heard of, witnessed, or even been a party to a sad story like this one. Why does this sort of thing happen as often as it does? What causes a fall like this? How do you know that what happened to Brad and Veronica won't happen to you?

I believe that those of us with artistic temperaments are more susceptible to sin than are any other group of people. It seems as though sin is always crouching at our door (Gen. 4:7). The gifts and talents of the artistic temperament often put us in the thick of God's activities. Many of us are on the front lines, very much like the musicians who led the nation of Israel into battle. That makes us targets of attack from the Evil One. Like Brad in our opening scenario, many of us have up-front visibility because we're in a position of leadership and/or we perform onstage in front of a lot of people. Satan targets anyone who has a public witness for Christ. He's going to do everything he can to bring us down, because he knows that a fall like Brad's can damage the cause of Christ. (Just think of all those disillusioned young people from Brad's youth choir.) Like Brad, many of us spend a great deal of time rehearsing and performing with members of the opposite sex. And Satan tries to use that opportunity to break up our marriages. Remember, Satan always prowls about like a roaring lion, looking to devour any artists he can (1 Peter 5:8).

The artistic temperament makes us easy victims for "the cravings of sinful man, the lust of his eyes and the boasting of what he has and does" (1 John 2:16). Many of us are in touch with our feelings. When lustful desires are combined with highly charged emotions, it's like putting gasoline on a fire. Many of us are also very aware of our senses. We like to be stimulated, especially visually, which opens us up to all sorts of sinful desires. We are passionate people who need to make sure that our passions don't get out of control. Because we're often in the spotlight, we end up dealing with all sorts of pride and arrogance issues.

We can also be very self-centered, even preoccupied with ourselves, resulting in selfish motives. Our being sensitive causes us to be hurt more easily and more often. I think this is why so many artists carry around a great deal of anger, bitterness, and resentment. As we've discussed earlier, our introspection also tends to make us more negative and critical.

We also have vivid imaginations. It's the nature of creativity to let your mind drift and be free, but a renegade imagination can also lead to sin. Most of us would be embarrassed if people saw our thoughts flashed on a movie screen. Jesus made a connection between our thoughts and our behavior (Matt. 5:27–28). You can't have an X-rated fantasy life and G-rated behavior. Even if we never do a fraction of the things we fantasize about, we still do damage to our souls by entertaining ungodly thoughts.

I don't know the reason for this, it's just an observation, but I've seen people with artistic temperaments struggle more with obsessive, compulsive, escapist, and addictive tendencies. Many are escaping to alcohol to avoid dealing with the pain in their lives, and there is among our ranks a growing number of men becoming addicted to pornography. They refuse to get help because they don't want to tarnish their image or because they think they can handle it on their own. So they hypocritically try to lead a double life—being a devout Christian in public but living with guilt and shame in private.

So there you have it. We are people who are more susceptible to lust of the flesh, lust of the eyes, pride, arrogance, selfish motives, anger, bitterness, resentment, a negative and critical spirit, impure thoughts, compulsive and addictive behavior, and hypocrisy and duplicity. Taking everything into account, it's not a great recipe for godly living! Those of us with artistic temperaments have an uphill battle when it comes to living holy lives.

The Seriousness of Sin

Let me affirm right at the top here that we need to take sin seriously. It's what separates us from God. It's why Jesus came to die on the cross. It's why our world is in such a mess. It's why there's a heaven and a hell. We cannot be cavalier about sin. There are no special exemptions just because you're an artist. Second Timothy 2:21 says that if we cleanse ourselves from sin, we will be a "an instrument for noble purposes, made holy, useful to the Master and prepared to do any good work." You can't make allowances for sin in your life and expect God to use you to your fullest. Make no mistake about it. Sin grieves the Holy Spirit and quenches the power of God in our lives. The Lord longs to be gracious to us (Isa. 30:18). Why would we want to jeopardize his fullest blessings on our lives with willful disobedience?

We deceive ourselves if we think we can live in sin and get by on talent alone. It's a deadly deception because at first it seems true. You can go far on talent alone. I've known a few artists who were living a double life and using their talents with seeming success—that is, until their secret life caught up to them. So you can go far, but you can't go long. Eventually your sin will find you out (Num. 32:23). Besides, it is much more fulfilling to have God work through you than around you. In your life right now, is there any sin that could keep God from using you to your fullest?

When we take sin lightly, we also underestimate the value of a clear conscience (1 Tim. 1:5, 19; 3:9). Having a clear conscience doesn't mean that we're perfect. It means that we know we're doing everything we can to intentionally obey Christ. The person who has a clear conscience is free from guilt and shame; he or she is quick to repent when convicted of sin. In your life right now, is there any sin that is keeping you from having a clear conscience?

Obviously the stakes are high if you have an up-front, highly visible ministry, as many artists do. Paul tried to avoid sin "so that our ministry will not be discredited" (2 Cor. 6:3). There is a lot of responsibility associated with being a public person. One of those responsibilities is dealing with the sin in your life. If you don't tend to this area, you could end up like Brad and Veronica and lose everything you have. Because we live in a society that has lost its moral compass, we've abandoned our sense of right and wrong. I've run across a number of Christian couples, for example, who try to justify living together outside of marriage. Let's state clearly that it is wrong for you to be living with your boyfriend or girlfriend. It is wrong to flirt with immorality. It is also wrong to gossip and slander. It is wrong to pamper your pride with arrogant thoughts and behavior. No matter how talented you are, you are not above God's laws, and you need to take responsibility for sin in your life. If you don't, it bears repeating—your sin will find you out and so will everyone else.

I realize that I'm talking to people who have strong perfectionistic tendencies, so let me say that I'm not talking about being perfect. I'm not talking about good works as your ticket to heaven or as the assurance that you'll be a successful artist. I'm talking about obedience as a response to what Christ did for you and me on the cross. I'm talking about living with every intention of obeying God. When your intention is complete obedience to the Word of God, you don't want to willfully disobey.

I shared that once with someone in my ministry, and he was incredulous. "You really don't expect everyone in our ministry to stop sinning, do you?" he asked.

"Well, I'd like to think that we're winning a majority of our spiritual battles," I replied, "and choosing a life of obedience because we are dead to sin and alive to Christ."

He shook his head in disbelief and said, "That's supposed to be enough to get me not to sin? Do I just brainwash myself into thinking I'm dead to sin? I sure don't feel very dead to sin."

"No, you don't have to brainwash yourself," I assured him, "because it's true. You've just chosen to believe otherwise, and what you believe determines how you live." I happened to know that this man was fighting a losing battle with a certain sin in his life. He had done what many Christians do, and that's give up. Hiding behind the claim that no one's perfect, he had lost all hope of getting his sinful appetite under control. To him, it was perfectly normal for Christians to have at least one area of willful disobedience in their lives. Sometimes it just can't be helped, he reasoned. He had tried but had given up. He knew in his mind that Christ's death on the cross freed him from the power of sin, but he hadn't experienced this power in his life.

It is true that no one's perfect—no one's "arrived"—but this should not be our rationale for excusing willful disobedience in our lives. "No one who is born of God will continue to sin" (1 John 3:9). Every act of willful disobedience is an attempt to meet our needs apart from God and distracts us from experiencing greater intimacy with Him. Now, I understand that we are all in different places in our spiritual journey, but when it comes to sin, we must never give up the fight. If we continue to grow in Christ, sin will continue to lose its appeal. My fellow artists, let's not tolerate this notion that it's okay to willfully disobey God in one or two areas of our lives. Fellowship with a holy God is impossible without obedience to His Word. Fruitfulness in ministry is impossible without complete submission to God's will. Having a strong moral fiber is a sign of character.

A Word to Those Battling Addictions

I know that in our fallen world addictions abound. Our dear brothers and sisters who are suffering with an addiction often feel helpless and ashamed. Yet Jesus died to free them too. We don't have to live in bondage to sin. Paul said that "sin shall not be your master" (Rom. 6:14; 1 Cor. 6:12). You can, with God's help, be delivered. Our "God is to us a God of deliverances" (Ps. 68:20 NASB). The road to recovery is not easy. Any addiction is easy to get into but difficult to get out of. Recovery begins by admitting you have a problem and then doing something about it. Remember, it is your responsibility to get help. Don't wait until you take a fall to finally seek help. If you're involved right now in some secret sin or addiction that's holding you in bondage, please see a Christian therapist, counselor, or pastor. Cornelius Plantinga Jr. writes, "An addict stands a chance of recovery only if he is finally willing to tell himself the truth. The only way out of the addict's plight is *through* it. He has to face it, deal with it, confess it. With the firm and caring support of people important to him, he has to rip his way through all the tissues of denial and self-deception that have 'protected his supply.' The addict has to take a hard step, the first of the famous twelve steps. Paradoxically, he must help himself by admitting that he is helpless. He must perform the courageous, difficult, and highly responsible act of acknowledging the hopelessness and wholesale unmanageability of his life" (italics in original).[1]

Accountable Relationships

In my experience in working with artists, I would say that we are consistently weak in two areas: setting up accountable relationships and doing spiritual battle. The most important thing we can do in addressing the sin in our lives is to be accountable to someone. James 5:16 says, "Confess your sins to each other and pray for each other so that you may be healed." Confessing sin is a good way to help us avoid it in the future. Knowing we'll have to confess a sinful act later makes us less apt to engage in it now. Whether you're accountable to one person or a group of people, accountability is an absolute must.

This is difficult for those of us with artistic temperaments. Because many of us are more introverted, we tend to shy away from relationships. We think we can handle life on our own, but that is such a lie. When we underestimate our need for accountable relationships, we give Satan an open invitation to knock us off. Some of us who are more introverted tend to be more private about our thoughts, and when we sin, we withdraw. Instead of confessing our sin to one another with vulnerable transparency, we hide it from others. It's a huge risk to expose our dark side to another person. There are huge trust issues here. We think, *What if people find out I'm struggling in this area? What would they think of me? What if they get to know the real me and don't like me anymore?* As difficult as it is, as risky as it is, the alternative is worse. I've seen artists fall simply because they were unwilling to establish or follow through with accountability. When I've talked with those who have had to step down from ministry due to sin, they're always deeply sorry that they didn't call out to someone sooner for help and support. It's ironic that they were so afraid to be transparent, because when they fell, their sins were made public and they were ashamed and embarrassed. They were too proud, too afraid, too stubborn, and they paid a high price. Paul tells us to make whatever changes we need to make to avoid being disqualified from ministry (1 Cor. 9:27). High on that list of changes is our need for accountability.

I can speak from firsthand experience about the value of accountable relationships. I honestly don't know if I would still be in ministry if I didn't have people with whom I could share my struggles. The Bible says that "as iron sharpens iron, so one man sharpens another" (Prov. 27:17). That's the beauty of accountable relationships. We can help each other and keep each other sharp. As a young Christian, I can remember being accountable to a small group of friends about having regular quiet times. Playing off the idea that a quiet time provided food for the soul, we developed a little code: "What did you have for breakfast?" meant "Did you have your quiet time this morning?" That's how we greeted each other every day in the hallway at school. I became very serious about having my quiet times, because I knew I was going to run into somebody that day who was going to ask me about it. As a young man, I was also accountable to a group of guys who wanted to help each other deal with lust. Every men's group I've been in has had to deal with this issue in some way. We were brutally honest with each other, called each other when we needed help, and prayed regularly for each other. Part of what kept me from doing something stupid was knowing that I had guys in my life who were going to ask me, "How are you doing with lust this week?"

To this day I still have people in my life for accountability because the potential to fall lies in all of us and I don't want to fall. Don't be deceived and think you can make it on your own. "If you think you are standing firm, be careful that you don't fall!" (1 Cor. 10:12). Christians stronger than you and me have fallen simply because they thought they were above the need for accountability. Don't let this happen to you. Find someone or a group of people to whom you can be accountable.

I've also seen accountability abused. All involved in an accountability group must agree that whatever is shared stays within the group. It's highly inappropriate for anyone to take something said in confidence to someone outside the group. When trust is violated in this way, it is hard—and sometimes impossible—to build it back up again. If something is said in private, keep it private. Accountability also doesn't work if you're not serious about it. Find someone who won't be soft on you. You need friends who care enough to be in your face about your fatal flaws and relentless about checking in. I've also seen artists enter into accountable relationships without really being committed to truth telling. They share just enough to give the illusion that they're being vulnerable, but they withhold important details about themselves. Those details often involve some sin they're struggling with. Whether they're avoiding the truth or just downright lying, the result is still deception. Proverbs 28:13 says that "he who conceals his sins does not prosper, but whoever confesses and renounces them finds mercy." Let's not hide our sins from those to whom we're accountable. Let's be open and honest. All the artists that I've ever seen take a fall and disqualify themselves from ministry either refused to cultivate accountable relationships or abused them.

Learn How to Do Spiritual Battle

Another area that artists are weak in is doing spiritual battle, fighting off the temptations that come into our minds. Whenever we face temptation, there is a spiritual battle that's waged in our minds. You would think that people like us, with all our creativity, would be able to do spiritual battle, but for all the reasons I've already stated, we seem to be losing the battle for the artistic mind. Paul tells us that renewing our minds will transform our lives (Rom. 12:2). If you want to live a holy life, it starts with your mind. If you want to change bad habits, begin changing how you think. If you want to overcome temptation or break free from the bondage of sin, you've got to start with your thought patterns.

Ephesians 6:12 says that "our struggle is not against flesh and blood, but against the rulers, against the authorities, against the powers of this dark world and against the spiritual forces of evil in the heavenly realms." The word *struggle* is significant. The King James Version uses the word *wrestle*. Both words underscore the need for us to be proactive when it comes to sin. We need to resist temptation instead of letting ourselves be pulled along by it. Doing spiritual battle is serious business. It's warfare! We are instructed to wear armor (Eph. 6:11, 13). We are told to gird our minds for action (1 Peter 1:13 NASB). Yet many of us go through our day completely oblivious to, or unprepared for, the spiritual battles ahead of us. James 4:7 tells us, "Resist the devil, and he will flee from you," but how many of us really do that? How many of us know *how* to resist Satan? Many of us struggle with the sins that easily entangle us (Heb. 12:1). These are the sins that we find difficult to shake, the ones we keep asking forgiveness for over and over again. The good news is that the weapons of our warfare are powerful enough to destroy such strongholds (2 Cor. 10:4), but we have to know how to use them. We have to know how to do spiritual battle, and then do it.

Many of us artists don't know how to stand up to the evil thoughts that pop into our minds. My wife and I have a car with a stick shift, and it drives her crazy when I'm thinking about something other than driving and forget to shift. The car's working hard but going nowhere because it's stuck in a lower gear. A person who doesn't know how to do spiritual battle will eventually fall into sin or stay stuck spiritually in a lower gear.

Another reason for our lack of ability in doing spiritual battle is that we just don't want to. We've grown accustomed to those sins that so easily entangle. Instead of fleeing or abstaining, we enjoy seeing how close we can get to sin without really doing it. So we fantasize about "how to gratify the desires of the sinful nature" (Rom. 13:14). We window-shop when it comes to evil; we enjoy thinking about it, meanwhile forgetting that Jesus made a connection between our thought life and our behavior (Matt. 5:21–32).

For a large part of my life, I've been plagued with a thought life that would have enabled me to compete with Paul for the title Chief of Sinners (1 Tim. 1:16). I didn't do most of the things I thought about, but I knew I had a thought life that didn't please God. For a while I wrote it off as the inevitable consequence of the fertile imagination that comes with being an artist. My delusion was such that I feared that cleaning up my thought life would make me less creative. I was afraid that if I submitted my thought life to Jesus Christ, I would start thinking rigidly instead of freely; I would lose my edge creatively. What a lie. I found the opposite to be true, because God wants to expand our creativity, not confine it. He's the Chief Creator. Doing life His way always brings more freedom, more power, more creativity.

Jesus in Spiritual Battle

Let's look at how Jesus did spiritual battle (fig. 1). The text is from Matthew 4:1–11. Notice first that Satan tried to appeal to Jesus' physical needs. Jesus had been fasting for forty days and forty nights, and He was hungry. Satan said, in effect, "Come on, Jesus. You've been working so hard. You deserve a break today. Turn these stones into bread." Satan will always try to get us to meet our needs apart from God. Jesus didn't entertain the notion Satan put into His head, as we sometimes do. He didn't fantasize about eating a full-course meal at Satan's table. Jesus quickly answered by quoting Scripture.

Satan knows Scripture, too, and he twisted it around to tempt Jesus a second time. He took Jesus to the pinnacle of the temple and told Him to throw Himself down. This would have created a huge spectacle, with a host of angels coming to Jesus' rescue. Talk about making an entrance! What a spectacular scene that would have made. Satan wanted Jesus to use His supernatural power for personal gain. That's the same temptation artists face—using our talents and abilities to glorify ourselves. This temptation is aimed at our human tendency to be self-centered and self-glorifying. Jesus again didn't even give it a second thought but instead responded to Satan's lies with the truth of Scripture.

Satan didn't give up. His next temptation appeals to our human tendency to desire fame, fortune, and power. He took Jesus to the top of a mountain, showed Him the kingdoms of the world, and said, "I will give You all this if You worship me." He offered Jesus what he tries to offer us artists: fame and fortune if we compromise our beliefs, our morals, our convictions. Jesus said, "Be gone, Satan" and renounced the sin of idolatry by once more quoting Scripture.

Notice three things about how Jesus handled these temptations: (1) He countered quickly, (2) He countered with truth, and (3) He renounced sin.

FIG. 1
Jesus Doing Spiritual Battle
Matthew 4:1–11

Counter Quickly

Jesus opposed Satan's attack immediately; He didn't let Himself fantasize about the thoughts Satan put in His mind. This is where we often go wrong. As I've stated earlier, we artists have very fertile imaginations, and we have no business entertaining some of the ungodly thoughts that come our way. Sin starts in the mind. We can't be passive about this. We shouldn't let sinful thoughts linger in our minds. We are instructed to "resist the devil" (James 4:7). That's not always easy for us. We live in a culture in which we're encouraged to indulge instead of resist. C. S. Lewis points out that even the arts are caught up in this mind-set: "In the first place our warped natures, the Devils who tempt us, and all the contemporary propaganda for lust, combine to make us feel that the desires we are resisting are so 'natural,' so 'healthy,' and so reasonable, that it is almost perverse and abnormal to resist them. Poster after poster, film after film, novel after novel, associate the idea of sexual indulgence with the ideas of health, normality, youth, frankness, and good humour. Now this association is a lie."[2]

Paul instructs us to "take captive every thought to make it obedient to Christ" (2 Cor. 10:5). This means that every bad attitude, every ungodly motive, and every negative thought that isn't from God needs to be taken captive to the obedience of Christ. This verse has become very dear to me, and this concept has revolutionized my life more than I can probably put into words. When a sinful thought tries to settle in my mind, the Holy Spirit often reminds me of this verse. And I'll find myself praying, *Lord, I want to take every thought captive to the obedience of Christ, so instead of entertaining this thought of* (whatever the sin is), *I bring it to you.* Writing in the seventeenth century, the Puritan author William Gurnall gives us this time-proven advice: "Christian, this is imperative for you to realize: When wicked or unclean thoughts first force their way into your mind, you have not yet sinned. This is the work of the Devil. But if you so much as offer them a chair and begin polite conversation with them, you have become his accomplice. In only a short time you will give these thoughts sanctuary in your heart. Your resolve—not to yield to a temptation you are already entertaining—is no match for Satan and the longings of the flesh."[3]

Counter with Truth

Jesus resisted the attacks of the Evil One with truth—more specifically, biblical truth. The psalmist says, "I have hidden your word in my heart that I might not sin against you" (Psalm 119:11). Don't ever underestimate the power of God's Word to correct sinful behavior. For example, Psalm 84:11 says, "No good thing does He withhold from those who walk uprightly" (NASB). On numerous occasions when a sinful thought invaded my mind, I'd remember that verse. It prevented me from doing something I would have later regretted because I don't want to miss out on any of God's blessings to "those who walk uprightly."

When Satan puts a tempting thought into our minds, we've got to counter it quickly with something powerful. Our counterattack may be something we say out loud or to ourselves, or it might take the form of a prayer. It doesn't always have to be Scripture, but it has to be truth based on God's Word. In *The Pursuit of Holiness* Jerry Bridges writes, "If we truly desire to live in the realm of the Spirit we must continually feed our minds with his truth. It is hypocritical to pray for victory over our sins yet be careless in our intake of the Word of God."[4]

This is one of the reasons why I'm a firm believer in Scripture memory, because it's such an effective way to store God's Word in our hearts and minds so we can draw on it quickly when facing temptation. I've memorized some verses that I pray or say to myself when I'm being tempted, and it's helped me a great deal.

Renounce Sin

Enticing as they were, Jesus rejected Satan's offers as sin. Because we're contending with our old nature, sin can sometimes look so good to us. There are also some ungodly thoughts that have become so ingrained in us that we don't question whether they're right or wrong anymore. That's why we need to renounce sin whenever the Holy Spirit brings it to light. Renouncing sin simply means that we forsake it. We say either out loud or silently, to God and to ourselves, that the sin we're contemplating is wrong. We distance ourselves from it. We remind ourselves how harmful, how awful, it really is. We remind ourselves that no matter how tempting it is, sin jeopardizes our ministry, our relationships with others, and our relationship with God. Sin never satisfies. It always leaves us empty and destitute. The more you tell yourself that something is not good for you, the more your whole body will believe it, and it eventually will lose its grip on you. Satan tries to make bad things look good to us and good things look bad to us. He is the father of lies (John 8:44), so when we renounce sin, we strike a major blow in his continuing efforts to deceive us.

The early Christians had a good understanding of the importance of renouncing sin: "In an ancient Christian baptismal liturgy, the candidate is asked, 'Do you renounce Satan and all the spiritual forces of wickedness that rebel against God? Do you renounce the evil powers of this world that corrupt and destroy the creatures of God? Do you renounce all sinful desires that draw you from the love of God?' The proper response to each question is a resounding 'I renounce them!'"[5]

Adam and Eve

Now let's look at how Satan tempted Adam and Eve (fig. 2). This time the text is from Genesis 3:1–6. The first thing Satan said to Eve was, in effect, "You poor woman. God said you couldn't eat from any of these fine-looking trees here in the garden." That, of course, was a lie. God didn't say to stay away from all the trees, just one. Satan often tries to get us to focus our attention on what we don't have as opposed to all we do have.

In her response Eve minimized the importance of the tree, much the same way we minimize sin, making it sound as if it's no big deal. Instead of referring to it as the Tree of Knowledge of Good and Evil, she said something like, "Yeah, God said to stay away from some tree out there in the middle of the garden or we'll die."

"You're not gonna die!" Satan assured her. "That God of yours is a killjoy! He's withholding wonderful things from you because he doesn't want you to be like him. Go ahead. Nothing bad will

FIG. 2

Satan Tempting Eve

Genesis 3:1–7

happen." That's just like Satan, isn't it? He tries to distort our concept of who God is. He will always try to get us thinking that God
doesn't really love us or care about us. He will tell us God is being
unfair. He also wants us to think that our sin is no big deal, that it
certainly is not going to hurt anything.

Adam, by the way, didn't fare any better than his wife. The Bible
records no running dialogue with Satan on his part. It appears
Adam didn't put up much of a fight at all. He gave in willingly and
impulsively. So how would you evaluate how well Adam and Eve
handled the temptation? First of all, did they counter quickly? Eve
did at first, but it was downhill from there. They were not persistent
in countering with truth, and they never reached a point where
they renounced sin and said, "No, this is wrong!"

Application to Real-Life Situations

Before we come down too hard on Adam and Eve, let's put ourselves
in some common situations we face and see how we do. Figure 3
deals with some of the thoughts leading to the sin of bitterness.
Notice that the right side is blank. No comebacks. No responses.
No standing up to temptation. Unfortunately that's the way it is for
too many of us when ungodly thoughts pop into our minds. This is
why I feel so urgent about this. Like Adam, we don't put up any fight.
We're not taking every thought captive to the obedience of Christ.

Take some time right now to fill in the right side of figure 3,
keeping in mind the need to counter quickly, counter with truth,
and renounce sin. You can do this as a group, with some artist friends,
or by yourself. Then do the same for figure 4, which deals with lust;
figure 5, which deals with envy; and figure 6, which deals with something sadly common among male artists these days: pornography. I
took a stab at filling in the blanks in figures 7–10 at the end of the
chapter, but remember, there is no set way of responding. Everyone
will have a different approach from one situation to another. The
important thing is to counter quickly, counter with truth, and
renounce sin.

FIG. 3

Doing Spiritual Battle Against Bitterness

FIG. 4
Doing Spiritual Battle Against Lust

FIG. 5

Doing Spiritual Battle Against Envy

FIG. 6

Doing Spiritual Battle Against Pornography

What Happens If I Fail?

I fail every day, and I take comfort in knowing that if I confess my sins, God is faithful and righteous to not only forgive my sins but cleanse me from all unrighteousness (1 John 1:9). When we fail, we must not run away from God, thinking He doesn't want us or love us anymore. We must run into His loving arms. Julian of Norwich said, "Our courteous Lord does not want his servants to despair because they fall often and grievously; for our falling does not hinder him in loving us."[6]

I often see artists get very emotional when confronted with their sinfulness. However, we need to beware of emotionalism without true repentance. There's nothing wrong with emotion. James says that we have every reason to mourn and to weep when it comes to our sin (James 4:9). When Isaiah came face to face with a holy God and acknowledged his sinfulness, he exclaimed, "Woe to me! ... I am ruined!" (Isa. 6:5). However, emotionalism without genuine repentance defies the seriousness of our sin. We need to do more than just skim the surface with our emotions; we need to let the seriousness of our willful disobedience sink deeply into our souls. I've seen artists show more emotion over being caught in sin than over the fact that they had offended a holy God. It's the difference between feeling embarrassed about a sin and being truly repentant. True repentance involves more than just feeling bad. It involves sincere remorse for having grieved the Holy Spirit. It involves taking responsibility for sin and renouncing it. Saying over and over again, "Oh, God. I'm sorry. I'm sorry. I'm sorry. I promise I'll never do it again" is from the shallow end of the pool compared with David's prayer after the Bathsheba affair. Listen to a few excerpts.

> Have mercy on me, O God,
>   according to your unfailing love;
> according to your great compassion
>   blot out my transgressions.
> Wash away all my iniquity
>   and cleanse me from my sin.
>
> For I know my transgressions,
>   and my sin is always before me.

Against you, you only, have I sinned
    and done what is evil in your sight,
so that you are proved right when you speak
    and justified when you judge.
. . . .
Create in me a pure heart, O God,
    and renew a steadfast spirit within me.
Do not cast me from your presence
    or take your Holy Spirit from me.
Restore to me the joy of your salvation
    and grant me a willing spirit, to sustain me.
. . . .
The sacrifices of God are a broken spirit;
    a broken and contrite heart,
    O God, you will not despise.

(Psalm 51:1–4, 10–12, 17 NIV)

That's genuine repentance. It's not mere emotion without substance. You can sense David's remorse. You can feel his brokenness and shame. Notice that David acknowledges his sin and renounces it. He puts himself back into submission to the Lord. It's obvious that his emotion is sincere, and it's coupled with true repentance. Paul also shows us that true repentance can be an emotional experience but also involves being earnest to change our ways and get right with God.

> Now I am happy, not because you were made sorry, but because your sorrow led you to repentance. For you became sorrowful as God intended and so were not harmed in any way by us. Godly sorrow brings repentance that leads to salvation and leaves no regret, but worldly sorrow brings death. See what this godly sorrow has produced in you: what earnestness, what eagerness to clear yourselves, what indignation, what alarm, what longing, what concern, what readiness to see justice done. (2 Corinthians 7:9–11)

Repentance is a change of heart that with God's help produces a change in our behavior. Sometimes restitution is involved. We need to make it up to the people we've offended. That's what happened to Zaccheus, the tax collector. He repented and wanted to pay back those he had cheated: "Zacchaeus stood up and said to the Lord, 'Look, Lord! Here and now I give half of my possessions to the poor, and if I have cheated anybody out of anything, I will pay back four times the amount'" (Luke 19:8).

I hope and pray that you never fall in such a way that you have to step down from ministry. I've seen that happen too often, and each time it's gut-wrenching for me to watch fellow artists disqualify themselves from ministry because of some sin that had too strong a hold on them. If you ever do fall, I would strongly recommend that you submit yourself to the restoration process. Be committed to it, no matter how hard it gets. The church should take disciplinary action with the goal in mind of restoring the individual to a right relationship with God, restoring the person to fellowship, and hopefully restoring him or her to ministry. However, the responsibility for restoration falls squarely on the shoulders of the one who fell. So follow through on your responsibility to get yourself right with God. I've seen artists restored to fellowship and ministry who had fallen to drugs, homosexual behavior, and adultery. Each time it was a lot of work and a long process, but each time it was extremely moving to celebrate the restoration of a fallen brother or sister.

Obedience

I've heard people who minister among athletes say that athletes are a lot more spiritual when they are injured. They fervently attend Bible studies and prayer groups because their injury has put their career in jeopardy and they're in crisis mode. While they worry and fret over whether they can come back or whether their career is over, everything suddenly takes on spiritual overtones. Then when their injury heals and they go back to playing, they pretty much forget all about God. They put their talent ahead of God. God was a means to an end. Now, of course, that's a generalization, but before we come down hard on athletes, we artists need to face the fact that we can be just as guilty of using God to advance our talent instead of obeying His commandments because we love Him.

Why Do You Obey Christ?

I'd like to zero in on a question facing all Christians in the creative and performing arts. The question is this: Why do you live a godly life? In other words, Why do you obey Christ? What motivates you to obey? Why are you "good"? Now I want to ask you another question: Why do you *really* live a godly life? It's not a trick question. What's the real reason?

When I pressed myself to be totally honest about why I obey Christ, I found out that my motives were often self-serving. I realized there are parts of me that obey because I want God to help me write a hit song. I'm not saying that it's wrong to obey because we want God's fullest blessings on our lives. However, some of us artists treat obedience as a means to an end. We obey because we don't want to lose the lucky rabbit's foot that God has become to help us make it as artists. When this happens, everything revolves around us and our talent instead of around the Lord. As a result, our obedience is strong when we feel we're close to our goal but wavers if the goal appears out of reach.

To complicate things even more, there is a kind of mystery going on behind the scenes when God uses us. After a service or performance, people might come up to us and say, "I felt the Spirit moving very strongly this morning when you were onstage," and we may not have felt the Spirit moving at all. Then there are times when we go to great lengths to be centered and focused on the Spirit, and we don't get any comments to verify that God even showed up. So why should we obey Christ if it doesn't "work"? If you're a writer, you know all too well how mysterious this thing called inspiration really is. When you write a successful story, poem, or song that God uses, you always try to go back and re-create the inspiration that led up to that. I imagine visual artists go through the same thing. You analyze your state of mind, your emotional and physical condition, and even what you ate for dinner the night before, with the hope of re-creating the conditions that led you to create successfully. Then if the magic doesn't return, you say, "It worked before, God. I did everything the same way. Why didn't it work this time?" We want our obedience to pay dividends according to our terms, and when it doesn't, we lose our motivation to obey. In fact, if the truth were known, some of us want God to bless our singing careers more than we want Him to bless those to whom we're singing. We say we want God to bless our drama ministry, but what we really mean is for God to give us the lead in the next big presentation.

Again, I'm not trying to challenge the notion that we need to abide in Christ if we minister in His name, because we most certainly do. And of course if God is going to use us to our fullest, we need to live lives of obedience and trust. I'm simply asking, What's driving our obedience? In John 14:21 Jesus says, "Whoever has my commands and obeys them, he is the one who loves me." For too long I read that verse and thought, *I gotta obey more.* But the verse is really saying that Jesus is inviting me to love Him more and to let my obedience flow out of that love. There's a relationship between how much we love Jesus and how willing we are to obey. When we have a sin problem, we have a love problem. Jesus makes that very clear when He says, "If you love me, you will obey what I command" (John 14:15). Now let me go back to my original question: Why do you obey God? Is it because you love Jesus or because you love using the gifts and talents He gave you? If you weren't able to serve God with your gifts and talents, would you still obey Him? Would you continue to have devotions and obey Christ if you couldn't write, create, or perform? Do you love performing, writing, or creating for Christ more than you love Christ? These questions are at the heart of what motivates artists to live a godly life.

Enjoying the Gifts More Than the Giver

I love to write music. I'll often write music that I know we won't use at church because I enjoy the creative process and I feel most alive when I'm writing. If I didn't do what I do professionally, I'd probably write music as a hobby. However, there have been times when I have wondered, *Do I love writing music more than I love Jesus?*

There was a period during my ministry at Willow Creek when over the course of two years I didn't write a single song. The reason was mainly because of time. My job responsibilities were getting out of hand and I had so little time to write. It wasn't that I wasn't getting any ideas. I had song ideas, just no time to develop them. As a result, I had a lot of "half-baked" songs. I felt like an injured athlete looking on from the sidelines as others played the game I love to play. It was a very difficult time for me. I wondered if I would ever write again. I struggled in my relationship with God, and I must admit that there were times when the day-to-day challenges to live a life of obedience to Christ were met with, "Why, what's the use?" Then one night something touched me deeply during a worship time at church, and I wept as I drove home. I realized that I had been taking for granted what Jesus did for me on the cross. I told the Lord that if I never wrote again, that would be difficult, but I'd be okay because I would always have Him. That was not an easy thing for me to say, but I had been through a desert experience artistically. Not being able to write for two years had boiled life down to the basics. I came to the point where I was so hungry for God that I finally understood what the psalmist was feeling when he wrote, "As the deer pants for streams of water, so my soul pants for you, O God" (42:1). Things that I thought I couldn't live without (such as music) paled in comparison with knowing Christ. Paul says, "I consider everything a loss compared to the surpassing greatness of knowing Christ Jesus my Lord, for whose sake I have lost all things. I consider them rubbish, that I may gain Christ" (Phil. 3:8). I felt as if I were truly laying my talent on the altar, and I told the Lord that if He would allow me to write again, I would never again take Him for granted.

You see, I thought I loved Jesus more than I loved music, but I really didn't. My passion for my work was greater than my passion for God. In fact, music was distracting me from being fully devoted to Christ (1 Cor. 7:35). My obedience to the Lord was more motivated out of a love for music than out of a sincere love for Jesus. Is it okay to love music? Is it okay to love what you do in the arts? Of course it is. God made us to be artists and gave us the arts to enjoy. However, if I were completely honest, the payoff to me for living the Christian life was a secure job, a chance to write music, and a certain amount of notoriety among my peers. Ah, "the good life." But God is calling us to live the abundant life, not "the good life." The abundant life is a life of sacrifice, self-denial, and commitment to the lordship of Jesus Christ. Life becomes abundant when we abide. I loved the blessings of God more than I loved God. To be honest, music was more important to me than my relationship with Christ.

This is a common trap that befalls many an artist. It can be easy for us to enjoy the gifts more than the Giver. Some people even approach art with a kind of romanticism that can make art itself seem like a religion. When that happens, the arts become the overriding "spiritual experience" of our lives and take the place of a vital, dynamic relationship with the Lord Jesus Christ. We're in trouble when that happens. Art must never take the place of God in our lives. That's the kind of idolatry Paul describes: "Although they knew God, they neither glorified him as God nor gave thanks to him, but their thinking became futile and their foolish hearts were darkened. Although they claimed to be wise, they became fools and exchanged the glory of the immortal God for images made to look like mortal man. . . . They exchanged the truth of God for a lie, and worshiped and served created things rather than the Creator" (Rom. 1:21–23, 25).

The Bigger Payoff

I've heard a lot of sermons on the benefits of godliness. These benefits far outweigh the alternatives. But do you know what the real payoff for obedience is? It's found in the second half of John 14:21: "Whoever has my commands and obeys them, he is the one who loves me. He who loves me will be loved by my Father, and I too will love him and show myself to him."

The real payoff for being obedient is that God will reveal Himself to us. "Blessed are the pure in heart, for they will see God" (Matt. 5:8). When we obey, God reveals more of Himself to us. Why would you want to trade that kind of intimacy with God for the passing pleasures of sin?

What does it mean to experience more of God? That's not very tangible, is it? Does it mean God feels closer? Does it mean I sense

Him moving more in my life? Does it mean something undeniably supernatural? Do I hear voices? Do I see signs? This all seems pretty vague and nebulous because it's describing life in the spiritual realm. Someday that spiritual realm will be more real to us than the temporal world we can see, hear, taste, touch, and smell (1 Cor. 13:12). For now we walk in faith, which is "being sure of what we hope for and certain of what we do not see" (Heb. 11:1). Experiencing as much of God's presence as we can this side of heaven is the reward of those who obey His Word.

This leads us to another set of disturbing questions: Is intimacy with God something I really want? Do I truly want more of Him in my life? Or would I really prefer success and fulfillment as an artist? These are good questions for us to be asking ourselves consistently, because they get at the heart of why we do what we do.

Jesus tells us to love Him with all our heart, soul, and mind (Matt. 22:37). He says it is the greatest commandment (v. 38). If we don't love Jesus, everything else is out of place. All our priorities, our motivations, even our good deeds will be wrong. If your love for Jesus doesn't feel as deep as the love that He described, the good news is that you can ask God to deepen your love for Him. Jesus prayed that the love God has for Him would also be in us (John 17:26), so every day for two years I prayed that same prayer. It was another one of my daily dangerous prayers, which I talked about earlier. I asked God to deepen my love for Jesus. I asked Him to help me to love Jesus more, to love what Jesus loves and hate what Jesus hates, to love others as Jesus loves others. I asked God to let my obedience flow out of my love for Jesus, just as John 14:21 says: "Whoever has my commands and obeys them, he is the one who loves me."

Grace-Driven Obedience

It was at this point that I discovered grace-driven obedience. There is a moral power behind salvation, and I'm a little embarrassed that it took me so long to really understand it, but when I finally got it, it was as if this huge light went on inside my head. This passage in Titus came alive to me like never before: "The grace of God that brings salvation has appeared to all men. It teaches us to say 'No' to ungodliness and worldly passions, and to live self-controlled, upright and godly lives in this present age, while we wait for the blessed hope—the glorious appearing of our great God and Savior, Jesus Christ, who gave himself for us to redeem us from all wickedness and to purify for himself a people that are his very own, eager to do what is good" (Titus 2:11–14).

At salvation God begins a remarkable work of transforming us into the image of Christ. He invites us to live a godly life. He redeems us from all wickedness and purifies our hearts. He gives us the power over sin, the freedom not to sin. We don't have to sin. We're free from sin (Rom. 6:7). Even though our natural desires cause us to struggle against temptation, we're still dead to sin (Rom. 6:11). Dallas Willard explains it this way:

> To be dead to sin with Christ is not to be lacking in these natural desires, but to have a real alternative to sin and the world's sin system as the orientation and motivation for our natural impulses. In our new life, we are capable of standing *beyond* sin's reach as we choose what we will do and in that sense we are unattached from it, we are dead to it. It *is* still possible in the abstract for us to sin, but we see it as the uninteresting or disgusting thing it is.... People without the new life have no choice. But we have a new force within us that gives us choice. In this sense we are free *from* sin even if not yet free *of* it. Doing what is good and right becomes increasingly easy, sweet, and sensible to us as grace grows in us (italics in original).[7]

Sometimes we forget that and give in to our old nature. Whenever we give in to the old nature, we're trying to keep a dead man or woman alive. God has fulfilled His end of the bargain. Jesus paid the penalty for our sins. Now it is our responsibility to cooperate with the Spirit's work in our lives. "Live by the Spirit, and you will not gratify the desires of the sinful nature" (Gal. 5:16). That means I must submit to the lordship of Jesus Christ and yield to the Spirit's direction of my life. Sometimes when a temptation comes along, I'll remind myself that I am dead to that sin. I don't have to let that lust, that evil desire, that sinful thought, or that negative feeling rule over me. That's in the past. That's the old me. The new me has come (2 Cor. 5:17).

I've found that the closer I draw to Christ, the more I want to obey Him. Yielding to Christ, while not always easy, becomes easier when I'm in fellowship with Him. I don't focus on obedience; I focus on being intimate with Christ. When we do that, our obedience begins to flow willingly out of our love for Christ. It's a process; it doesn't happen overnight and we will still struggle. There will be many testings along the way. We will stumble and fall and get back up, but over time sin will begin to lose much of its appeal. I've discovered that the closer I get to Jesus, the less attractive sin is. Sin just doesn't look as good to me as it used to. That's not to say that I am without sin, because I'm not. I'm just trying to be intentional about presenting the members of my body to God as instruments of righteousness, presenting myself as someone who is dead to sin and alive to Christ (Rom. 6:13). Even those nagging, entangling sins have started to lose their luster in light of His love. They're just passing pleasures that can't compare with knowing Christ (Heb. 11:25). And do you know what? I can't take any credit for that. It was God who was at work in me "to will and to act according to his good purpose" (Phil. 2:13). I know full well that God is the one who has given me not only the desire but the power to do His will. That's grace-driven obedience. Praise God!

I hope you will join me in praying that God will deepen our love for Jesus, that we would be artists who hunger for God and His righteousness. Don't let your obedience stem from obligation. Let it flow naturally and bountifully out of your love for Jesus. Let it grow out of your intimacy with Him. Let your holiness be rooted in your relationship with Him. Don't use your gifts out of any motivation other than that you love the One who gave you the gifts. God wants to use us to impact the world for Him. Just think what God could do with a team of artists who loved Him wholeheartedly. If we truly loved Jesus with all our heart, soul, and mind, I firmly believe we could change the world!

Follow-Up Questions for Group Discussion

1. Do you agree that people with artistic temperaments are more susceptible to sin? Why or why not?

2. Have you ever had accountable relationships in your life? Do you presently have accountability in your life?

3. If you've had accountability in your life, was it a good experience for you? Why or why not?

4. What would you expect from an accountable relationship? What kind of person would you feel comfortable being with in an accountable relationship?

5. Do you think most artists deal adequately with temptation? Why or why not?

6. How can memorizing Scripture help in the battle with temptation?

7. How can you tell when repentance is genuine?

8. Have you ever seen a church leader fall into sin? How did the church handle it? Do you agree with how the church handled it?

9. What causes an artist to love the gifts more than the Giver?

10. If something happened (such as a career-ending injury) and you couldn't function as an artist anymore, how else could you serve God?

Personal Action Steps

1. Determine what areas Satan would concentrate on and attack if he were to try to get you to fall. In other words, identify the temptations to which you are most vulnerable.

2. If you don't have an accountable relationship with anyone right now, find someone with whom you could initiate such

a relationship. Set up a meeting with that person and ask him or her to hold you accountable regarding the areas of potential sin identified in step 1.

3. If you do have an accountable relationship with someone right now, evaluate how it's going. Determine whether the two of you are being completely honest with each other about your struggles. Decide whether the two of you are being too soft on each other and not asking probing or difficult questions. Ask yourself personally whether you are hiding from your partner any sin that you need to confess and for which you need prayer support.

4. Choose an area of temptation that you often struggle with. Fill out figure 11, putting on the left some of the thoughts that pop into your mind that you know are not from God, and on the right some responses based on truth. Feel free to photocopy figure 11 and do this exercise with different sets of responses and with other areas of struggle. Remember to counter quickly, counter with truth, and renounce sin.

5. Memorize at least three Scripture passages to help you deal with the temptations you face most often.

FIG. 7

Possible Responses to Bitterness

FIG. 8
Possible Responses to Lust

FIG. 9
Possible Responses to Envy

FIG. 10
Possible Responses to Pornography

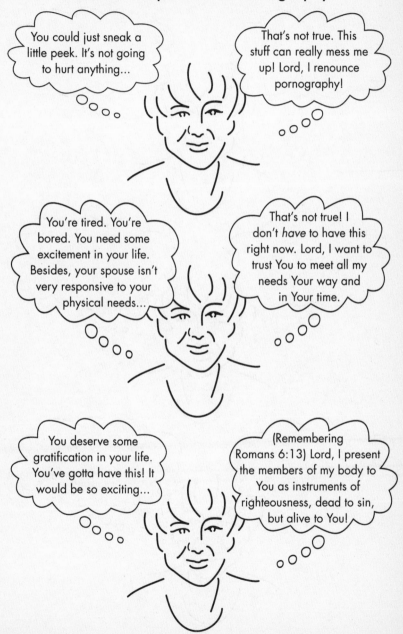

FIG. 11
Fill in the Blanks

Behind Every Fantasy

Fooled again. What I thought was paradise
Turned out to be nothing more than lies
I've learned my lesson, now I read between the lines
'Cause the truth is sometimes hard to find

Behind every fantasy
Is a harsh reality
And what looks good to me
May not always be the best for me
If I'm tempted to go along
With what I know is wrong
Help me see the reality
Behind every fantasy

Peace of mind for tomorrow and today
All depends on the choices that we make
All that glitters is not always gold
And what's hidden eventually gets told

Behind every fantasy
Is a harsh reality
And what looks good to me
May not always be the best for me
If I'm tempted to go along
With what I know is wrong
Help me see the reality
Behind every fantasy[8]

Rory Noland

Lord, not you,
it is I who am absent.
At first
belief was a joy I kept in secret,
stealing alone
into sacred places;
a quick glance, and away—and back,
circling.
I have long since uttered your name
but now
I elude your presence.
I stop to think about you, and my mind
at once
like a minnow darts away,
darts
into the shadows, into gleams that fret
unceasing over
the river's purling and passing.
Not for one second
will my self hold still, but wanders
anywhere,
everywhere it can turn. Not you,
it is I am absent.
You are the stream, the fish, the light,
the pulsing shadow,
you the unchanging presence, in whom all
moves and changes. How can I focus my flickering,
perceive
at the fountain's heart
the sapphire I know is there?[1]

Denise Levertov, "Flickering Mind"

Ten

The Spiritual Disciplines of the Artist

Darlene is an internationally acclaimed poet and is recognized as one of the leading writers of American contemporary poetry today. She rose to fame overnight with a collection of poems titled *Death and Life in the Garden*. The poems became very popular among poetry lovers as well as some who didn't love poetry. It's been almost five years since *Death and Life* hit the *New York Times* best-seller list, and since then Darlene has been on the fast track, reaping the fruits of her success. The lecture circuit, book deals, job offers, command performances for the president, and even television appearances have kept her extremely busy these last several years. This is what she's always dreamed about since she seriously started writing poetry in high school.

Tonight, though, as Darlene drives back to her hotel room after speaking at another literary convention, she's about as low as she's ever been in her life. She knows something's not right with her. Feelings of anxiety and emptiness have been gnawing at her for some time now. She felt a tinge of anger when a reporter from a local university newspaper asked, "What have you written since *Death and Life*?" It was an innocent question, and she's been asked that before, but this time the question irritated her. She responded by mumbling something about being busy with another collection of poems to be released next year. That's a half-truth—or a half-lie, depending on how you look at it. She has a book deadline that's been moved to next year after having been moved five previous times. The truth is, she hasn't even started that book. The reporter was taken aback by Darlene's abruptness and didn't venture any more questions.

Darlene has been telling herself for a while now that she doesn't have time to write anymore, but as she drags her tired body back to the hotel this cold winter evening, she knows it's not true. She's written bits and pieces on planes and in hotel restaurants, but she knows it's not her best writing. No, it isn't for lack of time that she's not turning out work of the same caliber as *Death and Life*. What's missing is a "soulish lifestyle," and deep inside she knows that. You see, Darlene is a committed Christian who used to spend a lot of quality time with the Lord.

Even though *Death and Life* is not a religious work, it has spiritual overtones. And Darlene knows that it grew out of her times of solitude with her Lord and Savior. She knows full well that her quiet times, as she calls them, enabled her to listen to God and hear the deeper truths of His Word. During those times of solitude she heard the plight of her fellow human beings and was able to write poignantly and powerfully about it. Her quiet times were a safe place for her where she could experience God and feel deeply. Her quiet times would call her to live life below the surface and to be centered on God's Word and His presence in her life. That's the kind of life she was living before she encountered success. That's the richness from which she used to write.

Darlene has no more quiet time in her life these days. She misses being on her knees as the early morning sunrise beams warmly across her face. She misses that old rocking chair by the fireplace, where she would read her Bible and discover passage after passage that came alive to her as if God were there, speaking directly to her. She used to journal about what God was doing in her life and sometimes would lose track of time and write for hours on end. She felt excited about the Lord back then and sensed His presence so much more easily.

She fights back tears as she sits in her hotel room. She's not sure how she ended up so far from God. It certainly wasn't intentional. At first she was so busy, she never gave her need for God a second thought. Because God seemed to be blessing her, it never crossed her mind that He might be missing her and yearning to spend time with her. She felt bad about not spending time with the Lord but didn't feel an urgency to do anything about it. After all, everything in her life appeared to be going so well. On some days she would rationalize by saying to herself that people couldn't tell if she hadn't had her quiet time that morning, but they would surely know if she was late for a speaking engagement. Now she feels guilty about neglecting her quiet time but doesn't know how to get back to the way her relationship with God used to be. Life is so much more complicated now than it was then. There are so many demands and expectations.

Darlene is suddenly startled by the telephone. She pulls herself together and picks up the phone. On the other end is a radio talk show host. Darlene quickly realizes she had forgotten that she had agreed to do a live interview after her speech this evening. She's on the air live over a Christian radio network. Though she's tired, Darlene manages to catch her second wind, do the interview, and even take a few calls from listeners. Off the air the DJ thanks her for her time, expresses admiration for her work, and closes by saying, "Darlene, you are an inspiration to all of us. Whenever I read *Death and Life,* I feel as if I'm reading the journal of someone who walks close to God. I wish I were more like you."

At this moment Darlene feels like the biggest hypocrite. She hangs up the phone and cries herself to sleep.

Questions for Group Discussion

1. What were some of the benefits Darlene experienced when she spent time with the Lord?

2. If Darlene's quiet times meant so much to her, why weren't they part of her regular routine anymore?

3. The opening scenario implies that Darlene equated her success with God's blanket approval of everything she did. Do you see any danger in this type of thinking?

4. Do you agree with Darlene that people couldn't tell whether she was having regular quiet times or not?

5. What percentage of Christians would you guess have a regular quiet time?

6. What, in your opinion, keeps Christians from regularly spending time with the Lord?

7. Why does the issue of spiritual disciplines produce so much guilt among today's Christians?

8. Isn't going to church every week enough for Christians to get by?

9. Do you think it's important for artists to have a regular quiet time? Why or why not?

10. Are there any other spiritual disciplines that you feel are important for artists to consider?

Are We Really That Undisciplined?

I had an interesting discussion once with a professional counselor who pointed out that his experience with people with artistic temperaments was that they were highly undisciplined. He referred to us as free spirits who are usually messy, highly unorganized, always late for appointments, and irresponsible with personal finances. Is that true? Do you think artists are undisciplined people?

I'm not sure I agree. I mean, think about it. What does it take to become an accomplished artist? It takes hard work. It takes practice. It takes—you guessed it—discipline. Think about all the rehearsing and training that goes into being an artist. A recent study of musicians resulted in the calculation that "up to the age of 21, a talented pupil will have spent about 10,000 hours in purposeful practice."[2] There's no denying the fact that being an artist calls for an unusual amount of discipline. Why do some parents insist that their kids take piano lessons? For the discipline. There's a lot of mind-over-matter that goes into being an artist. We didn't get to where we are today without investing large amounts of time and effort.

The concept of discipline is much maligned in our world of fast food, instant access, and immediate gratification. The misconception surrounding discipline is that it's a lot of work for nothing and is never any fun. But I think we in the arts know better, don't we? Who understands the value of discipline more than an artist? For us, it's just common sense. If you want to become an accomplished artist, you have to have a fair amount of discipline. In fact, discipline is a way of life for us. We know from firsthand experience that discipline reaps rewards. There is always a payoff for the hard work you put in, something enjoyable and completely wonderful waiting at the end. We would never attempt to play a violin concerto or sing an aria without disciplined practice. We would never try to act the lead part in a full-length play without memorizing lines and blocking. Practicing scales, vocalizing, warm-up exercises, and studying are all disciplines that we've come to accept as part of the process for anyone who wants to achieve anything in the arts. We know that any time spent in these kinds of disciplines is never in vain. It can sometimes be hard, but if you enjoy what you're doing, it can also be fun. Discipline allows you to do things you could never do before.

So it is with the spiritual disciplines. You know how discipline in the arts pays big dividends? How much more so when it comes to spiritual disciplines, which pay exceedingly huge dividends for all of this life as well as for the next. That's why Paul tells Timothy, "Train yourself to be godly. For physical training is of some value, but godliness has value for all things, holding promise for both the present life and the life to come" (1 Tim. 4:7–8).

Spiritual disciplines pay benefits not only for the future; they can benefit us right now. Solitude, Bible reading, prayer, fasting, Scripture memory—all have long-lasting, far-reaching benefits. You will not grow spiritually, be everything God wants you to be, or experience everything God wants you to experience without discipline: "Do you not know that in a race all the runners run, but only one gets the prize? Run in such a way as to get the prize. Everyone who competes in the games goes into strict training. They do it to get a crown that will not last; but we do it to get a crown that will last forever. Therefore I do not run like a man running aimlessly; I do not fight like a man beating the air. No, I beat my body and make it my slave so that after I have preached to others, I myself will not be disqualified for the prize" (1 Cor. 9:24–27).

Even though most artists understand the value of discipline, I can't totally deny my friend's observations about our lack thereof. As disciplined as we are about our talents, we can be equally undisciplined in other areas. Even though we understand the value of discipline, we don't apply it as we should to much else beyond the arts. I've come to the conclusion that we artists are selectively disciplined; we're disciplined about the things we want to be disciplined about. We invest time and energy in the things that matter most to us. In the same way, we must make the spiritual disciplines a regular part of our lives.

My Ministry Is the Product of My Relationship with Christ

Early in our ministry here at Willow Creek, Bill Hybels taught us a principle that penetrated deeply into my soul and still captivates me. The principle is this: My ministry is the product of my relationship with Christ. In John 15:4–5 Jesus says it like this: "Remain in me, and I will remain in you. No branch can bear fruit by itself; it must remain in the vine. Neither can you bear fruit unless you remain in me. I am the vine; you are the branches. If a man remains in me and I in him, he will bear much fruit; apart from me you can do nothing."

Abiding in Christ means that we are in right relationship with Him, that we're growing in Him, that our lives reflect His love, and that our hearts are full of His Word. Ministry that flows out of a relationship like that is dynamic ministry. In Colossians 3:16 notice that ministry in the arts comes *after* we're filled with God's Word: "Let the word of Christ dwell in you richly as you teach and admonish one another with all wisdom, and as you sing psalms, hymns and spiritual songs with gratitude in your hearts to God."

We're missing something if we think all we have to do to have an effective ministry for Christ is be a great writer or performer and catch a few breaks. There's so much more to it than that. There is a correlation between knowing God and bearing fruit. Ministry is most powerful when it flows naturally out of a life that's spent in intimate fellowship with the Father. You can tell when someone spends time with God. His or her ministry bears fruit in a deeply spiritual and powerful way. The older I get, the less impressed I am with flash and glitz, and the more I'm drawn to men and women who spend time with God. They're people whose ministry is indeed the product of their relationship with Christ. When they create or perform, it's obvious that they walk close to God. They fellowship with the Lord and it shows. God reveals Himself to them and they minister powerfully in the Spirit. Before the disciples went out to do ministry, they spent time with Jesus (Matt. 10:5–42). The church started as a product of their relationship with Christ.

Colossians 1:10 tells us to "live a life worthy of the Lord and ... please him in every way: bearing fruit in every good work, growing in the knowledge of God." When we walk close to the Lord, we will bear fruit in every part of our lives, not just the artistic part. Since Bill Hybels first taught this principle in the early days of Willow Creek, I've applied it to other areas of my life as well. For example, my parenting is the product of my relationship with Christ. I can't strive to be an involved and loving father without regular fellowship with my compassionate and gracious heavenly Father. My marriage is the product of my relationship with Christ. I can't love my wife as Christ loved the church unless I'm in daily contact with Jesus. My relational world is the product of my relationship with Christ. My leadership of the ministry I've been given is the product of my relationship with Christ. I am being shaped and molded by the time I spend at the feet of Jesus.

It is dangerous for an artist to do the work God assigned us detached from Him. George Frideric Handel was a deeply spiritual man who walked with Christ. As he wrote the glorious "Hallelujah Chorus," he broke down in tears and cried out, "I did think I did see all Heaven before me, and the great God Himself."[3] But today, except in a few rare cases, when the "Hallelujah Chorus" is performed, we focus on the singers, the soloists, the orchestra, the conductor, the period or nonperiod instruments, the recording, the acoustics— everything but God Himself. We've somehow managed to take God out of the "Hallelujah Chorus." It's become religious music without God. My urgent warning is that we Christian artists can fall into exactly the same trap: doing religious music without God, or doing Christian art without being intimately connected with Christ.

Nurturing a Relationship

If my ministry is the product of my relationship with Christ, I need to nurture that relationship. The best way I've found to do that is to have a regular quiet time. When I talk about having a quiet time, I'm referring to a time that is set aside regularly for Bible reading and prayer. What I'm calling a quiet time others might call devotions. Still others might refer to it as their daily appointment with God. It doesn't matter what we call it; all that matters is that we engage with the Lord on a regular basis. Our highest priority should not be our art. It should be our relationship with Jesus. For what would it profit an artist to have the world by the tail and lose his or her soul because the person wasn't living in a relationship with God (Luke 9:25)?

A regular quiet time allows you and me to experience God in a personal way. The God of the universe wants to spend time with us (1 Cor. 1:9). First John 1:3 says that "our fellowship is with the Father and with his Son, Jesus Christ." Fellowship is meant to be an intimate experience. If you want to read a passage of Scripture that poignantly describes how intimate God wants to be with us, read 2 Corinthians 6:16–18. Here we learn that God wants to dwell in us and walk among us. He wants us to be His people. He welcomes us into His presence. He wants to be a father to us and wants us to be sons and daughters to Him. Did you know God is that relational? He wants to spend time with us, not just once a day but throughout our day. He's the one drawing us to Himself. He's the one telling us to turn off the car radio and talk to Him. When your head hits the pillow, He's the one saying, "Talk to Me, My child." He's the one saying, "Come to Me. Whether you're happy, sad, angry, confused, lonely, discouraged, it doesn't matter. Come to Me."

Any time spent in God's presence will refresh your heart and renew your soul (Acts 3:19). That's why the psalmist says, "As for me, it is good to be near God" (Ps. 73:28). When we spend time one-on-one with the Lord, we also put ourselves in position to hear something personal from Him—something meant just for us. What compels me most to spend time with the Lord is that He might say something to me personally. After all, "he rewards those who earnestly seek him" (Heb. 11:6; see also Deut. 4:29). There are so many outstanding books available today about achieving intimacy with Christ, yet so few experience it for themselves. Reading about solitude is never the same as having solitude.

A quiet time can be a vehicle to help us to know Christ better. How important is that? Paul says that knowing Christ is more important than anything else: "I consider everything a loss compared to the surpassing greatness of knowing Christ Jesus my Lord, for whose sake I have lost all things. I consider them rubbish, that I may gain Christ" (Phil. 3:8). David reiterates that the most important thing we can do in life is to draw close to God: "One thing I ask of the LORD, this is what I seek: that I may dwell in the house of the LORD all the days of my life, to gaze upon the beauty of the LORD and to seek him in his temple" (Ps. 27:4).

Knowing God is even more important than being an artist. Here's what an artists' version of Jeremiah 9:23–24 might look like: "'Let not musicians boast about their music, and let not thespians boast about their acting, let not artists boast about their art, let not dancers boast about their dancing, and let not writers boast about their writing, but let anyone who boasts boast about this, *that they understand and know me,* that I am the LORD, who exercises kindness, justice, and righteousness on earth, for in these I delight,' declares the LORD."

I like how J. I. Packer puts it in his book *Knowing God:* "What were we made for? To know God. What aim should we set ourselves in life? To know God. What is the 'eternal life' that Jesus gives? Knowledge of God. 'This is life eternal, that they might know thee, the only true God, and Jesus Christ, whom thou hast sent' (John 17:3). What is the best thing in life, bringing more joy, delight, and contentment, than anything else? Knowledge of God."[4]

Philip was the disciple who said to Jesus, "Lord, show us the Father and that will be enough for us" (John 14:8). Jesus sounds a little frustrated with Philip when He replies, "Don't you know me, Philip, even after I have been among you such a long time? Anyone who has seen me has seen the Father. How can you say, 'Show us the Father'?" (v. 9). Philip had been a disciple for so long and still didn't know Jesus. Too many of us are the same way. We're religious, we're involved in a lot of church activities, but we still don't know Christ. Remember, Christianity is not a religion. It is a relationship.

Friendship with God

Jesus calls us friends (John 15:14–15). He calls us brothers or sisters (Heb. 2:11–12). Friends spend time together. They learn each other's thoughts. How can we know the thoughts of God unless we spend time with Him (1 Cor. 2:10–16)? Friends learn to enjoy each other's company. They grow in their relationship. We're talking about a God who draws near to us when we draw near to Him (James 4:8). He is not far away and aloof. "'Am I only a God nearby,' declares the LORD, 'and not a God far away?'" (Jer. 23:23). He is someone I can turn to for advice. He's someone I can celebrate with. He's even someone I can have fun with. He's somebody I can go to when I'm sad and lonely, and He's someone I can cry with. In his book *Surprised by the Voice of God,* Jack Deere captures the meaning of our friendship with Christ very eloquently:

> God comes to us like this because he wants a relationship. But sometimes we only want results. He wants to talk. But we only want him to fix things. It's not that he is against results or minds fixing things. He actually enjoys serving us. But he wants to be more than a servant. He wants to be a friend. Though I fear sometimes we want only a servant.
>
> Real friendships can't be forced. They must be chosen, and then pursued and purged of ulterior motives. Friends share secrets, and understanding of each other grows—so does trust and appreciation. If the friendship deepens, one day you wake up and realize that you love your friend for who they are, not for what they can do for you. In fact, they don't need to do anything for you. Just being with your friend is the highest joy. Yet the truth is that there is nothing you wouldn't do for your friend and nothing your friend wouldn't do for you. . . .

As long as we're primarily interested in our friend for what they can do for us, we'll never have a true friendship. Relationships can begin this way and then develop into true friendship, but until the relationship is purged of our desire to use each other, we'll never have a true friendship. And yet it is our truest friends who will do the most for us. . . .

One of the great mistakes of the church is to offer Jesus to people solely on the same basis that a salesman offers a product to consumers. Come to Jesus—he'll save you from hell, fix your marriage, get your kid off drugs, heal your diseases, take away your depression, make you powerful in word and spirit, give you a good job and a nice house. Jesus certainly saves people from hell, and he can do all the other things too.

It's not wrong to come to Jesus initially for what he can do for us. The problem is that many of us never progress beyond this stage. What if he doesn't fix our marriage or get our kids off drugs? What if he lets us go bankrupt? If our primary interest in Jesus revolves around what he can do for us, then when he "fails" to meet enough of our perceived needs, we'll leave him or become embittered. Many of us in the church can't seem to get past the stage of desiring Jesus for what he can do for us. We are so dazzled by Jesus' ability to provide for us that we can't see the loveliness of his Person. He is infinitely wonderful in himself, worthy to be loved and adored even if he never does a single thing for us. . . .

God makes it easy for us to reject him because he wants us to choose him for himself alone. It is perhaps one of the universe's greatest mysteries that the Son of God wants a friendship with us. He will not force himself on us. We must choose him for our friend and then pursue him for the rest of our lives if we want that friendship to grow.[5]

My Personal Lifeline

I've come to the conclusion that my quiet time is the most important appointment of my day. Direction for my life, vision for my ministry, Scriptures to help with temptation, even song ideas have all come out of my times of solitude with the Lord. I've come to realize that I couldn't live without God's Word. That's not being overly dramatic. I don't know where I would be if it weren't for those times with the Lord. Moses said that God's words "are not just idle words for you—they are your life" (Deut. 32:47). My quiet time is my lifeline. For this reason I consider having a regular quiet time to be a prerequisite for every artist involved in ministry.

I'm in a position in my life where I need the Lord daily, and I especially need His guidance and direction. In their book *Experiencing God* Henry T. Blackaby and Claude V. King encourage us to spend time with the Lord and find out what He's doing in and around us and then to adjust our lives to be a part of that:

> Right now God is working all around you and in your life. . . . The Holy Spirit and the Word of God will instruct you and help you know when and where God is working. Once you know where he is working, you can adjust your life to join him where he is working.
>
> Once you join God in what he is doing you will experience him accomplishing his activity through your life. When you enter this kind of intimate love relationship with God, you will know and do the will of God and experience him in ways you have never known him before. Only God can bring you into that kind of relationship, but he stands ready to do so.[6]

I'm not ashamed to say that I need the Lord in my life these days, probably more so than ever before. I need His wisdom and strength. I need to talk to Him and listen for His voice. Apart from Him I know I can do nothing (John 15:5). I wouldn't think of trying to do life without spending time with the Lord. I don't understand how non-Christians can live without Christ, but it is even further beyond me why Christians try to live without Him. I don't understand why we make a commitment to follow Jesus but then don't spend time with Him. I feel so strongly about this that if I were on my deathbed, my last words of advice to anyone who would listen would be, "Spend time with the Lord." It's the greatest privilege in all of life.

Where Our Character Is Formed

My quiet times have also been a vehicle for my own character growth. One reason for that is that we tend to become like those with whom we spend time. If you spend time with the Lord, you gain a new set of thoughts and priorities.

Philippians 1:6 says that "he who began a good work in you will carry it on to completion until the day of Christ Jesus." Our character growth is a process that God initiates and wants to be a part of. I distinctly remember as a young man telling John Allen, my spiritual mentor whom I mentioned in chapter 2, that I really wanted to grow in godly character. His response was, "Good. I'll pray that God will send you all sorts of problems to make you grow." And I remember thinking, "Gee, John, thanks a lot." I've since learned that while not every problem I encounter is God trying to build character in me, and while God is certainly not out to get me, it is true that God can use many of the problems I face to build character in me. Because I knew that "the Lord disciplines those he loves" (Heb. 12:6), my quiet times became for me that refuge I desperately needed when going through difficulty, a safe place where I could experience renewal from a God who loves me, where I could contritely ask, "Lord, what do you want me to learn from this problem?"

Most of my character growth has happened in the context of an ongoing relationship with the Lord. I could see I had a problem with perfectionism, for example, and I felt compelled to seek God's guidance and wisdom for dealing with it. Sometimes it felt like surgery. The Holy Spirit would point out the cancer threatening my spiritual life and say, "This has got to go." Sometimes it felt like therapy, as if I were talking to a friend about my problems. God was and always has been a safe place for me. He accepted me, warts and all. I found I could tell Him anything and He would always listen. I would pour my heart out to Him about a disappointment I was experiencing and ask, "God, how do you want me to respond to this?" Very often He has led me to something in His Word that spoke directly to my problem, something that ministered deeply to my soul.

In the process He would lovingly point out character flaws in me that were contributing to the problem. I don't know how many times I've said, "God, I'm weak in this area. Help me to grow." Scripture says that we are to "in all things grow up into him who is the Head, that is, Christ" (Eph. 4:15). What better place to do that than in the intimacy of a relationship with the One who made us and knows us better than we know ourselves? The Bible contains what we need to build our character. Hebrews 4:12 says, "The word of God is living and active. Sharper than any double-edged sword, it penetrates even to dividing soul and spirit, joints and marrow; it judges the thoughts and attitudes of the heart."

When God's Word is allowed to penetrate our thoughts, it can change our behavior. God's Word can get to the root of our problems if we let it. This is where character and integrity are forged—deep in the heart of who we really are. How can we assimilate the character of Christ into our whole being without saturating ourselves in God's Word? For when we behold Christ as revealed in God's Word, we are transformed into His image (2 Cor. 3:18). I'm not talking about some self-improvement program. I'm talking about genuine spiritual transformation that can only happen in the context of a loving, growing, vital, and intimately personal relationship with the Lord.

Bible Study and Prayer

It is not my intention to cover all the spiritual disciplines, just the ones that have been especially meaningful to me. Every spiritual discipline has benefits for this life and for the life to come, but the two most foundational disciplines are Bible study and prayer. These are the two that all believers should master before they go on to any others, and the two that the first-century church was especially devoted to (Acts 6:4).

The Artist As God's Mouthpiece

Participating in any arts-related ministry usually calls for the public expression of your talents. Hence you will often find yourself in the position of being God's mouthpiece. We often find ourselves in the same place as Jeremiah, to whom God said, "I have put my words in your mouth" (Jer. 1:9). I hope you don't take that lightly. I hope it never gets too easy to do Christian music, art, or theater. I hope the weight of that responsibility is sobering to all of us. If you're doing ministry in the name of Jesus, you need to be in the Word so you can communicate effectively His thoughts. It doesn't matter whether you're the front-and-center soloist or sing in the back row of the choir, whether you're playing the lead or a small part, whether your artwork hangs in the sanctuary or some obscure gallery. If we're God's mouthpiece, we have to know His thoughts. How can we know His thoughts if we don't spend time in His Word? Second Timothy 3:16–17 says, "All Scripture is God-breathed and is useful for teaching, rebuking, correcting and training in righteousness, so that the man of God may be thoroughly equipped for every good work." When we immerse ourselves in God's Word, we grow spiritually and He equips us to do what He's called us to do. We need to look at the discipline of the quiet time as part of our training to minister as God's mouthpiece.

We need to be students of God's Word the way we're students of our craft. We need to be able to discern biblical truth. We can't be waxing eloquent about heresy. We need to make sure that we sing, write, speak, and play God's truth. When I run across a song lyric that contradicts Scripture, it tells me that the writer either doesn't know his or her Bible or is purposely ignoring it. We need to be in the Word so we can discern what is scriptural and what is not.

Every artist needs to "do your best to present yourself to God as one approved, a workman who does not need to be ashamed and who correctly handles the word of truth" (2 Tim. 2:15). What if someone comes up to you after having seen you onstage and has a problem and wonders what the Bible has to say about it? At those times we need to be able to handle God's Word accurately. We don't have to be theologians. Most people don't want to know theology. They just want to know what the Bible says about their particular problem. If you're onstage, they assume you know. Peter tells us to "always be prepared to give an answer to everyone who asks you to give the reason for the hope that you have" (1 Peter 3:15). Could you lead someone to Christ by using God's Word? There is a responsibility that comes along with being God's mouthpiece. We need to know His Word and be able to use it accurately.

Conversational Prayer

I find prayer to be one of the most intimate aspects of my relationship with God. Because I've been adopted into the family of God, I can talk to Him as a son talks to his father (John 1:12; Rom. 8:15). I can come boldly, and of course reverently, into the presence of almighty God and talk to Him like a friend (Eph. 3:12). I can have a conversation with Him the way David or Joshua or the woman at the well did. There doesn't have to be anything fancy about it. I can tell God anything and everything.

I know many people who have benefited from using the acronym ACTS (adoration, confession, thanksgiving, and supplication) as a guideline for their prayer life. I found that when I had something written under each of those headings, it always generated enough material for a free-flowing conversation with the Lord.

I think it's interesting that when the disciples asked Jesus to teach them how to pray, He didn't give them a formula. He didn't say, "Do this, and then that, and then this." He simply prayed. He simply talked to His heavenly Father. That's the beauty of conversational prayer. It's a stimulating conversation with the One who created us. And it's not confined to the quiet time we set aside once a day. We can pray anytime, anywhere, throughout the day.

The Power of Prayer

I believe in the power of prayer to change things and/or to change me. In John 16:24 Jesus says, "Until now you have not asked for anything in my name. Ask and you will receive, and your joy will be complete." Remember, He is able. If we abide in Him, whatever we ask will be granted to us (John 15:7).

When I first started out in ministry, I was working in a start-up church out west, and we desperately needed musicians to serve in our ministry. I would pray daily that God would send us quality musicians. After all, He owns the cattle on a thousand hills (Ps. 50:10), so I figured He could bring us the musicians we needed. A woman at the church came up to me after a service and said that her brother was moving in from New York and that he played the trumpet. I didn't take it seriously. I never know what I'm getting into in these circumstances, and besides, everybody thinks their brother or sister or son or daughter is the greatest, right? Two weeks later she stopped me after the service and said that her brother had just moved in and would like to audition for me, so I obliged.

What I heard at that audition was the best trumpet player I had ever heard live. He had a great tone. He could play pop and classical. He could improvise and he had played professionally with a lot of big names. The problem was that he was as far from God as you could be. He didn't know the Lord at all. The next morning as I was praying, I said, "Lord, maybe I need to be more specific. I've been praying for more musicians, and you sent me this pagan trumpet player." I sensed the Lord saying, "Yes, I know. I brought him here all the way from New York so he could find Me. Are you going to invest time in him or not?"

Well, that put me in my place, so for several months I did everything I could to get alongside this guy. One time I had to visit him in jail because he had a drinking problem and got arrested for disturbing the peace. His language and behavior embarrassed me at first, but after a while I grew to love this guy, and my heart began to ache for him to know Christ. My friend eventually did come to Christ and now has a wonderful music ministry in the southwestern part of the country.

That early experience showed me that prayer is powerful. God can literally move people across the country if He wants them to be involved with a specific body of believers. It also taught me the value of listening. If I hadn't been on my knees, I would never have heard God say that He had brought this wayward musician to us so we could lead him to Christ. I can't pat myself on the back for that, though, because my prayers were self-serving. I started out wanting God to bring musicians to this music program I was building. My friend's sister was praying that he would find Christ. I hate to think where my friend would be—where so many others would be—if there weren't people faithfully praying for them.

For Those Just Starting Out

If you're just starting out in establishing a regular quiet time, I suggest that you first select a time in your schedule that you can count on to be free with a high degree of consistency. It doesn't matter whether it's in the morning, at night, or sometime in between. No time of day is more spiritual than another. Just pick a time of day when you can be fairly sharp. Also, find a time when you will encounter the least amount of distraction. A quiet time is best approached out of quietness.

Make it a reasonable time frame, too. An hour is too lofty a goal at the beginning. You'll get discouraged trying to fill the time. Start with ten minutes, then make it fifteen, then twenty, and keep expanding it as you grow in this discipline.

When you've settled on a time, next find a set place. It can be a room or a chair or a couch—anything that's comfortable and private. For me, in the summer it's a wicker chair on our back patio and in the winter it's a rocking chair by the fireplace. These are places that invite me back time and again for fellowship with my Savior.

Believe it or not, having a set time and place is half the battle. Now you're ready to dig in. Start by asking God to reveal Himself to you through His Word. Then read something from the New Testament. I would suggest one of the Gospels, say John. Read small sections at a time. Read slowly. Remember, this is not a contest to see how much you can read in one sitting. This is not some daily chore you get through as fast as you can. This is time alone with you and the Lord. As you read, keep asking yourself, "What does this tell me about what God is like?" Nothing fancy about that. Feel free to underline verses that are important to you. Some people like to keep a journal in which they write down what they learn from the Bible. If you want to try that and it works for you, do it. If it doesn't, don't. If you run across something you don't understand, skip it and move on. Don't let it discourage you or bog you down. There are some parts of the Bible that are so deep, even theologians wrestle with them. Besides, you can ask your pastor or your spiritual mentor about the troublesome passage later.

After you've spent time reading the Bible, spend a few minutes in prayer. You can start by praying about what you just read. Ask the Lord, "How can I apply this to my life?" I also suggest having a prayer list. I find that my mind wanders less if I have a list in front of me as I'm praying. You can use a different list for each day of the week, or you can use the same list every day, whichever works best for you. You might even want to keep a prayer journal so you can track how and when God answers your prayers. Pray about people or things that you're really interested in, that you feel passionate about. Also, keep your prayers simple. Remember, you're talking to God and He's there listening because He wants to be there. If it feels uncomfortable at first, you'll soon get over it. Prayer is something you learn by doing. J. Oswald Sanders says that "mastering the art of prayer, like any other art, will take time, and the amount of time we allocate to it will be the true measure of our conception of its importance. We always contrive to find time for that which we deem most important."[7]

You don't need to read another book about prayer. You just need to pray. You don't even need to be an expert to pray. You will become an expert the more you do it.

Variety Is the Spice of Life

Artistic people get bored easily, but there are ways to keep the spiritual disciplines from becoming ritualistic or mundane. If this truly is a relationship, we should be asking ourselves often, "What can I do to breathe life into my times with the Lord?" The psalmist says that being in God's presence brings joy (Ps. 16:11), so time with the Lord doesn't have to be drudgery. Don't get so rigid about your routine that you can't mix things up from time to time and have fun. Be flexible. Sometimes I'll start with prayer instead of ending with prayer, just to keep boredom from setting in. Sometimes I'll spend the entire time in prayer or in the Word. A few times I've sensed the Lord saying, "I want you to worship me this morning," so I've grabbed my guitar and spent the entire time worshiping. One summer my quiet times had become very stale, so I took a month off and walked around a nearby lake early every morning. It was a lot of fun. As I observed the beauty of the sunrise and the glory of God's creation, it was easy to enjoy His presence as we walked around that lake. After a month of that I went back to my usual routine with renewed vigor. You could also do a topical study from the Bible. You could write letters to God. You could write your own psalm. I know some people who use Bible commentaries or devotional guides to liven things up. A number of times I've gone through one of those fill-in-the-blank Bible study books. My point is, don't let your quiet time become a mindless and emotionless ritual. Make it enjoyable for you *and* the Lord.

Not every quiet time will be momentous. Some days you'll feel as if the heavens parted and God visited you in a powerful way. Other times it'll feel routine. However, if it seems that you got nothing out of it, you're still always better off for having been in the presence of Jesus. Rest assured that no time spent communing with God is ever wasted time.

If you've been faithful with your quiet time over a long period of time and it's starting to grow a little stale, take comfort in knowing that this happens to everyone. It's normal. We all go through periods like this. Any relationship, whether it be a friendship or a marriage or a family tie, needs a concerted effort to keep things fresh or it will become dull. If you're going through a dry spell, whatever you do, don't give up. Even though it doesn't feel as if you're moving forward, your roots are still being planted in the Word. The part of the tree that we never see growing is the roots, but the tree won't be healthy if the roots aren't firmly planted in the soil. Besides, you might be taking in spiritual truth that you'll need at a later time. Hosea tells us to "press on to acknowledge him. As surely as the sun rises, he will appear; he will come to us like the winter rains, like the spring rains that water the earth" (6:3). I've been through spiritual droughts in which I didn't get a whole lot out of my quiet times. That should never be a reason to stop. As Hosea says, God's presence will eventually break through, and that dry spell will be snapped as if a spring rain had just washed over your soul. Stay the course and be faithful to your commitment to fellowship with the Father.

Too Busy?

The main reason Christians don't have a regular quiet time is that we're too busy. One day when Martin Luther was faced with the prospect of another fast-paced day, he said, "I'm too busy not to pray." So it is with us. The busier we are, the more reason we have to spend time with God. The busier Jesus became, the more time He spent in prayer. In the middle of a busy schedule He would often withdraw to pray, sometimes spending long hours into the night on His knees (Matt. 14:23; 26:36; Luke 4:42; 5:16; 6:12). Listen to Henri Nouwen quote Mark 1:35 and then expound on it:

> "In the morning, long before dawn, he got up and left the house, and went off to a lonely place and prayed there." In the middle of sentences loaded with action—healing suffering people, casting out devils, responding to impatient disciples, traveling from town to town and preaching from synagogue to synagogue we find these quiet words: "In the morning, long before dawn, he got up and left the house, and went off to a lonely place and prayed there." In the center of breathless activities we hear a restful breathing. Surrounded by hours of moving we find a moment of quiet stillness. In the heart of much involvement there are words of withdrawal. In the midst of action there is contemplation. And after much togetherness there is solitude. The more I read this nearly silent sentence locked in between the loud words of action, the more I have the sense that the secret of Jesus' ministry is hidden in that lonely place where he went to pray, early in the morning, long before dawn.
>
> In the lonely place Jesus finds the courage to follow God's will and not his own; to speak God's words and not his own; to do God's work and not his own. He reminds us constantly: "I can do nothing by myself . . . my aim is to do not my own will, but the will of him who sent me" (John 5:30). And again, "The words I say to you I do not speak as from myself: it is the Father, living in me, who is doing this work" (John 14:10). It is in the lonely place, where Jesus enters into intimacy with the Father, that his ministry is born.[8]

We all know the story of Mary and Martha (Luke 10:38–42) and how Martha was so caught up in her duties as a hostess that she was unable to enjoy fellowship with Jesus. In fact, God was right there in front of her, but all she could see was the things on her to-do list. Because she was so task driven, she became angry at Mary and scolded Jesus for not reprimanding her: "Lord, don't you care that my sister has left me to do the work by myself? Tell her to help me!" (v. 40). Isn't it true that if you're trying to serve the Lord and you're not close to Him, you're going to be more resentful of others, more prone to anger? You can't serve the Lord with joy if you don't spend time with Him.

Mary, on the other hand, chose "what is better" (v. 42). Jesus would have surely rebuked her if she was being lazy. But she wasn't. She was simply choosing fellowship with God over busyness. In fact, throughout the Bible whenever we see Mary, she is always at the feet of Jesus (John 11:32; 12:3). She had a friendship with Christ because she made intimacy with the Savior a priority over her tasks. It seems she was never too busy for Jesus.

Back to Martha. She always seems to get the bad rap whenever this story is taught, doesn't she? But wasn't she being a good and faithful servant? She had a house full of hungry fishermen. What else was she supposed to do? I ask that because we all face that question quite often. What are you supposed to do when noble causes keep you from spending time with God? In Martha's case, she did a good thing but didn't do the *best* thing. I figure she had two valid options. She could have waited to serve dinner. It wouldn't have hurt the disciples if they'd had to wait an hour or two to eat. That way she could have sat at the feet of Jesus, been filled spiritually, and then served the meal. Besides, Jesus proved He could feed a small army. If the situation got desperate, He could always whip something up for them all to eat. The other option would have been for Martha to fix dinner for everyone and then spend time with the Lord, foregoing cleaning up right away if she had to. Either way she would have been able to spend time with Him, and either option would have spared her from getting angry at both Mary and Jesus.

I know it's not easy to find time to spend with the Lord. Our schedules are already so tight, but I've found that making my quiet time a priority has actually increased my capacity to get things done. I don't know how to explain that either, but the Lord seems to redeem the time spent with Him. It's not because the tensions subside, that's for sure. The "tyranny of the urgent" will always be staring us in the face. But maybe we end up working more efficiently because we gain a peace that passes all understanding from being in His presence (Phil. 4:7). Perhaps our soul is in a better place to face the heavy demands of life because we have spent time at the feet of Jesus.

Some of you are already convinced of the importance of having a regular quiet time, but you still haven't done it. My response to you is, Take responsibility now! Don't wait for someone else to come along and do it for you. Don't wait for someone else to tell you how to fit it into your schedule. Take control of your life and find a way to schedule a regular quiet time with the Lord.

Memorizing Scripture

Another spiritual discipline that I heartily recommend for the artist is memorizing Scripture. I believe that memorizing Scripture is a helpful step along the way to spiritually mature thinking. First Corinthians 14:20 says, "Stop thinking like children.... In your thinking be adults." As a very young Christian, I quickly realized that God's ways were far from my natural, dysfunctional way of thinking. "'My thoughts are not your thoughts, neither are your ways my ways,' declares the LORD" (Isa. 55:8). Indeed, thinking as a Christ follower should think didn't come naturally to me at all. I can remember being so discouraged, I would complain out loud, "I'll never grow spiritually. I just can't think like a Christian, let alone act like one."

Then I met an older man who knew large amounts of Scripture by heart. When asked his opinion or for advice, he would rattle off some passage that spoke directly to the situation. He wasn't showing off, either. He was one of the most humble men I've ever met. I remember thinking, *Wouldn't it be great to know that much Scripture from memory so you could instantly recall a passage whenever you needed it?* Right then and there I decided to memorize some Scripture. I need to have the Word of God readily available to me when up against the daily challenges of life.

I needed to have my mind renewed (Rom. 12:2), and I knew that memorizing Scripture would help. Sure enough, God's Word has been the biggest agent of change in my life. I've memorized certain verses that have literally changed the way I think. I wholeheartedly concur with Dallas Willard when he says, "As a pastor, teacher, and counselor I have repeatedly seen the transformation of inner and outer life that comes simply from memorization and meditation upon Scripture. Personally, I would never undertake to pastor a church or guide a program of Christian education that did not involve a continuous program of memorization of the choicest passages of Scripture for people of all ages."[9]

Insights are gained whenever we treasure God's Word in our hearts (Ps. 119:11). I didn't have to work all that hard at meditating on God's Word, because it started to happen naturally (almost accidentally) as I found myself unwittingly thinking about some verse I was memorizing (Ps. 1:2). Very often I'll see something in a verse I've memorized that I had never noticed before. That's the richness of God's Word.

I started to memorize Scripture because I wanted to, not because I had to. I began with the Navigator's "Topical Memory System," a series of booklets containing Scripture memory assignments. Eventually I decided to come up with my own memory verses—those that were especially meaningful to me. So I memorized verses to help me worship, verses to help me during times of temptation, verses to assist me in doing ministry, and verses to remind me of my commitment and priorities. I put them on little cards and memorized them as I drove to work each day. I still review them every morning as I make my breakfast and lunch. Scripture memory involves some work, so be sure to memorize verses that you feel passionate about.

The Daily Dangerous Prayer

Another spiritual discipline, which I've already alluded to, is what I fondly call my daily dangerous prayer. This is a short, one-line prayer, usually based on a Scripture verse, that I like to pray daily (normally at breakfast) for about a year. It's dangerous because I try to pick a verse that threatens the status quo in me, a verse that can shake me out of my spiritual complacency and revolutionize my life. In other words, if I really lived what a particular verse was saying, I'd be a brand-new person. Here are some examples of my dangerous prayers.

"Lord, help me to die to self" (from John 12:24).
"Lord, I present my body, and the members of my body, to you as instruments of righteousness" (from Rom. 6:13).

"Lord, help me to love Jesus the way you love Jesus" (from John 17:26).

"Father, grant me the kind of obedience that flows out of my love for Jesus" (from John 14:21).

"Lord, help me to put the needs of others ahead of my own" (from Phil. 2:3–4).

"Lord, have your way with me" (from Ps. 139:23–24).

"Lord, help me to do all that I do to your glory today" (from Col. 3:23).

"Give me the strength to do all You want me to do" (from Phil. 4:13).

You might ask, "Doesn't it get monotonous, praying the same prayer over and over?" No, it doesn't. First, I make sure that my dangerous prayer is something I feel passionate about. Second, the verse might remain the same, but my daily prayer changes as the needs change. I'm not praying the same prayer over and over. That one verse gets applied to my life in so many different ways. For example, as I'm writing this, my current daily prayer is, "Lord, stretch out your hand and work among us" (from Acts 4:30). I've been praying this for my family ("Lord, stretch out your hand and work in the lives of my two sons") and for the lives of some people I'm praying for ("Lord, stretch out your hand and reconcile that marriage, . . . heal that infirmity, . . . save that lost brother. . . ."). The prayer takes on different forms as I apply it to different needs. Just because I've prayed something for a year doesn't mean I've "arrived" and conquered my character flaws forever. In fact, quite the opposite happens. The more I grow, the farther I see I have to go. In the process, though, I move an inch closer to the image of Christ than I was before.

Avoid Legalism

Nothing produces more guilt in Christians than when someone starts talking about spiritual disciplines. Because we tend to be more sensitive, those of us with an artistic temperament are already walking around with our fair share of guilt. But there is a big difference between guilt and conviction.

Guilt is a feeling. We talk about *feeling* guilty. For this reason guilt has never been a healthy motivation to follow any of the spiritual disciplines. When the feeling wears off, there is no lasting incentive for change. Guilt is the work of the Evil One. He accuses us before God day and night (Rev. 12:10). Remember, "there is now no condemnation for those who are in Christ Jesus" (Rom. 8:1). Some people dread talking about the spiritual disciplines, because they always end up feeling down about themselves afterward. That's not how God works. He doesn't browbeat us into spending time with Him. When you start doubting your salvation because you haven't had a quiet time in a while, that sounds more like guilt than anything else. It's wrong to conclude that God doesn't love you anymore because you missed a few quiet times. Any spiritual discipline followed out of guilt will be quickly abandoned when the guilty feelings wear off.

Conviction, on the other hand, is more subtle because it is the work of the Holy Spirit (John 16:7–8). It is that still small voice that can be accompanied by deep emotion, especially tears, but has a more lasting impact than emotion. Having a quiet time or memorizing Scripture is not something you have to do. It's something you want to do. You sense God inviting you into deeper fellowship with Him and you respond. People who have a healthy outlook on spiritual disciplines won't go into turmoil if they don't have a quiet time for a few days. They'll feel bad about it because they genuinely miss meeting with the Lord, but they feel drawn to God instead of alienated from Him. One way to discern whether you're following a spiritual discipline out of guilt or conviction is to ask yourself, "Am I following this discipline because I feel God might be angry with me if I don't, or am I following it because deep inside it draws me closer to Christ?"

Avoid legalism when it comes to the spiritual disciplines. Having your quiet time in the morning doesn't make you more spiritual than someone who has his or hers at night. Don't use the spiritual disciplines to measure your spirituality or that of someone else. And don't follow these disciplines out of guilt and obligation. If you've been faithful with your quiet times, it's not the end of the world if you miss one now and then. Some of you might be in a season of life when the spiritual disciplines are going to be especially difficult. If you absolutely can't keep your usual appointment with the Lord, try to find another pocket of time somewhere else in the day, even if it means turning off the car radio and talking to Him as you're driving to work. I also know that it's really tough on a young mom with infants and toddlers to find any time alone with God. The Lord understands that. He had a mother once. Do whatever you can to spend time with Him, but be reasonable about it. Don't get down on yourself and withdraw from God. He knows that your time limitations will only last for a season.

The Greatest of These Is Still Love

During my days as a youth pastor, I heard one of our students say something that has deeply troubled me, even to this day. He said, "I don't know why my dad reads the Bible. It sure doesn't make him a more loving person." The father in question happened to be a pillar in the church and someone who was known for his spiritual discipline. Yet all his son could see was a deeply religious and spiritually disciplined man who was as cold as ice, even cruel at times. I wish I could say this was an isolated experience, but it's not. I've seen this happen more than just a few times, and to me it's the ultimate in hypocrisy. How can we read the Bible and still be lacking in love? Why are Christians in America regarded as self-righteous and judgmental instead of loving? How can I emerge from a deeply meaningful quiet time with the Lord and within ten minutes snap at my wife and kids?

In John 5:39–47 Jesus denounces the Pharisees for being disciplined in the Scriptures but not having the love of God in their hearts. They knew the Scriptures inside out and yet they never saw Jesus in them. They knew great amounts of Scripture from memory and still missed the point of it all. Don't let this happen to you. When you read the Bible, think about how you can apply it to your life. Ezra was a man in the Bible who set his heart not only to study God's Word but also to apply it to his life (Ezra 7:10). Spiritual transformation doesn't happen by filling our heads with all sorts of knowledge. It happens when we apply what we read to our lives.

Read God's Word with every intention of doing what it says, and it'll change your behavior.

The true mark of a Christian is not how disciplined you are but how loving you are. John Ortberg, one of our teaching pastors here at Willow Creek, says that "if we are not marked by greater and greater amounts of love and joy, we will inevitably look for substitute ways of distinguishing ourselves from those who are not Christians. This deep pattern is almost inescapable for religious people: If we do not become changed from the inside-out ... we will be tempted to find external methods to satisfy our need to feel that we're different from those outside the faith. If we cannot be transformed, we will settle for being informed or conformed."[10]

If spending time with God doesn't make you a more loving person, you're not spending time with the God of the Bible. The goal of Paul's ministry was "love, which comes from a pure heart" (1 Tim. 1:5). Jesus told His disciples, "A new command I give you: Love one another. As I have loved you, so you must love one another. By this all men will know that you are my disciples, if you love one another" (John 13:34–35). It wasn't really a new commandment for them, any more than it is for us. They had heard it all before and so have we. That's the problem. We've heard it a lot, but hearing it has not made us more loving people. What's true for the entire human race is also true of artists: if we have a boatload of talent, if we are successful artists, and if we read our Bible every day, but have not love, we have become just another noisy gong or clanging cymbal (1 Cor. 13:1–4). Dallas Willard, in commenting about the famous Love Chapter of 1 Corinthians, reminds us that following a bunch of rules won't make us more loving, but if we dwell in love, we will be more patient and kind and free of jealousy:

> Paul is plainly saying—look at his words—that it is love that does these things, not us, and that what we are to do is to "pursue love" (1 Cor. 14:1). As we "catch" love, we then find that these things are after all actually being done by us. These things, these godly actions and behaviors, are the result of dwelling in love. We have become the kind of person who is patient, kind, free of jealousy, and so on. ... It is very hard

indeed if you have not been substantially transformed in the depths of your being, in the intricacies of your thoughts, feelings, assurances, and dispositions, in such a way that you are permeated with love. Once that happens, then it is not hard. What would be hard is to act the way you acted before.

When Jesus hung on the cross and prayed, "Father, forgive them because they do not understand what they are doing," that was not hard for him. What would have been hard for him would have been to curse his enemies and spew forth vileness and evil upon everyone, God and the world, as those crucified with him did, at least for a while. He calls us to him to impart himself to us. He does not call us to do what he did, but to be as he was, permeated with love. Then the doing of what he did and said becomes the natural expression of who we are in him.[11]

Pursue love and dwell in it. If you're having your quiet time and one of the kids comes in and interrupts, don't lash out in anger against your child. Be reminded of your love for that child. Dwell in that love, listen to what he or she has to say, and then go back to your quiet time. If you're in the middle of your quiet time and remember that a brother or sister has something against you, drop what you're doing and write, call, or get together with the person and work things out (Matt. 5:23–24). Love is more important than ritual or discipline. We don't need a bunch of legalistic rules to live by. We need to pursue love. "Let no debt remain outstanding, except the continuing debt to love one another, for he who loves his fellowman has fulfilled the law" (Rom. 13:8). Don't fall into the trap of becoming more disciplined and less loving. "Let us not love with words or tongue but with actions and in truth" (1 John 3:18). Your quiet time should be a time when you dwell in the love of God. Soak in all the peace, joy, and love that always accompanies His presence; take in as much of it as you can. Sit in the solitude of His unconditional love. Dwell there in it. Let it wash over you. Let it transform your heart. And then come back to that place often in your mind as you go throughout your day. Now abides faith, hope, and love, but the greatest of these is, and always will be, love (1 Cor. 13:13). "Do everything in love"(1 Cor. 16:14).

Follow-Up Questions for Group Discussion

1. What kinds of activities are vital for any relationship between two people to grow?

2. What kinds of activities are vital for our relationship with the Lord to grow?

3. What are some of the challenges people face in establishing a regular quiet time with the Lord?

4. Do you think journaling is a good idea? Why or why not?

5. Do you think using a prayer list is a good idea? Why or why not?

6. Do you have any other suggestions for those just starting out in establishing the routine of a regular quiet time?

7. Do you have any other suggestions for those whose quiet times have become dry and dull?

8. Right now, where are you spiritually? Do you feel connected to God or far away? What can you do to get connected again?

9. What sorts of things cause you to feel close to God? (For example, reading the Bible, walking at sunset, listening to tapes or worship music, going to church, and so on.) How often are these things part of your regular routine?

10. How can we keep from becoming legalistic about spiritual disciplines?

Personal Action Steps

1. Identify which of the spiritual disciplines you would like to see more personal growth in this next year.

2. In the early church, the leaders were so devoted to prayer and God's Word that they went out of their way to protect those two disciplines as regular parts of their schedule. In Acts 6 they

even changed the entire serving structure of the church so as to assure the leaders more time for prayer and God's Word. Determine whether there are any radical changes you need to make to give yourself more time to commune with God.

3. Decide which Scripture verses you would like to memorize and have on the tip of your tongue. Choose someone to whom you can be accountable regarding Scripture memorization.

4. If you're willing to take the risk, write down a one-line prayer, based on a verse from Scripture, that you would like to pray earnestly every day this next year. Choose someone to whom you can be accountable concerning your daily dangerous prayer.

5. Find ways to show love tangibly to the various people you're going to see today.

On My Knees

When so many voices surround me
Screaming for attention all at once
Makes me long for some time with my Lord
And that old chair by the window where I go
To be with Him alone

On my knees
Is where I wanna be
When this life overwhelms me
I can pour my heart out
And bear my soul to the One who loves me
On my knees

Just me and the Lord in a quiet place
That's the best way I could ever start my day
So when life moves so fast I can't catch my breath
That appointment tends to be the first to go
And it's what I need the most

On my knees
Is where I wanna be
When this life overwhelms me
I can pour my heart out
And bear my soul to the One who loves me
On my knees[12]

Rory Noland

Notes

Introduction: Those "Artsy Types"

1. Rudolf and Margot Wittkower, *Born under Saturn* (New York, London: W. W. Norton & Co., 1963), 102.
2. Ibid.
3. Ibid.
4. Ibid.
5. Ibid.
6. Ken Gire, *Windows of the Soul* (Grand Rapids: Zondervan, 1996), 20.
7. Frank E. Gaebelein, *The Christian, the Arts, and Truth* (Portland, Ore.: Multnomah, 1985), 124.
8. Francis A. Schaeffer, *Art and the Bible* (Downers Grove, Ill.: InterVarsity Press, 1973), 12.
9. Patrick Kavanaugh, *The Spiritual Lives of Great Composers* (Nashville: Sparrow, 1992), 6.
10. Charlie Peacock, "The Nine Pursuits of the True Artist," excerpted from the Arthouse World Wide Web site at www.arthouse.org.
11. Leland Ryken, *The Liberated Imagination* (Wheaton, Ill.: Harold Shaw, 1989), 51.
12. John Fischer, *What on Earth Are We Doing?* (Ann Arbor, Mich.: Servant, 1996), 122.
13. Kent Nerburn, *Letters to My Son* (San Rafael, Calif.: New World Library, 1994), 139.

Chapter One: Proven Character

1. John Wooden, *They Call Me Coach* (Waco, Tex.: Word, 1972), 64.
2. David Jeremiah, *Turning Toward Integrity* (Colorado Springs: Victor, 1993), 7.
3. Rory Noland, "He Is Able," music by Rory Noland and Greg Ferguson (San Juan Capistrano, Calif.: Maranatha Praise, 1989).

Chapter Two: Servanthood Versus Stardom

1. C. S. Lewis, *The Screwtape Letters* (New York: Bantam, 1982), 41.
2. Patrick Kavanaugh, *Spiritual Moments with the Great Composers* (Grand Rapids: Zondervan, 1995), 80.
3. C. S. Lewis, *Mere Christianity* (New York: Touchstone, Simon & Schuster, 1996), 110.
4. Richard Foster, *Celebration of Discipline* (San Francisco: Harper, 1978), 130.

5. C. H. Spurgeon, *The Treasury of David*, vol. 2 (McLean, Va.: MacDonald, n.d.), 144–45.

6. Thomas à Kempis, *The Imitation of Christ,* ed. Paul M. Bechtel (Chicago: Moody Press, 1980), 180.

7. Frederick Buechner, *Wishful Thinking, A Theological ABC* (San Francisco: Harper & Row, 1973), 95.

8. Philip Yancey, *Open Windows* (Westchester, Ill.: Crossway, 1982), 211.

9. Greg Ferguson, "Audience of One" (South Barrington, Ill.: Ever Devoted Music, and San Juan Capistrano, Calif.: Maranatha! Music, 1991).

Chapter Three: The Artist in Community

1. Anthony E. Kemp, *The Musical Temperament* (Oxford, New York, Tokyo: Oxford University Press, 1996), 66.

2. Howard Gardner, *Creating Minds* (New York: BasicBooks, 1993), 195–96.

3. Pat Riley, *The Winner Within* (New York: G. P. Putnam's Sons, 1993), 21.

4. John Wooden, *They Call Me Coach* (Waco, Tex.: Word, 1972), 101.

5. Rory Noland, "Holy Spirit Take Control" (South Barrington, Ill.: Ever Devoted Music, 1984).

Chapter Four: Excellence Versus Perfectionism

1. Brennan Manning, *Abba's Child* (Colorado Springs: NavPress, 1994), 22–23.

2. Manning, *Abba's Child,* 19.

3. Franky Schaeffer, *Addicted to Mediocrity* (Westchester, Ill.: Crossway, 1981), 62.

4. Schaeffer, *Addicted to Mediocrity,* 45–46.

5. George Solti, *Memoirs* (New York: Alfred A. Knopf, 1997), 204.

6. Francis A. Schaeffer, *Art and the Bible* (Downers Grove, Ill.: InterVarsity Press, 1973), 14.

7. Peggy Noonan, *Simply Speaking* (New York: HarperCollins, 1998), 8.

8. "Marvelous Mark Morris," *BBC Music Magazine,* special issue, *Ballet from Ritual to Romance* (1996), 64.

9. Rory Noland, "Let the Lord Love You" (South Barrington, Ill.: Ever Devoted Music, and San Juan Capistrano, Calif.: Maranatha! Music, 1989).

Chapter Five: Handling Criticism

1. Neil T. Anderson, *Victory over the Darkness* (Ventura, Calif.: Regal, 1990), 215.

2. Rory Noland, "Open to the Truth About Myself" (South Barrington, Ill.: Ever Devoted Music, 1992).

Chapter Six: Jealousy and Envy

1. *Webster's New Twentieth Century Dictionary,* unabridged, 2nd ed. (Cleveland, New York: World, 1964).
2. Henri Nouwen, *Reaching Out* (New York: Doubleday, 1975), 70.
3. Dallas Willard, *The Divine Conspiracy* (San Francisco: HarperCollins, 1998), 151.
4. Dante Alighieri, *Divine Comedy: Purgatorio,* trans. John Ciardi (New York: Random House, 1996), canto 14, p. 148.
5. Gordon MacDonald, *The Life God Blesses* (Nashville: Nelson, 1994), 143.
6. Rory Noland, "I'm Amazed" (San Juan Capistrano, Calif.: Maranatha Praise, 1991).

Chapter Seven: Managing Your Emotions

1. Jane Stuart Smith and Betty Carlson, *The Gift of Music* (Wheaton, Ill.: Crossway, 1995), 164.
2. Rudolf and Margot Wittkower, *Born under Saturn* (New York, London: W. W. Norton, 1963), 74.
3. Jimmy Webb, *Tunesmith* (New York: Hyperion, 1998), 370.
4. Richard Foster, *Celebration of Discipline* (San Francisco: Harper, 1978), 102.
5. William Temple, *Readings in St. John's Gospel,* vol. 1 (London: Macmillan, 1939), 68.
6. John Piper, *Desiring God* (Sisters, Ore.: Multnomah, 1986), 76.
7. C. S. Lewis, *Reflections on the Psalms* (San Diego, New York, London: Harcourt Brace, 1958), 94.
8. Franky Schaeffer, *Addicted to Mediocrity* (Westchester, Ill.: Crossway, 1981), 59–62.
9. Rory Noland, "Praise God on High" (South Barrington, Ill.: Ever Devoted Music, 1998).

Chapter Eight: Leading Artists

1. Rainer Maria Rilke, *Letters to a Young Poet* (San Rafael, Calif.: New World Library, 1992), 64–65.
2. C. S. Lewis, *Mere Christianity* (New York: Touchstone, Simon & Schuster, 1996), 75.
3. J. Oswald Sanders, *Spiritual Discipleship* (Chicago: Moody Press, 1990), 110.
4. J. Oswald Sanders, *Spiritual Leadership,* (Chicago: Moody Press, 1967), 44.
5. Rory Noland, "Ever Devoted" (South Barrington, Ill.: Ever Devoted Music, 1988).

Chapter Nine: The Artist and Sin

1. Cornelius Plantinga Jr., *Not the Way It's Supposed to Be* (Grand Rapids: Eerdmans, 1995), 135.
2. C. S. Lewis, *Mere Christianity* (New York: Touchstone, Simon & Schuster, 1996), 92.
3. William Gurnall, *The Christian in Complete Armour,* abridged by Ruthanne Garlock et al. (Edinburgh, England: Banner of Trust, 1986), 197.
4. Jerry Bridges, *The Pursuit of Holiness* (Colorado Springs: NavPress, 1978), 78.
5. Ruth Goring, *The Creative Heart of God* (Wheaton, Ill.: Harold Shaw, 1997), 55.
6. Brennan Manning, *Abba's Child* (Colorado Springs: NavPress, 1994), 17.
7. Dallas Willard, *Spirit of the Disciplines* (San Francisco: HarperCollins, 1988), 115.
8. Rory Noland, "Behind Every Fantasy" (South Barrington, Ill.: Ever Devoted Music, and San Juan Capistrono, Calif.: Maranatha! Music, 1991).

Chapter Ten: The Spiritual Disciplines of the Artist

1. Denise Levertov, "Flickering Mind," *A Door in the Hive* (New York: New Directions), 1989.
2. Anthony E. Kemp, *The Musical Temperament* (Oxford, New York, Tokyo: Oxford University Press, 1996), 25.
3. David Ewen, *The Complete Book of Classical Music* (Englewood Cliffs, N.J.: Prentice Hall, 1965), 142.
4. J. I. Packer, *Knowing God* (Downers Grove, Ill.: InterVarsity Press, 1973), 29.
5. Jack Deere, *Surprised by the Voice of God* (Grand Rapids: Zondervan, 1996), 331–33.
6. Henry T. Blackaby and Claude V. King, *Experiencing God* (Nashville: Broadman & Holman, 1994), 45.
7. J. Oswald Sanders, *Spiritual Leadership,* (Chicago: Moody Press, 1967), 123.
8. Henri Nouwen, *Out of Solitude* (Notre Dame, Ind.: Ave Maria Press, 1995), 13–14.
9. Dallas Willard, *Spirit of the Disciplines* (San Francisco: HarperCollins, 1988), 150.
10. John Ortberg, *The Life You've Always Wanted* (Grand Rapids: Zondervan, 1997), 33–34.
11. Dallas Willard, *The Divine Conspiracy* (San Francisco: HarperCollins, 1998), 183.
12. Rory Noland, "On My Knees," (South Barrington, Ill.: Ever Devoted Music, and San Juan Capistrano, Calif.: Maranatha! Music, 1991).

WILLOW CREEK RESOURCES

Vision,   Training,   Resources,

This resource was created to serve you and to help you in building a local church that prevails! It is just one of many Willow Creek Resources copublished by the Willow Creek Association and Zondervan Publishing House.

Since 1992, the Willow Creek Association (WCA) has been linking like-minded, action-oriented churches with each other and with strategic vision, training, and resources. Now a worldwide network of over five thousand churches from more than eighty denominations, the WCA works to equip Member Churches and others with the tools needed to build prevailing churches. Our desire is to inspire, equip, and encourage Christian leaders to build biblically functioning churches that reach increasing numbers of unchurched people, not just with innovations from Willow Creek Community Church in South Barrington, Illinois, but from any church in the world that has experienced God-given breakthroughs.

Willow Creek Conferences

In the past year, more than 65,000 local church leaders, staff, and volunteers—from WCA Member Churches and others—attended one of our conferences or training events.

Conferences offered on the Willow Creek campus in South Barrington, Illinois, include:

Prevailing Church Conference—Foundational training for staff and volunteers working to build a prevailing local church; offered twice each year.

Prevailing Church Workshops—More than fifty workshops cover seven topic areas that represent key characteristics of a prevailing church; offered twice each year.

Promiseland Conference—Children's ministries; infant through fifth grade.

Prevailing Youth Ministries Conference—Junior and senior high ministries.

Arts Conference—Vision and training for Christian artists using their gifts in the ministries of local churches.

Leadership Summit—Envisioning and equipping Christians with leadership gifts and responsibilities; broadcast live via satellite to sixteen cities.

Contagious Evangelism Conference—Encouragement and training for churches and church leaders who want to be strategic in reaching lost people for Christ.

Small Groups Conference—Exploring how small groups can play a key role in developing authentic Christian community that leads to spiritual transformation.

Prevailing Church Regional Workshops

Each year the WCA team leads seven, two-day training events in cities across the United States. Workshops are offered in topic areas including leadership, next-generation ministries, small groups, arts and worship, evangelism, spiritual gifts, financial stewardship, and spiritual formation. These events make quality training more accessible and affordable to larger groups of staff and volunteers.

Willow Creek Resources

Churches can look to Willow Creek Resources for a trusted channel of ministry tools in areas of leadership, evangelism, spiritual gifts, small groups, drama, contemporary music, financial stewardship, spiritual transformation, and more. For ordering information, call 800-570-9812 or visit www.willowcreek.com.

WCA Membership

Membership in the Willow Creek Association as well as attendance at WCA Conferences is for churches, ministries, and leaders who hold to a historic, orthodox understanding of biblical Christianity. The annual church membership fee of $249 provides discounts for your entire team on all conferences and Willow Creek Resources, networking opportunities with other outreach-oriented churches, a bimonthly newsletter, a subscription to *Defining Moments* monthly audio journal, and more.

WillowNet (www.willowcreek.com)

This internet service provides you with access to hundreds of Willow Creek messages, drama scripts, songs, videos, and multimedia suggestions. The system allows you to sort through these elements and download them for a fee.

Our website also provides detailed information on the Willow Creek Association, Willow Creek Community Church, WCA Membership, conferences, training events, resources, and more.

Willow Creek Association
P.O. Box 3188
Barrington, IL 60011-3188
Phone: 800-570-9812
Fax: 888-922-0035
Web: www.willowcreek.com

We want to hear from you. Please send your comments about this book to us in care of the address below. Thank you.

GRAND RAPIDS, MICHIGAN 49530

www.zondervan.com